Adolf Galland

The First
and
The Last

The Rise and Fall of
the German Fighter
Forces, 1938-1945

Translated by Mervyn Savill
From the German Die Ersten und Die Letzten

Buccaneer Books
Cutchogue, New York

International Standard Book Number: 0-89966-728-7

For ordering information, contact:

Buccaneer Books, Inc.
P.O. Box 168
Cutchogue, N.Y. 11935

(631) 734-5724, Fax (631) 734-7920
    www.BuccaneerBooks.com

Publisher's Note

Adolf Galland was born in Westerholt, Westphalia. His father was bailiff to the Graf von Westerholt, a post that successive heads of his family had held since 1742 when the first Galland, a Huguenot, had emigrated to Westphalia from France. Galland began his aeronautical career at 17, flying gliders on the Borkenberge, a heath near Westerholt. In 1932, after a successful tour of gliding, Galland was admitted to an airline pilot training school in Brunswick. Joining the then-unofficial Luftwaffe, he was secretly trained in Italy in 1933. Although a crash during a training flight in Germany severely injured one eye, Galland managed to memorize an eye chart, pass a physical examination, and continue flying.

In 1937 Galland volunteered for service in the Cóndor Legion, the name for the German Volunteer Corps serving with Francisco Franco's forces in the Spanish civil war. He sailed from Hamburg with 370 other German soldiers, garbed in civilian clothes, masquerading as a Strength-Through-Joy tourist group. In Spain he was assigned to a fighter squadron near Vittoria, on the Northern Front. Galland wore the uniform of a Spanish Captain, customary with pilots of the Cóndor Legion. His baptism of fire came in June, 1937, when he engaged the Loyalist fighters in a Heinkel He-51 fighter. Although Messerschmitt Me-109 fighters had been introduced in Spain, a few flights still used the slower He-51s. These planes were no match for the Curtiss and Rata fighters of the Loyalists, and it was Galland's policy to avoid dogfights with the enemy; his activities were restricted to the strafing of ground targets. In Spain the Germans learned a good deal about ground-support operations. Galland firmly believes that the Russians, who used close support most effectively in World War II, copied the techniques first used by the Cóndor Legion.

Galland was recalled to Germany in the summer of 1938. He had flown over 300 sorties. The command of his flight was taken over by Werner Mölders, who was destined to become one of Germany's leading aces in World War II. Shortly before the end of the Spanish civil war Mölders became the youngest Wing commander in the Luftwaffe.

In Germany Galland was assigned to a desk job in the Air Ministry. His work consisted of working out directives for the organization and training of fighter pilots for ground-support operations. He detested the work and longed to return to flying. His first task was to organize and equip two new fighter groups. This was accomplished at record speed, but not without certain sacrifices in the quality of training and equipment. Many of the pilots were insufficiently instructed in the operation of their new aircraft and the planes themselves, old He-51s, Me-123s, and Me-45s, were hardly the last word in performance.

These new fighter groups were created to support the imminent occupation of the Czechoslovakian Sudetenland. On September 29, 1938, however, the Munich Pact eliminated the need for their immediate use.

On August 23, 1939, the German-Soviet Nonaggression Pact was signed. The invasion of Poland became only a matter of time. On September 1, 1939, Galland, who had joined a ground-support unit, was at an airfield at Reichenau in Silesia. In the darkness preceding dawn he took off with his squadron. World War II had begun.

The collapse of the Polish armies is now history. The Polish Air Force was destroyed on the ground. Communications were bombed out of existence. Transport was halted by strafing operations and the Polish troops were demoralized by the Ju-87 Stukas. In 27 days the war was over: the Polish Army capitulated. Warsaw was in flames. The Red Army had rumbled to the Bug River.

Galland, who had flown over two sorties a day during the campaign, was awarded the Iron Cross Second Class. On October 1, 1939, he was promoted to Captain. Shortly afterward he was reassigned to a fighter unit—the 27th Fighter Wing at Krefeld. The stage was set for battle in the West.

CONTENTS

1

The First

After the Blitzkrieg in the east followed the sit-down war in the west. It was a terrific nervous strain for all concerned. I commanded all three squadrons of our wing in turn for a fortnight while the respective commanders were on leave. There were continuous take-off alarms—false ones, of course, because the ominous siren wail or control tower orders that sent us zooming into the air, consuming considerable amounts of material and fuel, were usually based on errors or illusions. One radar report of a mass approach of enemy aircraft, for example, turned out to be a flight of birds. One day, however, in the lower Rhine area somebody was really shot down during one of these alarms. It was one of our planes, an FW-58 *Weihe*. She was piloted by the squadron leader. Nothing else happened.

We were delighted when at last the war of nerves changed into a shooting war. Behind the scenes at German army H.Q. there had so far been a confusing indecision. Originally Hitler wanted to turn westward soon after the conclusion of the Polish campaign, in order to have his rear free against the archenemy, which in spite of the temporary pact was after all the Soviet Union. The elder generals, however, led by Halder, Chief of the General Staff, and von Brauchitsch, Commander-in-Chief of the Army, were violently opposed to such a step. Facing the 85 French, 23 Belgian, and 8 English divisions were 62 German divisions ready for action, but these had also to guard the eastern frontier of the Reich. Halder and von Brauchitsch not only threatened to resign but were already seriously considering the idea of a *coup d'état*.

The postponement some dozen times of the German offensive on the Western front, between November, 1939, and May, 1940, was due not only to weather considerations, politics, personnel, armaments, etc., but also to chance. This could be qualified as lucky or unlucky according to the time and the point of view under consideration. On January 10, a Luftwaffe major flew from Münster to Bonn, carrying with him the entire plan of operations for the offensive in the west. In bad weather he was blown off his course and made a forced landing on Belgian soil. He did not manage to destroy the documents in time and they fell into the hands of the Allies. A new plan had to be worked out which after a further delay caused by bad weather was finally put into execution on May 10, 1940.

On the morning of May 12 when I flew in company with another plane over the front, our troops had already penetrated deep into Holland and Belgium. During those first days of the campaign in the west, together with the 8th Flying Corps we gave fighter cover to the German advance at Maastricht. As a Number 1 of our wing I was so overburdened with staff work, intelligence orders, changes of base, and conferences that I had literally to steal away on any sortie I wanted to make. What the others regarded merely as a daily duty was for me something I had to get to by tricks and ruses. On the third day of the campaign, May 12, 1940, I managed to score my first kill.

It is true to say that the first kill can influence the whole future career of a fighter pilot. Many to whom the first victory over the opponent has been long denied either by unfortunate circumstances or by bad luck can suffer from frustration or develop complexes they may never rid themselves of again. I was lucky. My first kill was child's play.

We did not see much of the English in those days. Occasionally we met a few Blenheims. The Belgians for the most flew antiquated Hurricanes, in which even more experienced pilots could have done little against our new ME-109E. We outstripped them in speed, in rate of climb, in armament, and above all in flying experience and training.

Therefore it was not particularly heroic when some five miles west of Liége my flight companion and I dove from an altitude of about 12,000 feet on a flight of eight Hurricanes flying 3000 feet below us. The route had been practiced innumerable times. The Hurricanes had not yet spotted us. I was neither excited nor did I feel any hunting fever. "Come on, defend yourself!" I thought as soon as I had one of the eight in my gun sight. I closed in more and more without being noticed. "Someone ought to warn him!" But that would have been even more stupid than the strange thoughts which ran through my head at that moment. I gave him my first burst from a distance which, considering the situation, was

2

still too great. I was dead on the target. The poor devil at last noticed what it was all about. He took rather clumsy avoiding action which brought him into the fire of my companion. The other seven Hurricanes made no effort to come to the aid of their comrade in distress, but made off in all directions. After a second attack my opponent spun down in spirals minus his rudder. Parts of the wings came off. Another burst would have been waste of ammunition. I immediately went after another of the scattered Hurricanes. This one tried to escape by diving, but I was soon on her tail at a distance of 100 yards. The Belgian did a half-roll and disappeared through a hole in the clouds. I did not lose track of him and attacked again from very close quarters. The plane zoomed for a second, stalled, and dove vertically to the ground from a height of only 1500 feet. During a patrol flight that afternoon I shot down my third opponent out of a formation of five Hurricanes near Tirlemont.

I took this all quite naturally, as a matter of course. There was nothing special about it. I had not felt any excitement and I was not even particularly elated by my success. That only came much later, when we had to deal with much tougher adversaries, when each relentless aerial combat was a question of "you or me." On that particular day I had something approaching a twinge of conscience. The congratulations of my superiors and my comrades left an odd taste in my mouth. An excellent weapon and luck had been on my side. To be successful the best fighter pilot needs both.

Two days later on May 14, the Dutch army capitulated. The Belgian army held out 14 days longer. The Belgian fortifications, which were known from World War I to be particularly hard nuts to crack, were taken in a few days, thanks to the extensive support given by the Luftwaffe, using Stukas and landing paratroops under fighter cover.

The taking of Fort Eben Emael gave the young German paratroopers the opportunity of causing a sensation by staging a classical example of a paratroop operation. This action, to which our wing gave cover, may give some indication of the very original tactics these troops employed. The sector where they were to be dropped lay deep inside Belgium, and the action could not be reconciled with the general plan of German operations, as far as this was known to us. What dropped from the transport planes and sailed down to earth were—dummies. On landing these invasion dummies set off a complicated mechanism which produced a good imitation of battle noises, The Belgians were deceived and flung consider-

3

able forces into the supposed danger area. Their absence from important defense positions was of great advantage to the attacking Germans.

The German army performed astonishing feats of war during their rapid advance. Again, as in Poland, the secret of these unbelievable successes was the cooperation between the fast-moving army and the Luftwaffe, where every move was carefully planned in advance and executed with precision.

Soon we pressed on to Charleville. Our aerodrome nestled among the foothills of the Ardennes. This was a very advantageous terrain for camouflage and defense, and this hidden position in the valley was once nearly fatal to my fellow pilot and myself. On May 19 as it was growing dark I shot down a Potez near the ground. This was during the so-called Operation *Abendsegen*. The French fighters used the twilight hour to strafe our advance routes.

The key to the success of the French campaign lay at Sedan. The breakthrough in the Ardennes by strong mechanized armored columns was one of the most daring and revolutionary and therefore successful ideas of the German war leaders during World War II. It emanated from Manstein, was rejected by von Brauchitsch and Halder, recognized by Hitler as excellent, and adopted against all opposition. Guderian put it into execution. Halder's original plan of operations was based on the Schlieffen plan of World War I and again entailed the risk that the offensive might come to a standstill on the Somme, while the strong right wing of the German army advancing through Belgium would meet the main force of the Allied army head on. The Allied General Staff believed as little as did Halder and von Brauchitsch in the possibility of a major breakthrough in the Ardennes. The unexpected success enabled the Germans to annihilate the superior forces of the enemy in rapid operations in which the army and the Luftwaffe combined.

The speed with which these operations were executed was a determining factor. The army therefore demanded energetic countermeasures against the French low-level attacks.

Following a suggestion of mine, the entire wing on a broad front combed the spearhead area at nightfall. Unfortunately without results. At last I spotted one of the French hedgehoppers. A wild chase began at the height of only a few feet. We raised the dust on the fields. The Frenchman flew with great skill, using all the cover the countryside offered. I had already hit him several times and shot away part of his tail. Nevertheless he still did his best to shake me off. I had to keep my eyes skinned because visibility was getting worse at each moment. The time was 21:45. Suddenly we were on top of a village. I still can see the church with its high steeple looming up in front of me. The Frenchman zoomed over the church. At that moment I got him, and he crashed on the far side of the village.

A few days later Milch came to visit us at Charleville, and decorated me with the Iron Cross 1st class in recognition of seven victories. I had only shot down French and Belgian planes. In addition to obsolete Hurricanes the pilots flew French types: Morane, Bloch, and Potez. Our ME-109E was technically superior to them all.

My first serious encounters with the R.A.F. took place during the battle of Dunkirk. Lord Gort with commendable skill rescued his defeated expeditionary force: with great loss of arms and equipment but nevertheless almost intact, together with 120,000 Frenchmen, making a total of 338,000 men, while the R.A.F. made a great and successful effort to provide air cover for the remarkable evacuation operation.

Although Dunkirk was a heavy blow for England and had a political rather than a military effect on her French ally, for Germany it was nothing like a total victory. Göring decided upon the destruction of the encircled British expeditionary force. After the victories over the Polish and French air forces he was more than ever a partisan of Douhet's Stuka idea. The army was amazed and alarmed by the irrevocable order given to the Panzer columns to halt their advance on Dunkirk. Some even thought that Hilter intended to spare the English foe in order to arrive at an honorable peace with Great Britain after the fall of France.

In addition to political grounds there were those of a military nature. In spite of the initial German successes Hitler still retained from World War I a great respect for his French antagonist. Therefore it was conceivable that he did not trust his own success. In any case he feared a threat to his armored divisions as they wheeled to the west and to the northwest from French forces, should they suddenly attack from the southeast—an intention Gamelin actually nursed although he was never able to carry it out. Hitler's knowledge of the battlefields of Flanders also originated from World War I. He regarded them as unsuitable for large-scale tank operations and saw in these fens a possible grave for his armored divisions. Ultimately it may have been Göring who was responsible for the fatal order to stop the advance. General Warlimont, Chief of Operations at German G.H.Q., in a

5

conversation with Captain Liddell Hart on this subject, informed him that he had heard Göring's reply to Hitler: "My Luftwaffe will complete the encirclement and will close the pocket at the coast from the air." Guderian remarked, "I believe it was Göring's vanity which caused Hitler to make this momentous decision."

In any case after this any sparing of the British enemy was out of the question. On the contrary, Göring made the greatest effort to solve this problem with his Luftwaffe. It merely proved that the strength of the German Luftwaffe was inadequate, especially in the difficult conditions for reinforcement created by the unexpectedly quick advance and against a determined and well-led enemy who was fighting with tenacity and skill. Dunkirk should have been an emphatic warning for the leaders of the German Luftwaffe.

On May 29 I flew a sortie with the staff flight in this sector. We spotted a formation of British Blenheim bombers below us. Two of them were shot down and crashed into the sea. The second one escaped me for some time by skillful evasive action, until low over the water my bullets ripped open her oil tank. She hit the water at a shallow angle and sank immediately. When I landed at Saint-Pol-sur-Mer, I found that my ME-109 was covered with oil. It was over Dunkirk too that I shot down my first British Spitfire.

During the embarkation of the British troops thick clouds of smoke lay over the battlefield. The huge stores of fuel and war material had been set on fire. As number 1A of our wing it was my duty to fly the aircraft on our commander's flank. Lieutenant Colonel Ibel had been a pilot in World War I. This gruff Bavarian was very popular with us. He was no longer a youngster, and the energy with which he tried to keep up to date with modern fighter aircraft and flying called for the greatest respect. I flew with him that day through the thick gray-black clouds of smoke, which rose to a great height, when suddenly a wing of Spitfires dove on us. We both saw them at the same time. Almost simultaneously we warned each other over the intercom. However we reacted differently, which normally should not have happened, since I was supposed to accompany the other aircraft. I saw my commander vanish in the smoke, and prayed that he might escape unscathed. I singled out the British pilot, blazing away with all I had, not seriously expecting much more than a strengthening of my slightly battered self-confidence. The Spits roared past me, tailing my commander, sure of their target. I could not find him again. He did not return with the

6

others to Saint-Pol, our base. We were already really worried when late at night he arrived on foot. The Spitfires caught him, but he had managed to get away with a lucky crash landing.

Dunkirk fell on July 4. The Dutch, Belgian, and British armies no longer existed. France stood alone, her Ninth Army beaten at Sedan. The First Army had capitulated at Lille. The German war machine rolled irresistibly through France. Gamelin was replaced by Weygand as commander-in-chief. Not the Oise, the Marne, nor the Seine proved to be a barrier capable of halting the German advance or of slowing it down in the least. The enemy air force was heavily damaged and greatly disorganized by the blows of the German Luftwaffe and the quick German advance. The extensive losses it had sustained began to make themselves felt. Resistance visibly decreased. We saw little of the R.A.F.

The death blow to the *Armée de l'Air* was supposed to be Operation Paula, large-scale attacks on the airfields and French aircraft factories in the sector of Paris, for which 300 bombers and Stukas were employed. We provided the air cover. The success of this undertaking is debatable. German and French reports agreed on the one point that 25 to 30 German planes were lost. Anyhow Operation Paula was the single attempt at strategic air warfare during the French campaign.

On June 3 I had just shot down an unidentified aircraft similar to a Curtiss, when we—I was flying with Captain Ankum-Frank—encountered two flights of Moranes. There was an incredible dogfight. The only thing to do was to attack first and then try to escape as best we could: I closed in on the tail-end plane and banked still steeper! The fellow flew well, but his aircraft was inferior to mine. At last, from a short distance, I managed to get in a broadside on a climbing turn. He burst into flame. I avoided him only by inches. I bent a blade on my propeller and the right astern against his wing. My aerial was shaved off: it had been about three feet long. The Morane spun down in flames and crashed into a forest not far from Meaux, north of Paris. No time to lose! I closed in on the next one! Well riddled, she went vertically down with a black smoke trail. I could not observe the crash because the rest of the Moranes were harassing me, so I could not register this kill. It would have been my thirteenth.

We entered Paris on June 14 without a shot being fired. German jack boots stamped down the Champs-Elysées. A guard of honor of the German Wehrmacht drew up at the grave of the unknown soldier. In the *bôites* of Montmartre

7

appeared signs *Man Spricht Deutsch.* The government had fled to Bordeaux. Marshal Pétain become president and proposed armistice on June 16.

Quite unexpectedly, as so often happens in the service, I was transferred to the 26th Fighter Group, *Schlageter,* before the French campaign was finished. I was to take over the command of the 3rd Squadron, stationed on a rather God forsaken and primitive airfield. It was a hot summer day when I arrived. I walked across the runway in my flying kit. No flags had been put out to welcome me. A few of the ground crew were standing by an old-fashioned well. I had a murderous thirst and a great need for a wash. I asked very politely if it were possible to get a pail of water. "Certainly," was the reply, "the whole well's full, only you'll have to wind it up yourself." The men could never have guessed that I was their new commander! I spared them the shock and wound up my pail of water as I had been told. This, by the way, was a better introduction to my new squadron than the fact that I went up the same afternoon and returned with a bag of two.

On June 22, 43 days after the start of the armed conflict, Marshal Pétain signed the truce in the Forest of Compiègne.

Our last action station was Villacoublay, which because of its closeness to Paris became quite a favorite.

After the signing of the truce our orders were, "Home to the Reich," and we were transferred to München-Gladbach to be refitted. Our losses in men and material had been small. Naturally I took every opportunity to go and see my parents, for my home was only a few flying minutes' time away. Then came a surprise transfer order to Döberitz. Was another Orlog about to start? No, we were to screen a state function at which Hitler in his well-known speech made the peace offer to England. One bomb on the Kroll Opera House would actually have eliminated the entire German High Command at one fell swoop, so the precaution seemed well justified. At that time we were still prepared to support Göring's claim: "My name is not Göring if an enemy aircraft is ever seen over Germany!" Later these words were to be quoted with steadily increasing bitterness.

After an investiture of army commanders at the Kroll Opera House, a wave of promotion ran through the entire force. It reached me on July 18, 1940, when I was made a major. At first my position and duties were unchanged. From Döberitz we returned to München-Gladbach.

On August 1, when Marshal Kesselring pinned the Knight's Cross on my tunic after my seventeenth kill and many completed low-level attacks, we were already stationed on the military airfields in the Pas de Calais area. Opposite lay the English coast, upon which a few days later the German Blitz was going to be unleashed.

Kesselring had his advanced base at Cap Gris Nez. During the investiture two fighter planes flew over at great height. "What are those?" he asked me. "Spitfires, Herr General-feldmarshal," I replied. He laughed. "The first to congratulate you . . ."

2

The Battle of Britain Starts

The strategic necessity for those operations which increased dramatically until the autumn and petered out in the winter of 1940-41, known in the history of the war as the "Battle of Britain," resulted from the political situation, in other words from the impossibility of reaching an agreement with England to put a stop to the war. The aims of these operations were:

1. The blockade of the British Isles in cooperation with the navy. Attacks on ports and shipping; mining of sea lanes and harbor entrances.

2. The achievement of air supremacy as a preliminary to the invasion (Operation Sea Lion).

3. Annihilation of England by total air warfare.

In retrospect one can state that the German Luftwaffe, despite its numerical strength and its technical equipment at the time, was not in the position to fulfill even one of the above-mentioned tasks.

Against the 2500 available German air force planes, according to German calculations, Britain disposed of about 3600 war planes, only 600 of which were fighter aircraft. Our numerical inferiority was roughly balanced by our technical superiority. This—at least with regard to the fighter force— was not necessarily the result of farsighted planning. The ME-109 was at the time the best fighter plane in the world. It was not only superior to all enemy types between 1935 and 1940 but was also a pioneer and prototype for international fighter construction. The ME-109 did not result from demands made by aerial warfare. On the contrary, it was a gift from the ingenious designer Messerschmitt, which was at first looked upon with great distrust and was nearly turned down altogether. It was put into mass production far too late. Had this stage been reached during the first two years of the war, it would have given the Germans absolute supremacy in the air.

The old fighter pilots from World War I, who were now sitting "at the joy stick" of the supreme command of the Luftwaffe, with Göring at their head, had a compulsory pause of 15 years behind them, during which they had probably lost contact with the rapid development of aviation. They were stuck on the idea that maneuverability in banking was primarily the determining factor in air combat. The ME-109 had, of course, much too high a stress per wing area and too great a speed to have such abilities. They could not or simply would not see that for modern fighter aircraft the tight turn as a form of aerial combat represented the exception, and further, that it was quite possible to see, shoot, and fight from an enclosed cockpit. In addition to other erroneous concepts it was feared that the higher take-off and landing speed of the ME-109 would set insoluble aviation problems. Of course all this was proved to be false in practice. Today this sounds almost like a legend from the stone age of aviation. However all these shortcomings were most painful realities at the time. They added decisively to the fact that the German fighter production started very sluggishly and only reached its peak when the war was practically lost. In the beginning of 1940 the monthly production figure for ME-109 fighters was approximately 125. While Udet was Chief of Aircraft Production this figure exceeded 375 and sank again to 250 at the beginning of 1942. Milch increased it to 1000 in 1943, and under Speer the peak was reached with a monthly production of 2500 fighters. That was in autumn, 1944!

At the end of 1944, therefore, we had a fighter production about 20 times higher that it had been at the time when the Luftwaffe entered the Battle of Britain. Had the fighter production of the year 1944 been reached in 1940, or even in 1941, the Luftwaffe would have never lost air supremacy and the tide of the war would have taken an entirely different course. And this production figure could have been reached! Neither technical reasons nor shortage of raw materials prevented it. Nor was it a question of the men who were entrusted at different times with the arming of the German air force. It was the fundamental ideology of the German leadership with regard to aerial warfare, about which some further explanation is needed.

Hitler's strategical thoughts were exclusively directed toward the offensive. His initial successes confirmed that he had been right, and undoubtedly strengthened his opinion still further. With regard to aerial warfare, therefore, the Stuka idea must have had a fascination for him. The idea of anni-

11

hilating the enemy from the air, of stifling any resistance by terrific bombing, approached his concept of the Blitzkrieg. The enemy had to be beaten, and all his means for a possible counteroffensive must be destroyed, before one was compelled one day to go over to the defensive. The same ideas were held by the first Luftwaffe Chief of Staff, General Wever, who up to then had been an army officer. He was killed in a crash during the summer of 1936. He was considered to be the German Douhet or Rougeron. In agreement with Hitler's and Göring's ideas he definitely stressed the bomber. The fighters played a subordinate role from the start. They were, so to speak, only tolerated as a necessary evil, a concession to the unpopular act of defense. The strategic concept current in Germany was to regard the Luftwaffe as an instrument of attack. Therefore bombers were needed first of all. If, contrary to all expectations, these bombers could not achieve air supremacy—according to Douhet this was to be done by annihilating the enemy air force on the ground by surprise attacks—then from sheer necessity the bomber attacks had to be flown with fighter cover. Yet allowance for this was made unwillingly, and in the case of eventuality, because the operational radius of the bomber—already not very convincing—would have been still further restricted and would have taken away the character of the bomber arm, which after all was to be a strategic and, for the war, decisive means of attack.

Thus it is no wonder that of the 1491 war planes produced in 1939, according to the official figures of the German quartermaster, there were only 449 fighter planes, i.e., only about a third. This ratio became even more unfavorable to the fighters in the following year, 1940. Out of 6618 aircraft, only a quarter were fighters, i.e., 1693. Aggravating, too, was the fact that not only the production side of the fighter air arm was pushed into the background but also questions of personnel. The nucleus of men Göring had available for the reconstruction of the Luftwaffe in 1933 consisted of about 300 fighter and a few dozen reconnaissance pilots. These were in part remnants from World War I, incorporated into the Secret Reichswehr, and in part newly trained men. At the outset bomber pilots had to be furnished from this number. When the Stuka units were formed, the strength of fighter pilots was again drained. From 1938 onward Göring started to create "destroyer" units, equipped with the twin-engined ME-110, which, having a wider range, could penetrate much deeper into enemy territory. These units were supposed to become "the operational fighter elite of the Luftwaffe." Once more the best pilots of the fighter arm were lost to them.

The JU-87 Stuka did not prove itself in the Battle of Britain, although no one can dispute its value especially for army support to land operation as given on the Eastern front in World War II.

The probability of hitting the target and the effect of the bombs themselves were highly overrated. Although the Stuka was most suitable for attacking vulnerable pinpointed targets such as ships, railway junctions, bridges, or power stations, it was soon proved that in order to achieve a lasting effect, saturation "carpet bombing" with bombs released from close formations in horizontal high-altitude attacks was much preferable. From the point of view of the defense it possessed this considerable shortcoming: the attacking Stukas had to leave their formation and descend low into the range of ground defenses, thus making a most vulnerable target for AA guns and enemy fighters. Their losses during the course of the Battle of Britain became catastrophic both on account of this and because of their incredibly low speed. They had to be taken out of the battle. I shall discuss this later in detail.

A decisive factor for the current prejudice against the fighter arm inside the German Luftwaffe lay in the development of German aircraft construction. During the years of 1935-36 the designers produced two technically first-class twin-engined bomber aircraft, the DO-17 and the HE-111. They were even faster than the AR-65, AR-68, and HE-51 fighters. When it was already believed that the fighter should play a secondary role according to the ideas of air strategy prevailing among the German High Command, this idea was only reinforced by the state of the technical development in Germany. What good could fighter protection be to the bombers if the accompanying fighters could not even keep up with them? Fighter aircraft simply did not fit into the picture of the strategical air arm, but were looked upon as tactical weapons. It was believed that their place was local air defense, the winning of air superiority over the front, or if necessary to assist the army in land operations in conjunction with ground support planes. When the German fighter pilots were given strategical tasks during the course of the Battle of Britain, there was surprise that they were not equal to the task, and people spoke of a "letdown."

The soldier of today is impelled more and more to become a mechanic, an engineer, subordinated to the technics and mechanization of modern warfare. One day the fighter pilot guided from the ground will chase, at supersonic speed, the atom-bomb carrier for scores of miles high up in the stratosphere. But science must not become an aim in itself. Only the spirit of attack borne in a brave heart will bring a success to any fighter aircraft, no matter how highly developed it may be.

The first year of the war confirmed to a certain degree the strategical concept of the German Luftwaffe, in which the fighter arm represented a *quantité négligeable*. In Poland as well as in France a greater part of the enemy air force had been destroyed on the ground, a minor part only in the air. Meanwhile it had become obvious that the Luftwaffe would not have a walk-over against the R.A.F. At the opening of the battle it showed, as it had done previously during the air battles of the French campaign, that the English had a fighter arm which was numerically stronger and better controlled because of their lead in the field of radar. With regard to crews and fighting spirit it was absolutely first class.

Already in the second phase of the Battle of Britain, therefore, a task was allotted to the German fighters that exceeded the operational limits fixed for it inside the German Luftwaffe. They were to defeat the British fighters in large-scale battles in order to win the total air supremacy necessary for the bombers which were to follow up the attack.

I should not care to say which one of the three following strategic aims was responsible for the order to gain air supremacy: the total blockade of the island, the invasion, or the defeat of England according to Douhet concepts. I rather doubt if the General Staff knew themselves, because during the course of the Battle of Britain the stress was put on all of them in turn.

Such an operation is rarely successful and it was quite alien to the usual German methods. The only answer I can find is that taken all in all the High Command at this period had no clear plans for the further pursuit of the war. Hitler's aim as before still lay in the east. The war against England was for him merely a necessary evil, with which he had to cope somehow—just how, he was not quite sure.

In the High Command there were enough voices to reject an attack on England, if for no other reason than because in their opinion even an occupation of England would never persuade the British Empire to terminate the war, and because the defense of the entire Continent, including the British Isles against Anglo-American air and sea power, would have been impossible for any length of time.

Another remarkable point of view was that the impending air offensive against England would reveal to the enemy the limitations and weaknesses of the German Luftwaffe and thus rob Germany of the strongest military-political trump she then held.

Instead of laying the cards on the table, it would perhaps have been better to continue to attack England on the periphery and to cut off one of her most important lifelines by closing the Mediterranean at the Strait of Gibraltar and at the Suez Canal. Such an operation, concentrated swiftly on a weak link of the enemy, should have succeeded, and the actual strength or weakness of the Luftwaffe would not thereby have been revealed. Such an operation would certainly have had a great influence on the further course of the war.

Hitler decided differently. In this he was mainly supported by Göring who, dismissing the qualms of individual commanders of the army and other branches of the forces, confronted Hitler once more with his classic argument: "Then I will do it with my air force."

During the midsummer weeks in 1940 the 2nd and 3rd Air Fleets were concentrated on the Channel coast. My squadron, the 3rd JG 26, was stationed on a well-camouflaged airfield near Guines. The commander of the JG 26 Wing was Major Handrick. This wing was subordinated to Jafu 2 under the command of von Döring, who in turn was under the 2nd Flying Corps (Lörzer), attached to the 2nd Air Fleet (Kesselring.) The units of the 3rd Air Fleet in Cherbourg and Le Havre sectors were commanded by Sperrle. The concentration of these forces incidentally took place contrary to all expectations without interference from enemy aircraft. The British seemed to be concentrating their forces on defense.

Establishing our aircraft in these positions brought to an end the first phase of the Battle of Britain on July 24, 1940. The action of the Luftwaffe was not directed against the Navy and merchant shipping. Soon after the beginning of the war isolated attacks without fighter support were made from northwest Germany, and from Norway after the occupation of that country, on British warships and the northern England ports. For these actions the twin-engined dive bomber JU-88 was particularly suitable but was not available in sufficient numbers. Its successes were limited. The sensational sinking of the aircraft carrier *Ark Royal* turned out to be an error caused by a misread report, which was unfortunately found out only after the alleged feat had been considerably exploited by propaganda. On Hitler's special orders we were not allowed to attack the battleship *Repulse* which was lying in a dry dock because at that time he was still anxious to avoid in all circumstances the dropping of bombs on English

15

soil. The Luftwaffe were to concentrate exclusively on military and maritime targets. Simultaneously intensive reconnaissance supplied the information for essential military objectives in the Britsh Isles.

With the opening of the Western Campaign the attack by the Luftwaffe on British merchant shipping was intensified. It acted in cooperation with the German navy, hoping to cut off the supply lines for the British troops, which had now entered into a shooting war with Germany. Neither the bombing attacks, with or without fighter cover against British supply ships, mainly off the east coast of England, nor the mining of ports brought any telling success. The forces employed were too small, as the bulk of the Luftwaffe was still tied down in the French campaign.

When this was brought to a victorious end, the first tentative plans for an invasion of England, the so-called Operation Sea Lion, were prepared. They received only dilatory attention as long as the English reply to Hitler's last peace offer of July 19, 1940, was still in abeyance.

The army, upon which the task of invasion would fall, had demanded from the navy the provision of the necessary shipping space, as well as the landing and supply craft. The navy on the other hand demanded from the air force the protection of the invasion fleet against air attacks as well as an air umbrella, implying air supremacy for the execution of the landing operations. Thus the army and the navy made their participation in this undertaking—to which for a variety of reasons they adopted a skeptical attitude—dependent on prerequisites which only the air force could fulfill. Added to the many doubts and objections of the generals and admirals there arose fundamental strategical considerations with the framework of the war leadership, which prompted Jodl to warn Hitler of the great risk of an invasion. General Warlimont said to Liddell Hart, "Hitler was only too willing to accept these objections." According to the same source General Blumentritt defined the current opinions held in army circles as follows: "We looked upon the whole thing as being a kind of war game." For the air force and especially for the fighter arm it became anything but a game. To the air force fell the main responsibility of parting the way for Operation Sea Lion. This order for preparation was adhered to long after the actual Battle of Britain was over. The Sea Lion, which at the second phase of the Battle of Britain, July 24, 1940, was ready to pounce over the Channel, was never let loose. The beast was finally recalled by Hitler on September 17, 1940, and died in a pigeonhole in the archives of the General Staff.

The second phase of the Battle of Britain, lasting from July 24 to August 8, 1940, was essentially a fighter battle. On its opening day I was with my squadron for the first time in action over England. Over the Thames Estuary we got involved in a heavy scrap with the Spitfires, which were screening a convoy. Together with the staff flight I selected one formation as our prey. We made a surprise attack from a favorably higher altitude. I glued myself to the tail of the plane flying outside on the left flank. During a right-handed turn I managed to get in a long burst. The Spitfire went down almost vertically. I followed it until the cockpit cover came flying toward me and the pilot baled out. I followed him down until he crashed into the water. His parachute had failed to open.

The modern Vickers Supermarine Spitfires were slower than our planes by about 10 to 15 mph but could perform steeper and tighter turns. The older Hawker Hurricane which was at that time still frequently used by the English compared badly with our ME-109 as regards speed and rate of climb. Our armament and ammunition were also undoubtedly better. Another advantage was that our engines had injection pumps instead of the carburetors used by the British, and therefore they did not conk out through lack of acceleration in critical moments during combat. The British fighters usually tried to shake off pursuit by a half-roll or half-roll on top of a loop, while we simply went straight for them, with wide-open throttle and eyes bulging out of our sockets.

During this first action we lost two aircraft. That was bad, although at the same time we had three confirmed kills. We were no longer in doubt that the R.A.F. would prove a most formidable opponent.

3

A Battle for Life and Death

*The German fighter squadrons on the Channel were in con-*tinuous action from then on. Two or three sorties daily was the rule and the briefing read: "Free chase over southeast England." The physical as well as the mental strain on the pilots was considerable. The ground personnel and the planes themselves were taxed to the limit.

After the take-off the formation used to assemble in the coastal area, still over land, at an altitude of 15,000 to 18,000 feet, in order to climb to between 21,000 and 24,000 feet when crossing the English coast. In the attempt to outclimb the opponent our dogfights occurred at ever-increasing altitudes. My highest combat at that time took place at 25,000 feet. But at 27,000 feet and more—close to the lower limits of the stratosphere—one could usually see the vapor trails of German or English fighters.

It used to take us roughly half an hour from take-off to crossing the English coast at the narrowest point of the Channel. Having a tactical flying time of only 80 minutes, we therefore had about 20 minutes to complete our task. This fact limited the distance of penetration. German fighter squadrons based on the Pas de Calais and on the Cotentin peninsula could barely cover the southeastern parts of the British Isles. Circles drawn from these two bases at an operational range of 125 miles overlapped approximately in the London area. Everything beyond was practically out of our reach. This was the most acute weakness of our offensive. An operating radius of 125 miles was sufficient for local defense, but not enough for such tasks as were now demanded of us.

In the Battle of Britain a powerful air force was to be used strategically on a big scale for the first time in the history of warfare. The bomber is the vehicle of strategic air warfare. It is therefore amazing that the opening of the battle was not allotted to them but to fighters, which previously had only been regarded as a tactical weapon. It was assumed that the

18

appearance of German fighter squadrons over England would draw the British fighters into the area within our range where they would be destroyed, beaten, or at least decimated in large-scale air battles. Although only a small portion of the English homeland was covered by the operational range of our fighters, it was hoped in this way to achieve air supremacy, or at least sufficient superiority in the air over the whole of the British Isles, to expose it to the attack of the German bomber force.

Things turned out differently. Our fighter formations took off. The first air battles took place as expected and according to plan. Due to the German superiority these attacks, had they been continued, would certainly have achieved the attempted goal, but the English fighters were recalled from this area long before this goal was reached. The weakened squadrons of the R.A.F. left their bases near the coast and used them only for emergency landings or to refuel. They were concentrated in a belt around London in readiness for our bomber attacks. Thus they evaded the attack *in* the air in order to encounter more effectively the attack *from* the air, which would logically follow. The German fighters found themselves in a similar predicament to a dog on a chain who wants to attack the foe but cannot harm him, because of the limitation of his chain.

As long as the enemy kept well back, our task could not be accomplished. Rather aptly we called the few bombers and Stukas, which from now onward accompanied our roving expeditions, "decoy ducks." Only with bombers was the war from the air over England a possibility, and to prevent such a development was the decisive aim of the British Command. To this end the R.A.F. called out the fighters again, but the German hope of attracting them into annihilating combats was never realized.

In the opening encounters the English were at a considerable disadvantage because of their close formation. Since the Spanish civil war we had introduced the wide-open combat formation in which great intervals were kept between the smaller single formations and groups, each of which flew at a different altitude. This offered a number of valuable advantages: greater air coverage; relief for the individual pilot who could now concentrate more on the enemy than on keeping formation; freedom of initiative right down to the smallest unit without loss of collective strength; reduced vulnerability, as compared to close formation; and, most important of all, better vision. The first rule of all air combat is to see the opponent first. Like the hunter who stalks his prey and maneuvers himself unnoticed into the most favorable position for the kill, the fighter in the opening of a dogfight must detect the opponent as early as possible in order to attain a superior position for the attack. The British quickly realized the superiority of our combat formation and readjusted their own. At first they introduced the so-called "Charlies": two flanking planes following in the rear of the main formation, flying slightly higher and further out, on a weaving course. Finally they adopted our combat formation entirely. Since then, without any fundamental changes, it has been accepted throughout the world. Werner Mölders was greatly responsible for these developments.

From the very beginning the English had an extraordinary advantage which we could never overcome throughout the entire war: radar and fighter control. For us and for our Command this was a surprise and a very bitter one. England possessed a closely knit radar network conforming to the highest technical standards of the day, which provided Fighter Command with the most detailed data imaginable. Thus the British fighter was guided all the way from take-off to his correct position for attack on the German formations.

We had nothing of the kind. In the application of radiolocation technique the enemy was far in advance of us. It was not that British science and technics were superior. On the contrary, the first success of radar must be recorded on the German side. On December 18, after the R.A.F. had previously tried in vain to attack Wilhelmshaven on September 4, 1939—the day following the British declaration of war—a British bomber formation approached the German Bight, making for the same target. An experimental Freya radar set sighted their approach in time for German fighters to intercept and practically destroy the enemy task force which flew without fighter protection; the attack was defeated. After this defensive success thanks to timely radio location, the British bombers never returned without fighter protection.

There could be no more singular proof of the importance of high-frequency technique for defense against air attacks. However, since the German Command was predominantly occupied with offensive plans, not enough attention was given to this technique. The possibility of an Allied air attack on the Reich was at the time unthinkable. For the time being we were content to erect a few Freya sets along the German and later along the Dutch, Belgian, and French coast; they had a range of 75 miles but gave no altitude reading.

20

Under the serious threat for England arising from the German victory in France—no one described it more forcefully than Churchill in his memoirs—the British Command concentrated desperately on the development and perfection of radar. The success was outstanding. Our planes were already detected over the Pas de Calais while they were still assembling, and were never allowed to escape the radar eye. Each of our movements was projected almost faultlessly on the screens in the British fighter control centers, and as a result Fighter Command was able to direct their forces to the most favorable position at the most propitious time.

In battle we had to rely on our own human eyes. The British fighter pilots could depend on the radar eye, which was far more reliable and reached many times further. When we made contact with the enemy our briefings were already three hours old, the British only as many seconds old—the time it took to assess the latest position by means of radar to the transmission of attacking orders from Fighter Control to the already-airborne force.

Of further outstanding advantage to the English was the fact that our attacks, especially those of the bombers, were of sheer necessity directed against the central concentration of the British defense. We were not in a position to seek out soft spots in this defense or to change our approaches and to attack now from this direction, now from that, as the Allies did later in their air offensive against the Reich. For us there was only a frontal attack against the superbly organized defense of the British Isles, conducted with great determination.

Added to this, the R.A.F. was fighting over its own country. Pilots who had baled out could go into action again almost immediately, whereas ours were taken prisoner. Damaged English planes could sometimes still reach their base or make an emergency landing, while for us engine trouble or fuel shortage could mean a total loss.

Morale too and the emotions played a great part. The desperate seriousness of the situation apparently aroused all the energies of this hardy and historically conscious people, whose arms in consequence were directed toward one goal: to repulse the German invaders at any price!

Thus, during the first weeks of our air offensive it was apparent that in spite of our good bag of enemy planes, this was not the way to achieve our air superiority. The German Command, which in any case lacked clarity in its aims, grew more uncertain. The order came for low-level attacks on English fighter bases. This was a difficult and costly undertaking. The sites were well protected by a host of heavy and light ack-ack guns. We also met with a novel defense: aerial cables, fired by rockets during our attack, which descended slowly on parachutes, protecting the lower air regions above the targets. The planes themselves were magnificently camouflaged, so that our efforts were out of proportion to the number of effectively destroyed enemy planes.

During this time we provided fighter cover for the attacks by bomber formations and Stukas on shipping and convoys. We could not miss the splendid opportunity of continuously attacking the convoys, so important to Britain's subsistence, under the protection of the German fighter squadrons stationed on the channel coast. Here the slow speed of the JU-87 turned out to be a great drawback. Due to the speed-reducing effect of the externally suspended bomb load she only reached 150 mph when diving. As the required altitude for the dive was between 10,000 and 15,000 feet these Stukas attracted Spitfires and Hurricanes as honey attracts flies. The necessary fighter protection for such sorties was considerable, and the task of the pilots was fraught with great difficulties. The English soon realized that the Stukas, once they peeled out of formation to dive singly onto their targets, were practically defenseless until they had reassembled. We made numerous attempts to counteract this shortcoming. With our greater speed it was impossible to follow the Stukas into the dive without a dive-brake. Equally impossible was the idea of providing fighter cover on all different levels between the start of the dive and the pull-out. The losses of JU-87s from sortie to sortie rose.

We fighter pilots were blamed. The Stuka was regarded as the egg of Columbus by the German Air Command. It was not born in the eyrie of the German Eagle, for Udet and other experts had brought it over from the New World. This type had been developed in the U.S.A. as a small, handy light bomber suitable for pinpoint attacks. The idea of the Stuka was taken up in Germany with enthusiasm because it promised the greatest success with a minimum expenditure of material and manpower. Single precision attacks on pinpointed targets instead of mass attacks on large areas became the motto of the German bomber strategy. The greatest effect was to be achieved with the smallest expenditure of material. This demand was imperative owing to the situation of German raw materials—a situation which would became dangerous in the event of a long war. Major General Jeschonnek, then Luftwaffe Chief of Staff, was a keen champion of this idea. In spring, 1939, he said to his colleagues of the Luftwaffe, "We must save more: not money but material."

Only the Stuka seemed to solve this problem. Thus originated the JU-87, which had contributed considerably to the successful Blitzkrieg in Poland and France, although in actual fact it encountered little opposition. Right until the end of the war it proved repeatedly its value as a tactical weapon in support of an army, especially against tanks. In the Battle of Britain it proved disastrous.

This did not deter the German Command from continuing with the idea of the Stuka. The accompanying fighter pilots were blamed for the painfully high losses, although the limitations of the Stuka in action were obvious enough in the Battle of Britain. The fighter pilots were blamed, not the designers who continued to base their entire production of medium and heavy bombers on the Stuka idea. They not only went on to produce a twin-engined Stuka, the JU-88, and the DO-217, but demanded full diving performance from all subsequent types of bombers, including the four-engined HE-177, which entailed high stability, the fitting of divebrakes, automatic pull-out apparatus, Stuka target-sighters, etc. Because of this blockheadedness—one cannot call it anything else—the development and production of the German long-range bomber was seriously delayed. To the claim that at the beginning of the war, four-engined bombers operating 500 miles to the west of Ireland accounted for no less than half the shipping losses in the North Atlantic, the famous North American air force expert P. de Seversky, replied, "Luckily Hitler allowed himself to be talked out of the idea of long-range bombers . . ." He should have added, ". . . and got all excited about the strategic Stuka idea." The realization of this idea was to be accomplished by the HE-177. I shall refer later to this problem.

The next phase starting on August 8, was the third phase in the Battle of Britain and had several objects in view. When the fighter force failed to achieve air supremacy, the bomber force was ordered to attack British fighter bases and to bomb aircraft and motor industries. While in particular Portsmouth, Portland, and numerous targets on the British east coast were bombed, the free chase of the fighters continued.

The bombing attacks on the British fighter bases did not achieve the expected success. Apart from the fact that it was purely coincidental if the respective fighter squadrons were grounded at the time of the attack, the quantity of bombs dropped on each target was by no means sufficient. Runways and buildings were usually only slightly damaged and could generally be repaired overnight. At Luftwaffe H.Q., however, somebody took the reports of the bomber or Stuka squadrons in one hand and a thick blue pencil in the other and crossed the squadron or base in question off the tactical map. It did not exist any more—in any case not on paper. Reports of fighter and other pilots regarding numbers of shot-down enemy planes were also exaggerated as happens on both sides during large-scale air battles. Thus it came about that one day according to the calculations in Berlin there were no more British fighters, while we were supposed to have achieved a certain superiority; but we were far from achieving air supremacy. One of the main reasons for this was the short range of the ME-109, allowing only little penetration and in consequence reducing the range of the bombers.

With additional fuel tanks, which could be released and discarded after use, as employed later by both sides and which we had already tried successfully in Spain, our range could have been extended by 125 to 200 miles. At that time this would have been just the decisive extension of our penetration. As it was, we ran daily into the British defenses, breaking through now and then, with considerable loss to ourselves, without substantially approaching our final goal.

Failure to achieve any noticeable success, constantly changing orders betraying lack of purpose, and obvious misjudgment of the situation by the Command, and unjustified accusations had a most demoralizing effect on us fighter pilots, who were already overtaxed by physical and mental strain. We complained of the leadership, the bombers, the Stukas, and were dissatisfied with ourselves. We saw one comrade after the other, old and tested brothers in combat, vanish from our ranks. Not a day passed without a place remaining empty at the mess table. New faces appeared, became familiar, until one day these too would disappear, shot down in the Battle of Britain.

In those days I often met my younger brother Wilhelm, who was an aide-de-camp in an AA training camp also on the Channel coast. The youngest of the family, Paul, was training as a fighter pilot. Fritz, the eldest, contemplated a changeover from AA to fighters and Wilhelm too soon decided to join us. In the end all four of us were fighter pilots and three of us often flew together in one squadron. At that time I expressed my conviction to Wilhelm quite openly that things could not go on much longer as they were. You could count on your fingers when your turn would come. The logic

24

of the theory of probabilities showed us incontestably that one's number was up after a certain amount of sorties. For some it was sooner, for some later.

The reproaches from higher quarters became more unbearable. We had the impression that, whatever we did, we were bound to be in the wrong. Fighter protection created many problems which had to be solved in action. As in Spain, the bomber pilots preferred close screening in which their formation was surrounded by pairs of fighters pursuing a zigzag course. Obviously the proximity and the visible presence of the protective fighters, gave the bomber pilots a greater sense of security. However, this was a faulty conclusion, because a fighter can only carry out this purely defensive task by taking the initiative in the offensive. He must never wait until he is attacked because he then loses the chance of acting. The fighter must seek battle in the air, must find his opponent, attack him, and shoot him down. The bomber must avoid such fights and he has to act defensively, in order to fulfill his task: war from the air. In cooperation between bomber and fighter, these two fundamentally different mentalities obviously clash. The words of Richthofen expressed during World War I, summarizing the task of the fighters, often came to our lips. Fundamentally they are still valid today. "The fighter pilots have to rove in the area allotted to them in any way they like, and when they spot an enemy they attack and shoot him down; anything else is rubbish."

We fighter pilots certainly preferred the "free chase during the approach and over the target area." This in fact gives the greatest relief and the best protection for the bomber force, although not perhaps a direct sense of security. A compromise between these two possibilities was the "extended protection," in which the fighters still flew in visible contact with the bomber force but were allowed to attack any enemy fighter which drew near to the main force.

In addition to this we introduced "Fighter reception": fighter squadrons or wings were sometimes sent right up to the English coast to meet the often broken-up and battered formations on their return journey, to protect them from pursuing enemy fighters. The Air Sea Rescue Service was carried out with boats and flying boats under fighter protection, with the aim of saving parachuted airmen or crews from ditched aircraft. This service was a boon, for it rescued many German and English pilots, even from the Thames Estuary.

It was of great interest to me after the war, in conversation with British or American airmen, to discover that they had been troubled with identical problems regarding fighter protection.

What we went through in 1940 they experienced in the years 1943 to 1945 during the large-scale daylight raids on the Reich. The points of view expressed by fighter pilots as well as by bomber pilots of both sides were identical.

After something like a month of action on the Channel coast neither the situation nor our mood was particularly rosy. It was then that I was ordered to attend a war conference at Karin Hall. I flew to Berlin and was taken from there by a staff car to Göring's estate in the most beautiful part of the March of Brandenburg. Germany presented a picture of peaceful serenity. The war had hardly made any difference to the daily life at home. Those who were not yet called up earned good money. Women of servicemen received generous subsidies. Money circulated freely. Theatres, cinemas, and places of amusement were crowded. No, the war had not even touched the outer husk of German life.

Was one to take this as a bad or a good omen? The I-could-not-care-less attitude at home and the general lack of interest in the war did not please me. I had come straight out of a battle for life and death, the brunt of which so far had been borne by the fighter force. Naturally we had no insight into the ramifications of this war, but we guessed fairly accurately that the battle we were fighting on the Channel was of decisive importance to the continuance and the final outcome of the struggle. We were aware that it needed a tremendous concentration of strength in order to emerge victoriously, and we felt that our own strength was being overtaxed. The colossus of World War II seemed to be like a pyramid turned upside down, balancing on its apex, not knowing which way to lean. And for the moment the whole burden of the war rested on the few hundred German fighter pilots on the Channel coast. Did not their number sink into insignificance, like a dot, in comparison with the millions of men under arms in Germany? Emotions are often illogical. Naturally, neither the army divisions that led a peaceful life in occupied territories or in garrison at home, nor those happy and carefree crowds bent on amusement could have been of any help to us in the fight against the R.A.F. And yet this contrast had a deeply depressing effect on me.

The frame of mind of those in the High Command and other offices was optimistic. In the cultured, luxurious atmosphere of Karin Hall one felt out of place with one's small troubles and scruples amongst all the self-assured, confident,

26

and yet both understanding and helpful generals and General Staff officers. After a general discussion of the situation Göring drew Mölders and me into a lengthy conversation. It opened with our being invested with the gold Pilot Medal with jewels and by an appreciation of our successes. But after this ceremony the Reichsmarshal let us know quite plainly that he was not satisfied to date with the performance of the fighter force and particularly not with the execution of fighter protection. He energetically called for greater efforts. He also had his own plan for reviving the alleged lack of aggression on the part of the fighters. To this end he wanted to introduce radically younger blood into the command of the fighter force.

At the beginning of the war all commanding officers were elderly men who had already seen service in World War I. During the western offensive it had already been obvious that they were neither physically nor mentally equal to the high demands aviation made upon them. Therefore many of them had been released. As a next step Göring wanted to put young and successful pilots in command of the fighter squadrons. He started with Mölders and me, and promoted us to squadron commodores.

I was not at all satisfied with this and said so openly to Göring: "My group is a pleasure to me and the responsibility sufficient; I am also scared of being tied to the ground and of not seeing enough action." "Don't worry," said Göring. He then explained that the main idea of his new measure was that the squadron should be led in the air by the commodore himself, and this commodore could only be the most successful pilot of the entire squadron.

Could such a revolutionary measure be imposed upon military tradition? Young fighter-pilot officers, well tested in solo fights and in the leadership of small formations, could come quickly and unconventionally into high-ranking and responsible positions. One or two failures were only to be expected. However, during the course of this increasingly difficult fight it was proved that the leader of a fighter squadron only received full recognition if he asked nothing from his men that he was not prepared to do himself. The Fighter Command was the first branch of the air force to introduce younger men into the leader corps. Two years later Bomber Command followed suit after overcoming the greatest resistance.

I did not entirely believe Göring's promise that I should see just as much flying. I was suspicious and annoyed. When he asked us finally if we had any request to make, I said, "Yes,

Herr Reichsmarshal: to remain a group commander." This was turned down.

On our journey back to Berlin Mölders and I naturally discussed all that had been said. Mölders had a splendid record of successfully destroyed enemy aircraft, and the figure had mounted since the battle of the West Wall, during the offensive against France and now over England. He was the ace of all German fighter pilots. Wieck, Balthasar, and I followed him at some distance in constant rivalry. Brilliant though Mölders was as a fighter, his actual abilities and ambitions lay more in the field of tactics and organization. He did not approve at all of my opposition to Göring's plan, which suited his wishes and inclinations perfectly. He alluded to the great fighter pair of World War I, Richthofen-Böleke, the former of whom was the more successful fighter, while the latter was—at least for the development of fighters as a weapon—the more important tactitian. "Well," he said finally with indignation, "as far as I am concerned, you can be the Richthofen of the Luftwaffe. I prefer one day to be its Böleke." He certainly would have been too, had his death not torn him away from his activities far too early.

A fortnight later we met the Reichsmarshal again. This time he came to visit us on the coast. The large-scale attacks of the bombers were imminent. The air supremacy necessary for these had not been achieved to the degree expected. The English fighter force was wounded, it was true, but not beaten. Our pursuit Stuka and fighter force had naturally suffered grievous losses in material, personnel, and morale. The uncertainty about the continuation of the air offensive reflected itself down to the last pilot. Göring refused to understand that his Luftwaffe, this sparkling and so far successful sword, threatened to turn blunt in his hand. He believed there was not enough fighting spirit and a lack of confidence in ultimate victory. By personally taking a hand he hoped to get the best out of us.

To my mind, he went about it the wrong way. He had nothing but reproach for the fighter force, and he expressed his dissatisfaction in the harshest of terms. The theme of fighter protection was chewed over again and again. Göring clearly represented the point of view of the bombers and demanded close and rigid protection. The bomber, he said, was more important than record bag figures. I tried to point out that the ME-109 was superior in the attack and not so suitable for purely defensive purposes as the Spitfire, which although a little slower, was much more maneuverable. He rejected my objection. We received many more harsh words. Finally as his time ran short he grew more amiable. He asked what were the requirements for our squadrons. Mölders asked for a series of ME-109s with more powerful engines. The request was granted. "And you?" Göring turned to me. I did not hesitate long. "I should like an outfit of Spitfires for my squadron." After I had blurted this out, I received rather a shock. It was not really meant that way. Of course fundamentally I preferred our ME-109 to the Spitfire. But I was unbelievably vexed at the lack of understanding and the stubbornness with which the command gave us orders we could not execute—or only incompletely—as a result of many shortcomings for which we were not to blame. Such brazen-faced impudence made even Göring speechless. He stamped off, growling as he went.

4

"Bombs on England"

In those days all the loud-speakers of the "Greater German Reich" from Aachen to Tilsit, from Flensburg to Innsbruck, and from the army stations of most of the occupied countries, blared out the song: *"Bomben auf En-ge-land."* By beating the big drum in strong and martial rhythm and blending it with the roar of aircraft, they expected a mass psychological effect. We pilots could not stand this song from the very start.

Moreover during the first and the second phase of the Battle of Britain there could be no question as yet of Bombs on England. Only with the third phase did bombers appear over England to assist the fighters in the battle for air supremacy. Until then they had only concentrated on shipping targets. This third phase of the Battle of Britain was fought between August 8 and September 7, 1940. In this action the bombers returned to the task allocated to them by Douhet: the enemy air force must be wiped out while still grounded. Douhet however envisaged for this task waves and waves of bombers, darkening the sky with their multitudes. He would have been gravely disappointed to see the realization of his strategic dream as it was put into practice over England at the time.

Unfortunately the English defense profited once more by the limited range of the German fighters. In effect the actual battle sector over England represented not even one tenth of the total area of the island. In the remaining nine tenths the R.A.F. could build aircraft, train pilots, form new squadrons, and build up reserves almost without interference. These forces could then be sent into the very limited front, mainly the sector around London. Churchill describes in his memoirs the difficult situation of the British faced by a superior German fighter force, especially with regard to personnel at the beginning of the Battle of Britain. The situation was only saved by concentrating all resources on the replacement of losses. All these efforts would have been of no avail had the whole island been the battlefield instead of this restricted tenth.

This unfortunate state of affairs could only have been changed effectively by an efficient German long-range bomber. If such machines could have carried the war from the air to the north, northwest, and west coasts, and into all corners of England, then the process of replenishing the already- damaged R.A.F. could have been prevented or at least hampered. Furthermore it would have forced the British defense to spread out. Instead of this it could only concentrate on the narrow sector against which we carried out a frontal attack.

The Luftwaffe, alas, had no heavy strategic bombers. General Wever, their champion, had demanded them energetically. The German aircraft industry delivered him a whole series of good designs. The choice at last fell on the HE-177, a four-engined aircraft in which two combined engines each drove a four-bladed propeller. Hitler, who often showed an amazingly correct intuitive judgment, especially in questions of engine techniques, raised his doubts about such a combination from the start. He proved to be right. This combination became the source of technical hitches, which—combined with other reasons—delayed the mass production of the HE-177 for about three years. Incidentally Hitler, acting on his correct judgment, later assumed the right to interfere in the technical development of the Luftwaffe, sometimes in a way that proved disastrous. More of this later. In any case the long-distance bomber was not available in 1940. Not until Dönitz became Commander-in-Chief of the Navy and demanded aircraft with a longer range for the protection of his U-boats was the HE-177 once more seriously considered. She went into service for the first time on the supply lines to Stalingrad, in the winter of 1942-43; contrary to her original purpose she was used as a troop carrier. Even on this run considerable technical faults came to light. On the death of Wever the development of a long-range strategic bomber force was stopped. It was considered sufficient to have Stukas and a large fleet of twin-engined medium-range bombers. Jeschonnek, the fourth Luftwaffe Chief of Staff after Kesselring and Stumpf, gave his specifications for a long-range twin-engined fast bomber as follows: 2500-pound bomb load, 600-mile range, and a speed of 435 mph. His demands held fire because of the impressive initial successes at the beginning of the war and because Hitler's dislike of a war with England made any new developments appear as of secondary importance.

We therefore had to get used to the fact that our offensive could only be directed against a small and extraordinarily well-defended sector of the British Isles. But this sector included the capital, the heart of the British Empire, London. The seven-million-people city on the Thames was of exceptional military importance as the brain and nerve center of the British High Command, as a port, and as a center for armament and distribution. The fact that London was within the range of day bombing attacks with fighter cover, however inefficient and disadvantageous the German offensive was, must be regarded as one of the positive sides of our offensive.

We fighter pilots, discouraged by a task which was beyond our strength, were looking forward impatiently and excitedly to the start of the bomber attacks. We believed that only then would the English fighters leave their dens and be forced to give us open battle.

The Commander-in-Chief appeared once more at the Channel to be on the spot and to give the order for the beginning of the operation in person. When on the afternoon of September 7 the German squadrons assembled over the Channel coast—bombers, Stukas, fighters, destroyers, more than 1,000 aircraft in all—and at the moment this air power, never before seen in such strength, set course for London, each of the participants realized the importance of the hour. The fourth phase of the Battle of Britain had started.

Today it is easy to smile at the expectations we nursed in those days as to the possible effect of such an attack. With two or three times the number of bombers carrying five times the bomb load, with improved bombsights and perfected methods of attack, the Allies could not destroy or even completely paralyze a city like Berlin. The step which we then took was leading us into unknown territory.

During the first of the 38 large-scale raids on London the targets were confined to London installations and oil depots on the Thames. Only later were the raids extended to targets in the London area. We used 150-, 750-, 1250-, and very rarely 2500-pound high-explosive bombs. In contrast to these the Allies later used bombs up to ten tons. The bomb load was between 2500 and 4500 pounds per aircraft and the total weight of bombs released in each attack was about 500 tons. The later practice of saturation bombing as employed by the Allies in their raids on the Reich could not be achieved with the means at our disposal. Moreover the bombs dropped were scattered over many single targets.

The raiding unit was generally one bomber wing, of between 50 and 80 planes, protected by a fighter wing. In the beginning of the fourth phase our total raiding strength was about 400 to 500 bombers and 200 Stukas. Protection was given by about

500 fighters and 200 destroyers. The enemy, according to German calculations at the time, had not much more than 200 front-line aircraft.

The assembly of the bombers and fighters took place in the vicinity of our fighter bases over some landmark on the coast at a predetermined altitude and zero hour. It happened more than once that the bombers arrived late. As a result the fighters joined another bomber formation which had already met its fighter escort and thus flew doubly protected; while the belated formation had either to turn back or make an unescorted raid usually resulting in heavy losses. Radio or radar guidance for such an essembly was not available; even our intercom did not work most of the time. These difficulties increased with the deterioration of the weather in the autumn and finally assumed the proportions of a tragedy.

All formations had to take the shortest route to London, because the escorting fighters had a reserve of only ten minutes' combat time. Large-scale decoy maneuvers or circumnavigation of the British AA zone were therefore impossible. The antiaircraft barrage around London was of considerable strength and concentration and seriously hampered the target approach of the bombers. The balloon barrage over and around the capital made low-level attacks and dive-bombing impossible. The bulk of the English fighters were sent up to encounter the German raiders just before they reached their target. I know of no instance in which they managed to prevent the bombers from reaching their target, but·they inflicted heavy losses both on them and the German escort fighters.

The types of bombers used were HE-111, DO-17, JU-87, and JU-88. They had all been put into service long before the outbreak of the war. The HE-111 and the DO-17 had already been used in the Spanish war. Even the JU-88, sometimes called the Wonder Bomber, had risen to fame in 1938 by putting up a world-speed record. Exposed to the vigorous and modern English defense and to new conditions, many insufficiencies came to light with regard to these planes. In addition to many other shortcomings all types showed that they were not sufficiently armed for defense. The existing armament was of morale value alone.

The AA batteries concentrated around London, and their accurate fire, sometimes directed from fighter planes, forced the German bomber formations higher and higher. In this way they exceeded their best operational altitude and became even slower.

The JU-87 squadrons had to be taken out of service after

the first large-scale attacks on London. The losses of the bombers were high enough but the Stuka losses could not be supported. Their pinpoint accuracy lost its effect because of the interference on the part of the defense. They changed over at last to dropping their load in horizontal flight, but in this way they were less efficient as bombers and more susceptible to the enemy's defense. The High Command of the Luftwaffe therefore gave orders that in the future they were only to be used for attacks on convoys and targets in the coastal regions. The renunciation of such a weapon of attack, from which it had expected so much, was certainly no easy decision for the German Command.

Nor did the destroyer units last through this phase of the battle. In view of the losses and previously recognized failings, the High Command converted a proportion of these destroyers into fast bombers, for use in the next phase of the battle. It was deplorable that these units were created so to speak at the expense of the fighters, and their failure indirectly caused a weakening of the fighter arm.

Any encounter with British fighters called for maximum effort. One day on my way back from London I spotted a flight of 12 Hurricanes north of Rochester. I attacked from 2500 feet above them and behind, shooting like an arrow between the flights. From ramming distance I fired on one of the aircraft in the rear line of the formation, tearing large pieces of metal out of the plane. At the last moment I pulled my nose up and leaped over her. I now flew right through the center of the enemy's formation. It was not a pleasant sensation. Again I fired my cannon and machine gun into one of the Hurricanes from close range. Luckily the English had had a similar or even bigger fright than I. No one attacked me. As I broke off I saw two parachutes open below the broken formation.

It was not as simple as this with another Hurricane I shot down west of Dungeness. I had damaged her badly and she was on fire. She ought to have been a dead loss. Yet she did not crash but glided down in gentle curves. My flight companions and I attacked her three times—without a final result. I flew close alongside the flying wreck, by now thoroughly riddled, with smoke belching from her. From a distance of a few yards I saw the dead pilot sitting in his shattered cockpit, while his aircraft spiraled slowly to the ground as though piloted by a ghostly hand.

I can only express the highest admiration for the British fighter pilots who, although technically at a disadvantage, fought bravely and indefatigably. They undoubtedly saved their country in this crucial hour.

The short range of the ME-109 became more and more of a disadvantage. During a single sortie of my wing we lost 12 fighter planes, not by enemy action, but simply because after two hours' flying time the bombers we were escorting had not yet reached the mainland on their return journey. Five of these fighters managed to make a pancake landing on the French shore with their last drop of fuel, seven of them landed in the "drink."

It turned out that a forced landing on the water was preferable to a parachute descent into the sea. After touching down on the water, the plane remained afloat for between 40 and 60 seconds, just about long enough for the pilot to unstrap himself and to scramble out. The lucky ones were fished out of the water by the tireless Air Sea Rescue Service. Mae West, rubber dinghy, colored flare bag, Very pistol, and other useful trifles may have weighed the pilot down like a Father Christmas, but they turned out to be excellent accessories.

I made my fortieth kill over the Thames Estuary on September 24. Our squadron was in the best of spirits. The JG 26 *Schlageter* had already made a name for itself in the Battle of Britain. No difference was made between my own successes and those of the squadron. I was the third member of all the armed forces—after Dietl and Mölders—to receive the oak leaves to the Knight's Cross. Apart from the Grand Cross, which was reserved solely for the Reichsmarshal, this was the highest military award in those days. It did not worry me a great deal that I was grounded at the same time. I would arrange things somehow. I had been ordered to Berlin for the investiture.

Hitler received me in the new Reich Chancellory. It was the second time I sat opposite him. On the first occasion, after my return from Spain with the Cóndor Legion, our meeting had been in the form of a collective reception. Now I was alone with him. Our conversation was a lengthy one. I expressed my great admiration for our enemy across the water. I was embittered by several insidious and false representations and commentaries by the press and on the radio, which had referred to the R.A.F. in a condescending and presumptuous tone. I expected contradiction or anger from Hitler when I gave him a different picture. On the contrary he did not interrupt me, nor did he try to change the subject. He nodded repeatedly and said that my description confirmed his beliefs. He too had the greatest respect for the Anglo-Saxon race.

The decision, he said, had been all the more difficult for him, to wage this life-and-death struggle, which could only end with the total destruction of one or the other. He called it a world historical tragedy and said that it had been impossible to avoid this war despite all his sincere and desperate attempts. If we won the war, a vacuum would be created by the destruction of Great Britain, which it would be impossible to fill.

In most convincing terms Hitler expressed not only his sympathy for the English race but also his admiration for the class of political and industrial leaders which down the ages had developed on a much broader basis than anything that had so far existed in Germany. In their political development, favored by different circumstances, the English were a hundred years ahead of us. All the virtues an eminent race had developed over long periods became manifest during critical phases in its history, as England was going through then. He regretted that he had not managed to bring the English and the German people together in spite of a promising start.

I must admit that I was highly impressed by the Führer's words at the time. He had managed to take the wind out of my sails. I no longer felt bitter.

At the Air Ministry a Luftwaffe liaison officer attached to the Ministry of Propaganda greeted me with the embarrassing news that representatives of the foreign press were waiting to interview me. It did not suit me at all, but it could not be avoided. What I had already heard from the German propaganda about the war front was not to my liking, as I have already mentioned. I had no intention of speaking now in the same vein. My answers were tape-recorded and the Ministry made me a present of the recording later. The last time I played them was on the day I was taken prisoner, and I noted that I had no desire to take one word back, nor did I wish that they had remained unsaid. After the war a U. S. interrogation officer began his conversation with the remark, "We are old acquaintances. I have interviewed you before." It was in the Theatersaal of the Ministry of Propaganda in the Wilhelmsplatz, Berlin.

From Berlin I flew to see Göring in East Prussia. At the gate of the Reichsjägerhof in the Rominterheide I met Mölders. As commander of the 51st Fighter Wing, also based on the Channel, he had received the oak leaves three days before me for his fortieth kill. To his annoyance he had been detained until now by Hitler and Göring. He was in a hurry to get back to his station. The obligation to defend your title as the most successful fighter pilot in the world was still taken very seriously. After a hurried farewell he called to me, "The Fat One promised me he would detain you at least as long as he did me. And by the way, good luck with the stag I missed."

The Reichsjägerhof was a log cabin made of huge tree trunks, with a thatched roof jutting far over the eaves. Göring came out of the house to meet me wearing a green suède hunting jacket over a silk blouse with long puffed sleeves, high hunting boots, and in his belt a hunting knife in the shape of an old Germanic sword. He was in the best of humor. Both the disagreeable memory of our last meeting and his worries about the Luftwaffe in the Battle of Britain seemed to have been spirited away. We could hear the stags out on the heath: it was rutting time.

After congratulating me he said that he had a special treat in store for me. He gave me permission to hunt one of the royal stags, which were usually reserved for him. It was a so-called "Reichsjägermeister-stag." He knew them all and each one had a name; he watched over them and was loathe to part with one of them. "I promised Mölders," Göring said, "to keep you here at least three days, so you've got plenty of time." That night no mention was made either of the war in general or the Battle of Britain in particular.

Next morning at ten o'clock I had bagged my stag: it was really a royal beast, the stag of a lifetime. There was no further reason to prolong my stay at the Reichsjägerhof.

Yet Göring kept his promise to Mölders and did not let me go. In the afternoon the latest front-line reports from the 2nd and 3rd Air Force Groups were brought to him. They were devastating. During a raid on London exceptionally high losses had been sustained.

Göring was shattered. He simply could not explain how the increasingly painful losses of bombers came about. I assured him that in spite of the heavy losses we were inflicting on the enemy fighters, no decisive decrease in their number or in their fighting efficiency was noticeable. At the great altitudes where aerial combats took place it was only possible in rare cases to follow the possible victim down to its final crash in order to verify the kill. Even if the German figures of enemy aircraft destroyed were perhaps overestimated, the fact that their fighter strength obviously did not diminish could only be accounted for in this way: England, by a great concentration of energy, was making up her losses in the peaceful nine tenths of her territory.

The achievements of a nation determined to assert itself would be exemplified a few years later by the Germans.

37

After this conversation, when I asked Göring to allow me to rejoin my squadron, he had no objection. I flew back to the Channel. Over Pomerania I had to make a forced landing. In the train, as I continued my journey, the stag caused more sensation than the oak leaves to my Knight's Cross. My fellow passengers insisted that the stag's head stank to high heaven, or that it was dangerous to travel with the horns unprotected. A few hunters opened their eyes in astonishment. All of them were right.

5

Between "Sea Lion" and "Barbarossa"

On September 27, 1940, during my visit to the Reichsjägerhof the German-Italian Axis was enlarged by the entry of Japan to a Triple Alliance. This pact made it suddenly clear that the war was not merely a European conflict but one of world-wide dimensions. From a political viewpoint this tripartite pact was another success for Hitler's foreign policy.

The pact with Japan was accepted in Germany more with the intelligence than with the heart, as in the case of the Russian pact. Japan represented a very real military factor in the world. Now that she was on our side her sea power in particular was looked upon as a feature which might dissuade the U.S.A. from entering the war—an important consideration in view of the increasingly hostile attitude of President Roosevelt toward Germany.

This Japanese trump card in the German hand also seemed advantageous in relation to the Soviet Union. The Russian invasion of Finland on November 30, 1939, had outraged the entire world. The brave resistance put up by this small heroic nation, which concluded in an honorable peace on May 12, 1940, had been looked upon with great satisfaction by everyone. The possible significance of the Finnish winter campaign as a maneuver to show the world the strength of the Red army, was probably only recognized by a few at that time. It was considered as a sign of the unsatiable Russian imperialism, whose appetite had been whetted by the partial successes in Poland. The fear that, following her old desire for ports which were not icebound, Russia would next turn to the Balkans and the Bosporus was confirmed on July 2, 1940, when Stalin occupied the Romanian part of Bessarabia and the Bukovina. In spite of the promise of aid to Romania made in April, 1939, England did not react to the Russian provocation.

A fortnight after Mussolini's unexpected attack on Greece, which was regarded abroad as a well-planned action on the part of the Axis combined headquarters, Molotov, the Russian foreign minister, appeared in Berlin to establish his government's claims in the new sector, which had now been drawn into the war. His discussions with Hitler between November 12 and 14, 1940, must have been of great importance to the further course of the war. Molotov demanded not only a free hand in Finland and the Baltic states, but also the occupation of Romanian territories—already tacitly ignored—plus the whole of Bulgaria and access to the Bosporus.

To fulfill these demands would mean to open the doors for Bolshevism to the Western world. To take a firm stand against them would be tantamount to an open declaration of war. The German-Soviet relationship had reached its limit: the tactical expediency to which Hitler had resorted in August, 1939, as a political move was now in danger of growing into a tie with incalculable consequences. Stalin's later relationship with the Western Allies would arrive at this critical point one day— actually at Yalta, where Stalin made far-reaching demands on the West. They were accepted by Roosevelt and Churchill. In this way Stalin laid the foundations of the powerful present-day position of Russia extending far into the Western world.

Molotov had to leave Berlin without achieving anything. It was certainly not easy for Hitler to come to such a decision. Had he satisfied the Kremlin's requests, especially the one regarding access to the Mediterranean, it would have forced England to the defense of one of her most important lifelines and would have placed her in an unavoidably aggressive position toward Russia. This would only have pleased Hitler had the Battle of Britain turned out as planned. Operation Sea Lion had been canceled and he did not really know how to force the British to their knees.

The Battle of Britain, of course, was never one of Hitler's original war aims. It was merely a stone which had rolled in his way; it had either to be removed or to be by-passed. In any case it was something which could not be allowed to interfere with the main objective, the destruction of Bolshevism.

Giving way to the Soviet request would have meant leaving this road. Russia could have put her foot in the door to the West which was already ajar, thanks to the temporary pact with Germany.

Hitler's decision meant for Germany the renunciation of a safeguarded rear, while the struggle with the West was still undecided. By rejecting the Russian requests he made up his mind to concentrate all his available forces in the east, the original aim of the war. The fate of our battle in the west against the R.A.F. was also decided at this moment.

Between the fourth phase of the Battle of Britain—which came to an end on October 20 with the aid of day raids—and the fifth and last phase, during which targets in the British Isles were bombed by night, came the first attacks by fighter-bombers, a novelty in the history of aerial warfare. The fighter supporting land operations of the army is exclusively a tactical arm, a kind of "flying shock troop," to attack, at low level, enemy positions and troop movements in the front line even with bombs, rockets, and small arms. The fighter-bomber within the framework of strategical air operations fulfills a most important task when used against targets far behind the front line. This was proved clearly at a later date, when the Allies used fighter-bombers in their offensive against the Reich. The countless locomotives on the West Germany Railway network damaged by American fighter-bombers toward the end of the war testify to this.

On the German side the fighter-bomber idea had a different origin. After completing its original task in the war in the air, i.e., after achieving air supremacy, the fighter was not used as an additional arm in the "war from the air," but was made into a fighter-bomber as a stopgap and a scapegoat. We started with the premise that the fighter was apparently unable to give sufficient protection to the bombers. This was true. But instead of accepting the front-line pilots' explanation and, if possible, eradicating the cause or, as an alternative, stopping these untenable raids, the following conclusions were drawn: If the fighter arm is unable to protect the bombers, it must deliver the bombs to England on its own account.

Political propaganda reasons may also have persuaded the leaders to make such a faulty decision. The raids on England had become a question of prestige. The day bombing could not be continued, and night raids were only in preparation. This gap was to be filled by fighters transformed into fighter-bombers. Not military expediency but a momentary political demand created the fighter-bomber. Instead of making it possible to achieve the goal of a raiding war on England—for the success of which air superiority was imperative—by a powerful strengthening of the arm, we weakened this by transforming fighter planes into bomb carriers. The operative value of fighter-bombers cannot be denied, but only by pre-supposing a surplus of fighter aircraft. To use a fighter as a fighter-bomber when the strength of the fighter arm is inadequate to achieve air superiority is putting the cart before the horse.

It started with the so-called Test Unit 210, flying ME-109s, ME-110s, and ME-210s. In about the middle of September they were transferred to the Pas de Calais and were to be escorted by my squadron. Simultaneously the seven fighter wings engaged in the Battle of Britain received the order to equip either one squadron per wing, or one flight per squadron, as fighter-bombers, which virtually meant the transformation of a third of the fighters into fighter-bombers.

We fighter pilots looked upon this violation of our aircraft with great bitterness. We had done everything possible to increase our performance in order to keep up with a progressive enemy. We had discarded everything dispensable in an attempt to squeeze another ounce of speed out of them. We had always demanded ejectable spare tanks in order to increase our range. Instead of that they now gave us bomb-release gadgets and we were forced to see a third of our aircraft drop out of air combat.

The fighter-bombers were put into action in a great hurry. There was hardly time to give the pilots bombing training. Most pilots dropped their first live bomb in a raid over London or on other targets in England. We had a total of 250 fighter-bombers. The ME-109 carried a 500-pound H.E. bomb; the ME-110 carried two of them and four 100-pounders, all together 1400 pounds. No great effect could be achieved with that. Even less so because the fighter pilots were annoyed at carrying cargo and were glad to get rid of the bomb anywhere.

The fighter-bomber raids were carried out in the following way: Each wing provided the escort for its own bombers. The altitude for the approach was about 18,000 feet. At the start we let the fighter-bombers fly in bomber formation, but it was soon apparent that the enemy fighters could concentrate fully on the bombers. Therefore we distributed the fighter-bombers in small units throughout the entire formation and thus brought them in fairly safely over their target area. This type of raid had no more than nuisance value. The passive behavior toward enemy fighters, the feeling of inferiority when we were attacked, because of loss of speed, maneuverability, rate of climb, added to the unconvincing effect of single bombs scattered over wide areas, combined to ruin the morale of the German fighter pilot, already low because of the type of escorting that had to be done.

We had an outspoken antipathy for the order to escort fighter-bombers. The Luftwaffe High Command countered our negative attitude sharply. Göring declared angrily that the fighter arm had failed to give adequate protection to the bomber squadrons and were now opposed to escorting fighter-bombers, a job which had resulted entirely from their own failure. If they were to prove unfit for this task as well it would be better to disband the fighter arm altogether. That was the limit! The fighter pilots who took part in the Battle of Britain were quite justly convinced that they had done their duty during the past weeks of heavy fighting. They had accepted heavy losses in unflagging action combined with outstanding successes, but never once did they question the final aim or how long this murderous battle was going to last. Morale having already been heavily taxed, and on top of that to be unjustly accused, put military discipline to a stiff test. In young flying officer circles the leadership was passionately and bitterly criticized. This was the first serious crisis in the relations between the fighter arm and the Luftwaffe Command.

The advance of autumn revealed another disadvantage for us: the weather. At one time we had expected a great deal from the famous London fog. The vision of the city and its suburbs covered with "pea soup," preventing the British fighters from taking off, and the picture of factory chimneys peeping out of it, like target markers for our bombers, was so tempting that I once mentioned it to Hitler as a consoling thought. The Führer waved this argument aside with a rather apathetic gesture, saying that we dared not rely on this. How right he was! Questions of weather were Hitler's specialty. In this respect he sometimes had lucky intuitions, but he also had very able meteorologists to whom it was no secret that, especially in autumn, the weather over the Channel is predominantly westerly, i.e. developing from east to west, which of course is a grave disadvantage to an attacker from the east. The defender therefore knew the actual weather and what to expect over the battle zone sooner than the attacker. The English could nearly always forecast the weather early enough to make provisions for it. We were always surprised by it. More and more often situations arose in which the assembling of bombers and fighters could be accomplished only partially or not at all. On account of this the bombers sustained higher losses. With the seasonal deterioration of the weather it became increasingly difficult to carry out the bigger raids according to plan.

Weather conditions over the Channel were the last of a series of reasons why the German Command eventually discontinued the day raids on London on October 20, 1940. They had lasted six weeks. The bombers had lost about 30 to 35 per cent of their strength, and the fighters about 20 to 25 per cent, during these actions. The over-all fighting strength of the Luftwaffe was reduced to three quarters compared with the beginning of the Battle of Britain. It is therefore wrong to speak either of annihilation or of a decisive defeat of the German Luftwaffe in this battle. Those who express the point of view that the back of our air force was broken and that it was never again in a position to recover from this blow misunderstood the real situation. This error must be contradicted in the interests of history. It is true to say that the cessation of German day raids on London was an outstanding and brilliant English success of both military and political importance. The last phase, too, of the Battle of Britain was to be a great worry to the English population and their war leaders. But the immediate, the mortal, danger was overcome. England had passed victoriously through one of the most serious ordeals in her history. She never lost her courage or her self-confidence. Staggering and bleeding, but with clenched teeth, she stood fast during the critical round.

With the German night raids, toward the end of October, 1940, the fifth and last phase of the Battle of Britain began. The German fighter arm, however, did not take part in this. Besides London there were raids on Liverpool, Birmingham, Manchester, Southampton, and nearly all the larger towns as far north as a line running from Edinburgh to Glasgow, at that time the limit of the German bomber range.

The change-over from day to night bombing took place without any loss of time. This was possible because the crews, as part of their peacetime training, had received complete instructions and practice in night and blind flying. The planes and their equipment remained nearly unchanged. An efficient bombsight for night bombing was as conspicuously absent as the radar eye.

During the later Allied air offensive against the Reich the R.A.F. could concentrate on night raids while the Americans took over the day raids. Germany on the other hand found herself in the position of the poor man who has to wear the same shirt day and night. Thus the same crews flew the same planes in which they had already been in action during the day offensive, up to three sorties in one night over England. In this way our attacking strength consisted of between 600 and 800 bombers. Our maximum bomb load of 5000 pounds was a little higher than during daytime. The loss of speed and height of approach could be borne at night. The total weight dropped per night per target reached the not inconsiderable figure of 1000 tons.

Unfortunately the accuracy of the attacks and the concentration of bombs were unsatisfactory. Often the targets could not be located because of bad weather conditions. Soon experiments were made with means of lighting up the targets as the English did later. Yet precision attacks remained embryonic in the absence of nearly every assistance, navigational or radar. Different methods of attack had to be invented, tested, and slowly developed during actual raids.

Approach and attack were made from between 9000 and 18,000 feet. Navigation was done by radio using coastal stations and by a beam directed from the coast onto the target. We flew singly and not in formation. The English defense was fairly powerless at the beginning against the German night raiders. The R.A.F. night fighters were still being developed, and in spite of feverish efforts achieved no results worth mentioning. Most dreaded were the AA guns, especially in the belt around London. On the other hand the exploding AA shells were a great help in locating the target in bad weather. Taken all in all, the German losses during the night raids remained within reasonable limits. Losses through weather conditions and errors of navigation were equal to those caused by the defense.

The best results of the night raids were achieved during periods of full moon, with good weather and a clear view of the ground. Such a night was November 14-15, 1940. The German squadrons had a particularly important target for this night, an industrial town in Warwickshire, where in addition to essential war factories there were important works of the vital aircraft industry: Coventry (population 205,000). The first waves managed to cause fires in the target areas which could be seen from a great distance. The squadrons which took part with about 800 aircraft made up to three sorties that night against Coventry. The total load of bombs released was 1000 tons, and as regards execution and effect it was the optimum of a concentrated night raid. The German Luftwaffe never again repeated this success in this form. Only much later with quite different resources did the English produce anything similar. Coventry was an accidental success. With insufficient aid in navigation and location of targets the night raiders over England, who were dependent on the weather during this time of the year, could not achieve any shattering effect despite their moderate losses. Slowly the German night raids faded out. In April, 1941, they were almost entirely stopped.

Without fanfares or fuss the Battle of Britain came to an end.

6

New Strategic Ground

After Molotov left Berlin without achieving anything, the German-Soviet relationships became noticeably cooler. With the preparations for Operation Barbarossa, interest waned in the aerial conflict with England. The cessation of the day raids on England, partly forced on us by the weather conditions, was also perhaps with the idea of nursing the strength of the Luftwaffe for the forthcoming blow against the Soviet Union.

What would have happened had Hitler not attacked Russia and had he used the pause in the Battle of Britain enforced by the weather to replenish and restrengthen his Luftwaffe, in order to end the interrupted struggle, which so far no one had won? What would have happened had the Battle of Britain been started immediately after the fall of France instead of only in July, whereby the Luftwaffe would have gained four or six weeks before the start of the unfavorable autumn weather? What would have happened had the Sea Lion—whose expected jump had been awaited in all seriousness by the English war leaders—not been recalled by Hitler? Could the English forces have withstood the German onslaught? Even today these questions are still difficult to answer. I do not believe, however, that the dilatory preparations for Operation Sea Lion, the delay in opening the Battle of Britain, the rejection of Molotov's requests in Berlin, and finally the breaking off of the Battle of Britain at a moment when the score was no more than equal can be traced back to Hitler's initial reluctance to fight a war in the west.

With the fading out of the Battle of Britain and the preparations for the campaign against the Soviet Union, Hitler now steered the German war machine on this course. We officers at the front could not and were not intended to know this. Hitler tried to hide his real intentions so that neither we nor the world should get a glimpse of them. On Christmas Eve, 1940, on a visit to our squadron at Abbeville he made a

46

half-hour speech. This was a different Hitler from the one I had talked with in the new Reichskanzlei. Here spoke the Hitler we knew from his broadcast speeches. He was absolutely convinced of victory. The war, he said, was as good as won. He had managed to confront and beat one adversary after the other, thus avoiding a war on two fronts. The danger of a Soviet attack had been arrested. By an unexpected stepping up of the U-boat war and by a huge drive in aircraft production, England would finally be subjected. No coalition of powers in the world could rob us of our victory.

In this little circle we believed that we had been let into the most closely guarded state secrets. This of course was not the case at all. On the contrary not a single sentence was intended to be a secret, but was meant to be repeated. It was a typical speech with a purpose, and it did not miss the mark.

Looking back on the discrepancy between what Hitler said then and the real situation, I could not help asking myself a question which I was going to ask myself many times later: Was Hitler able to give such an impressive and at the same time untrue picture of the situation by some kind of autosuggestion? Naturally he skipped over the Eastern Campaign, regarding it as already won. I am inclined to answer this question in the affirmative in view of the unbalanced relationship between the requirements for the conduct of the war and Hitler's conception of them—a relationship which grew worse as the war progressed.

In actual fact no one could have said at Christmas, 1940, that the war was rapidly coming to a victorious end. It had already spread to the Balkans and North Africa. The operations started in the summer, 1940, by the Italians, with the Suez Canal as a tempting goal, got under way again only when the German Afrika Korps was formed in the winter of 1940-41. Rommel's reinforcements crossing the Mediterranean needed to safeguard their increasingly stronger Luftwaffe detachments. Soon the eastern plains of Europe would become an additional battlefield to swallow up our forces. Roosevelt was prepared to throw the immense war potential of the U.S.A. into the balance of the war. Heavily wounded but far from conquered, England, the latest enemy in dominated Europe, sat tight on her island, which later was to become the aircraft carrier used for the destruction of Germany from the air.

It was not surprising that we found it impossible to force England to her knees with an active strength of only 600 medium bombers and 600 to 700 fighters of limited range.

One must not forget that the German air force was only four and a half years old when it was called upon to bear the great test of World War II. In that short space of time the strongest air force of the world had been created. Undoubtedly this represented an extraordinary feat—a feat to be admired all the more since at the time not only trained men were unavailable but also all the prerequisites for the creation of an air force: ground organizations, training facilities, units and their leaders, flying personnel and technicians, aeronautical science and research, planes and armaments, and an armament industry to produce them. And finally there was a shortage of raw materials for explosives and fuels; no plants existed to produce synthetically from coal the substitutes for the raw materials essential to a large air force.

During that same period the air force had to share the German war potential with the army and the navy. Furthermore, Germany was not living for rearmaments alone. The civil section of German production had a similar boom. Dwelling houses and official buildings were erected in the cities besides buildings for the armament industry and barracks. In the country, aerodromes and grounds for military maneuvers were laid out as well as farms and new settlements. The network of roads reached a greater degree of density and efficiency, not only because of the construction of the Autobahn, which has often been wrongly termed purely strategical. As a whole, the German nation manifested a deployment of strength which was unique.

It was unquestionably thanks to Hermann Göring, the creator of the Luftwaffe, that it was at all possible for the German air force to develop while such a vast program of construction and enlargement was taking place at the same time in all fields. It was estimated that the reconstruction of the Luftwaffe represented 40 per cent of the total German rearmament capacity during those years. With great energy and a passionate love for his arm, Göring knew how to create for it the place which in his mind was its due in the structure of a Continental military power. In any case, the importance of the air force in a future war had been recognized in Germany in good time, accurately, and fundamentally.

Without doubt, mistakes were made during the period of development. Doubtless everything suffered from undue haste and overoptimism. The effect of an air force and of its combat potential in those days was exaggerated, although of course the concept anticipated later technical developments. But the principles on which Hitler, advised and encouraged

48

by Göring, based the creation of an independent Luftwaffe were sound and correct.

Thus he wielded an instrument, which in cooperation with the motorized units of the army helped his Britzkrieg strategy to achieve its brilliant successes. This instrument did not yet represent the strategical air force as we know it today. When in the summer of 1940, contrary to the original plan of the German High Command, it had to be used for strategical purposes against England, its chances of success were limited by its numerical strength, its technical equipment, and the state of development of armaments. Experience was lacking as regards limitations, required strength, and methods of strategical air operations. The Spanish civil war had only yielded knowledge and experience in the technical and tactical fields. Strategically we broke new ground in the summer of 1940.

During the Battle of Britain the Luftwaffe carried out operations which were completely novel in the history of warfare. The most important of these were:

1. An unlimited struggle for air supremacy, independent of any army operations.

2. Strategical air warfare by means of daylight bombing with fighter escort.

3. Strategical air warfare by means of night raids.

4. The sending of fighter-bombers into action.

5. Strategical air warfare against supply ships.

None of these operations was really successful, simply and solely because it was impossible to complete them successfully with the means available to the Luftwaffe. In each of these fields new practical experience had to be gained, experience for which almost without exception, preliminary study and theory were no substitutes. The experience gained was not a German prerogative: all the nations at war profited from it. While the German war potential from now on had to satisfy other demands to a steadily increasing degree, ultimately to be more and more reduced until it was not enough to protect our own land, the Allies were slowly but surely increasing theirs and were busy mobilizing. Helped by this growing war potential, avoiding as far as possible the mistakes made by Germany, and utilizing all our experiences, Britain created a strategical air force which eventually crushed Germany.

The Luftwaffe had revealed her limitations and weakness to the whole world during the Battle of Britain. The myth of her invincibility had been exploded. But something else had occurred which nobody could have anticipated: The first step Germany had undertaken with the opening of the Battle of Britain led into uncharted fields of air strategy and became a hypothesis for the second, the finally successful step. This was taken by the Allies, following in German footsteps. The first step was full of risks and dangers. Germany stumbled but did not fall. Only the second step brought the success to the others—and destruction to Germany.

7

A Nightmare Becomes a Reality

At the end of 1940 we wing commanders on the Channel coast put in a joint petition, asking permission to withdraw our field squadrons one by one from the fighting in order to refit and also to give them a rest. The petition was granted. We were transferred to our west German home bases, where our aircraft were reconditioned and refitted. Göring granted a free skiing leave to all pilots. We enjoyed it to the full.

Outwardly and inwardly refreshed, sunburned, and in good spirits, we returned from Arlberg at the end of February, 1941. We were sent to Brittany to protect warships in Brest harbor and the U-boat pens which were under construction. Orders to protect fixed objects were very much disliked by fighter pilots. Their element is to attack, to track, to hunt, and to destroy the enemy. Only in this way can the eager and skillful fighter pilot display his ability to the full. Tie him to a narrow and confined task, rob him of his initiative, and you take away from him the best and most valuable qualities he possesses: aggressive spirit, joy of action, and the passion of the hunter. The fighter arm cannot be manacled, particularly when his fetters are determined by earthbound thinking. By its intrinsic properties the fighter arm belongs to the elite. The almost unbelievably expensive product of clever designers, precise technicians, and specialized workers, given into the hands of scientifically chosen and comprehensively trained experts, constitutes an arm of the highest efficiency, but also one of great delicacy. It can be compared with a razor blade which must be guided by a sensitive hand. The man who uses it like a hatchet must not be surprised if it turns jagged in his hand and finally becomes useless.

We went to Brittany without enthusiasm. "Air defense," our orders read; we did not expect much else but sitting around and waiting. It was exactly four months since I had shot down my last enemy plane. On the transfer flight from Düsseldorf to Brest I landed with my flight companion, Oberfeldwebel Menge, at Le Touquet, from where we made a private excursion over the British Isles. At first there was not an English fighter to be seen, but we provoked Fighter Command so long with our presence that they got fed up with us and sent up a flight of Spitfires. Lucky for me, I discovered them as they were climbing up to the attack. At an altitude of 3000 feet I made a surprise attack on one of them and managed to score many machine-gun and cannon hits until she went down in flames. The pilot baled out. Menge also shot down a Spitfire. Now, at last having ejectable extra fuel tanks, we flew back quite satisfied to Brest, where our wing had already arrived.

As I had expected, nothing happened there. Sometimes we bagged a reconnaissance plane, but this was, after all, no task for a fighter wing. I used the time in perfecting our training. Frankly I envied Mölders, who was stationed once more with his wing on the Channel coast and still had contact with the British fighters. He was far in the lead with the number of enemy aircraft to his credit. Wieck had been killed; Balthasar was wounded.

April 15 was Osterkamp's birthday (he was then a squadron leader at Le Touquet) and he invited me to come over. As a present I packed a huge basket of lobsters with the necessary bottles of champagne into my ME-109F and took off, with Oberfeldwebel Westphal piloting the companion plane. Again it was too tempting not to make a little detour on the way and to pay a visit to England. Soon I spotted a single Spitfire. After a wild chase fate decided in my favor. My tough opponent crashed in flames in a little village west of Dover.

A few moments later we saw a flight of Spitfires climbing ahead of us. One of them lagged behind the formation. I approached him unnoticed and shot him to smithereens from a very short distance. We flew right on close to the formation, where I shot down a third Spitfire, which I nearly rammed. I was unable to observe the crash. Westphal was now in a good firing position but suddenly all his guns jammed. Now it was time to bolt as the Spitfires waded in on us. Throttle full open in a power dive down to the Channel! We were heavily attacked. Westphal was noticeably faster than I. Something was wrong with my crate.

As I came in to land at Le Touquet the ground staff waved frantically and fired red light signals. At last I understood their gestures: I had nearly made an involuntary crash landing. When I worked the mechanism to let down the undercarriage it did not go down but retracted instead. It must have been down the whole time. I must have touched the button with my knee during the action over England. I remembered that I had had to do some readjusting and that the flying properties of the plane had definitely changed. Lobster and champagne bottles were safe. Hunter's luck! Together with the report of the Spitfires I handed the birthday present to Osterkamp.

Two days later, on April 17, the remnants of the Yugoslav army capitulated in the Balkans. This campaign too had not been part of Hitler's original plan. Now that Molotov had left Berlin with cold feet, there was need to interfere with the Soviet desire for expansion in the Balkans. The Reich offered protection to the Romanian government, which was accepted. The German army marched into Romania. On March 1, 1941, Bulgaria joined the tripartite pact. Yugoslavia joined a few weeks later. Another two days and the pro-German government in Belgrade was overthrown. The Reich had to intervene by force. Within a few days Weichs' army marched into Carinthia, Styria, and South Hungary; Kleist's armored corps occupied the Sofia sector; List's army was standing in the mountain region on the borders of Bulgaria and Greece. On April 6 the campaign in the Balkans began. This was the last time that motorized German army units, perfectly coordinated with the air force, decisively defeated in the shortest possible time a courageous and well-mobilized adversary. The 8th Flying Corps under von Richthofen, a specialist in cooperation, proved itself once wore. Strongly supported by Stukas, List broke through the well-designed and tenaciously held Metaxas Line. On April 9 he took Salonika. Weichs and Kleist advanced in a pincer movement from north and east toward the main concentration of the Yugoslav army. Nis fell on April 9 and Zagreb on the eleventh. Belgrade fell on April 13. With the unconditional surrender on the seventeenth this campaign came to an end. The Greek government together with the British troops, which had been in Greece since March, escaped to Crete on April 23.

On May 20 the invasion of Crete from the air started. So far it was the greatest operation of its kind in World War II. The conquest of Crete proved a brilliant success in spite of the heavy losses sustained by the Luftwaffe. On June 2 the last Englishman had been chased from the island. The German propaganda presented this venture as being a sort of dress rehearsal for the allegedly imminent invasion of the British Isles.

Göring spoke in the same strain in Paris at a briefing of the commanders of all the units stationed in France. He left us in no doubt that the Battle of Britain had only been an overture to the final subjection of the British enemy. This was to be effected by an immensely increased rearmament of the air force, an intensification of the U-boat war, and would be brought to a conclusion by the actual invasion itself. I must say that the plans Göring unfolded before us were convincing and that we took it for granted that the necessary war-industrial capacity was available.

At the end of the discussion Göring took Mölders and me aside. He beamed. He wanted to know what we thought of his speech. He chuckled softly and rubbed his hands with glee. "There's not a grain of truth in it," he said. Under the seal of greatest secrecy he disclosed to us that the whole discussion was part of a well-planned bluff, the aim of which was to hide the real intentions of the German High Command: the imminent invasion of the Soviet Union. It was a paralyzing shock! The dread which had been hanging over us like the sword of Damocles since the beginning of the war would now become a reality: war on two fronts. I could think of nothing else but the dark and sinister vision of starting a war with the Soviet Union, so tremendously strong in manpower and natural resources, while our strength had already proved insufficient to conquer the British in the first assault. Now we were to turn against a new, unknown, and in any case gigantic enemy, without having first cleared our rear. We thought, in view of our experiences, that to attack England again was a hard decision. But, after all, we knew our opponent and his potential power. It was no easy task but we knew how to hit him, and we could do it if we concentrated all our forces on this one aim. It went against the grain, it was contrary to the German concept of purpose and duty, to be satisfied with a half-measure of success when a task had to be accomplished, and worse to turn to a new aim while the first had not yet been achieved. It was absolutely contrary to what Hitler had told me personally and to what he said in his Christmas speech to our squadron: to avoid war on two fronts and to eliminate one enemy after another. I had admired that concept. This new one which Göring expounded to us filled me with the greatest mistrust, even with horror. I was stunned by the idea and did not hide my scruples. But no one shared my opinion. To my amazement not only Göring but Mölders was excited and enthusiastic. In the east, said Göring, the Luftwaffe would win new laurels. The Red air force was numerically strong but, from a point of machines and personnel, hopelessly inferior. It would only be necessary to shoot down the leader of a flight for the remaining illiterates to lose themselves on the way home. We could shoot them down like clay pigeons.

I listened to Göring, neither convinced nor sharing his enthusasm in the slightest. "And what about England?" I asked. Göring merely waved his hand disdainfully. In two months or at the latest in three, the Russian colossus would be crushed. Then we would throw against the west all our strength, enriched by the inexhaustible strategic resources of Russia. The Führer, he said, could not wage war against England with the full weight of our forces so long as the rear was threatened by a power which undoubtedly had offensive and hostile intentions toward us.

For the first four to six weeks of the Russian campaign Mölders and his wing would go to the Eastern front. In the west there would remain only the 2nd and the 26th Fighter Wings which were each to produce a training and a recruiting unit. After that I was to go to the East with my wing and relieve Mölders. "You will do the rest, Galland," said Göring in his fatherly and most optimistic tone. Then he dismissed me.

Full of qualms I returned to my base. I was deeply upset! There was no one with whom I could share my worries. Göring had given Mölders and me strict order² not to reveal his disclosure. Perhaps, I said to myself, I am seeing things only from my limited horizon of a wing commander. The danger from the east was obvious. The hope remained that the campaign against the Soviet Union would really go as smoothly and according to plan as all the previous Blitz campaigns. My greatest hope regarding Russia was the expected rottenness of the Soviet regime of terror. I had already mentioned this to Göring, whereupon he became very serious and shook his head violently.

"Don't talk to me about a possible internal collapse of the Bolshevist regime. The Führer regards such a possibility as absolutely out of the question. Don't court disaster by talking to anybody about this. Even in Germany any action by subversive elements would be a hopeless undertaking. In the Soviet Union, a regime twenty years older than ours, it would be madness and suicide to try a *coup d'état* to overthrow the government. Not even on the fringes of his calculations would the Führer allow such an idea to crop up. The Soviet Union cannot be beaten in any other way than by force. And that is what we are going to do. You can depend on that!"

In those days, when the approaching war with the Soviet Union overshadowed everything like a dark cloud on the horizon, Göring drew me into one of the most mysterious affairs of war. The star actor of this drama is at the moment behind bars in Spandau: Rudolf Hess.

Early in the evening of May 10, 1941, I got a telephone call from the Reichsmarshal. He was very agitated and ordered me to take off immediately with the entire wing. This did not make sense to me. To begin with it was already getting dark, and furthermore there were no reports of any enemy aircraft flying in. I pointed this out to Göring.

"Flying in," he repeated, "what do you mean by flying in? You are supposed to stop an aircraft flying out! The deputy Führer has gone mad and is flying to England in an ME-110. He must be brought down."

I asked for the probable course of the aircraft and the time it had taken off. Göring ordered me to call him back personally on our return. I put the receiver down and did not know who had gone mad, the deputy Führer, the Reichsmarshal, or me.

In any case the order I had received was mad. There were about ten minutes left till dark. At that hour many ME-110s were in the air on test flights or service trial flights in preparation for night sorties. How should we know which was the one Rudolf Hess was flying? Just as a token, I ordered a take-off. Each squadron leader was to send up one or two planes. I did not tell them why. They must have thought that I had gone mad.

In the meantime I looked at the map to work out the distance and flying time from Augsburg to England. If it was true that Hess had taken off from the Messerschmitt factories at Augsburg, he would only have a very small chance of reaching England, his alleged destination. Although he was a World War I pilot, such an undertaking needed a lot of skill, prudence, and flying ability—or sheer lunacy.

This was the theme of the telephone conversation I had with Göring, when I reported the failure of our mission. Should Hess really succeed in getting from Augsburg as far as the British Isles, the Spitfires would get him sooner or later.

His ME-110, of course, got to Scotland where Hess apparently ran out of fuel. He bailed out and was picked up by a farmer armed with a pitchfork near Paisley.

An official party communication on May 12 stated: "Party member Rudolf Hess recently managed to obtain an aircraft against the Führer's strict orders forbidding him to fly on account of an illness which had been growing worse for years. On May 10 at about 6 P.M. Hess took off from Augsburg on a flight from which so far he has not returned. . . . A preliminary check on the papers he left behind seems to indicate that he harbored the illusion that he could bring about a peace between Germany and England by a personal intervention through certain English acquaintances."

What ever lay behind this flight, someone had made a last-minute attempt to pull the emergency cord of a fast train speeding over the wrong points.

The mobilization for the east began. Wing after wing was transferred to eastern bases in readiness for action. The whole brunt of the fight against the R.A.F. now rested on the two wings which remained in the west. JG 2 moved south of the Seine, while the JG 26 returned to the Pas de Calais. My staff was at Audembert. The English began what they termed the "Nonstop Offensive." With its usual exaggeration the German propaganda called it the "Nonsense Offensive," which we at the front took a poor view of, but it was not so far wrong this time. The early fighter attacks developed into bombing raids with fighter escort, and these grew more intense after the opening of the Eastern front. No particular strategical purpose could be discerned in these once or twice daily raids. Only once were industrial targets in the sector west of Cologne attacked in a low-level surprise raid across Holland. We intercepted this force on its return and shot down eight bombers and a few fighters. However the roles were now changed. The R.A.F. did the attacking, and we defended as best we could. The numerical ratio had shifted to our disadvantage.

On May 1 our group commander, Fieldmarshal Sperrle, congratulated our wing on its five hundredth kill. By the end of the year we had nearly doubled this figure. During the weeks just before and just after the beginning of the Russian campaign the British increased their air activities considerably. The strong reduction of our forces on the Channel front had the effect of making the enemy feel his way first and then of trying to gain air supremacy in this sector which was now only weakly defended.

June 21: It was a sunny summer day, I remember quite clearly, and I shall never forget it. About midday the radar station reported, "Large formation of enemy aircraft approaching." As we found out later, it was a force of Bristol Blenheim bombers with a fighter escort of about 50 Spitfires and Hurricanes. They were raiding Saint-Omer, a favorite target of the British in those days. I gave the alarm and sent up all three squadrons. They soon engaged the enemy in a battle which cost both sides heavy losses.

At 12:24 o'clock I took off with the flight detailed as the

57

leading unit of the wing. At an altitude of 1100 feet we sighted the British formations which had just raided the airfield of Arques near Saint-Omer. From a greater height I dove right through the fighter escort on to the main bomber force. I attacked the right plane of the lower rear row from very close. The Blenheim caught fire immediately. Part of the crew bailed out. The plane exploded on crashing near the airfield of Saint-Omer. The time was 12:32: eight minutes after take-off. Kill number 68.

In the meantime my unit was struggling with Spitfires and Hurricanes. My flight companion and I were the only Germans at the moment attacking the bombers. Immediately I started my second attack. Again I managed to dive through the fighters. This time it was a Blenheim in the leading row of the formation. Flames and black smoke poured from her starboard engine. She broke away from the formation. I saw two parachutes open. The time was 12:36. Kill number 69.

But then Spitfires were on my tail. Tracer bullets whizzed past me. I tried to shake them off. A sharp downward bank and I got rid of my pursuer. A layer of haze enveloped me. But I caught a barrage. My right radiator was shot up and I was leaving a long trail of smoke behind me. A little later the engine seized up—emergency landing! Luckily the airfield of Calais-Marck was just below me. I made a harmless crash landing. Half an hour later an ME-108 collected me and brought me back to my squadron.

After lunch the dance continued. At four o'clock there was a new alarm: "Strong British fighter formations approaching from the Channel." All air-worthy machines were up again and at the enemy. My faithful flight companion, Rottenflieger Hegenauer, who had flown almost all sorties against England with me during the previous year, had been shot down almost at the same time as myself. So I started alone. Southeast of Boulogne I sighted my 1st Squadron, and decided to join them. Slightly lower and to port of them was a Spitfire formation. I immediately attacked one of the last planes of the formation. Unfortunately not the last! But the Spitfire I went after crashed in flames. Kill number 70. A nice even number, I thought as I followed her down to register the kill. I had no witness, as I was flying alone.

Hell broke loose in my crate. Now they've got me! That's what happens if I take my eye away for a couple of seconds! Something hard hit my head and arm. My aircraft was in bad shape. The wings were ripped by cannon fire. I was sitting half in the open. The right side of the fuselage had been shot away. Fuel tank and radiator were both leaking heavily. Instinctively I banked away to the north. Almost calmly I noticed that my heavily damaged ME still flew and responded tolerably well with the engine cut off. My luck has held once more, I was thinking, and I will try to glide home. My altitude was 18,000 feet.

My arm and head were bleeding. But I didn't feel any pain. No time for that. Anyhow nothing precious was hurt. A sharp detonation tore me out of my reverie. The tank, which up to then had been gurgling away quietly, suddenly exploded. The whole fuselage was immediately aflame. Burning petrol ran into the cockpit. It was getting uncomfortably hot. Only one thought remained: Get Out, Get Out, Get Out! The cockpit-roof release—would not work—must be jammed! Shall I burn alive in here?—I tore my belt open. I tried to open the hinged top of the roof. The air pressure on it was too strong. Flames all around me. I must open it! I must not fry to death in here! Terror! Those were the most terrible seconds of my life. With a last effort I pushed my whole body against the roof. The flap opened and was torn away by the air stream. I had already pulled her nose up. The push against the joy stick did not throw me entirely clear of the burning coffin, which a few minutes before was still my beloved and faithful ME-109. The parachute on which I had been sitting was caught on the fixed part of the cockpit roof. The entire plane was now in flames and was dashing down to earth with me. With my arm around the aerial mast I tugged, I pushed against anything I could find with my feet. All in vain! Should I be doomed at the last moment although I was already half freed? I don't know how I got free in the end. Suddenly I was falling, I turned over several times in the air. Thank God! In my excitement I nearly operated the quick harness release instead of the cord. At the last moment I noticed that I was releasing the safety catch. Another shock! The parachute and I would have arrived separately, and this would have done neither of us any good. A jerk and like a pendulum I was suspended from the opened parachute. Slowly and softly I floated down to earth.

Below me a column of black smoke marked the spot where my ME crashed. By rights I should have landed in the Forest of Boulogne like a monkey on a tree, but the parachute only brushed a poplar and then folded up. I landed rather luckily in a soft, boggy meadow. Up to now I had been under high tension of nerves and energy. I collapsed. I felt as wretched as a dog. Shot and bleeding profusely from head and arm,

59

with a painfully twisted ankle which started to swell immediately, I could neither walk nor stand up. Suspicious and unfriendly French peasants came at last and carried me into a farmhouse. The first Germans I saw were men of the *Todt Organisation* from a nearby building site. They packed me into a car and took me back to my base at Audembert.

Everybody was already considerably worried about me, and my reception was correspondingly warm. After I had drunk an extra large cognac and smoked a cigarette, essential after any kill, I felt much better. In the naval hospital at Hardingham I was repaired by my good friend Marine-Geschwader Arzt Dr. Heim. I am especially grateful to him for allowing me to smoke on the operating table and for not detaining me at the hospital, but letting me return to my base. I could continue to conduct operations from the ground, at least for the time being.

The news of the day's events—the *Schlageter* Wing recorded a bag of 14—traveled fast. Congratulations poured in from all sides. My birthday and my seventieth kill were celebrated in a befitting manner. Osterkamp came over from Le Tourquet. What he had to tell me besides his congratulations struck me like a bolt from the blue. No one had expected anything like it, least of all I. So far the oak leaves to the Knight's Cross had been the highest award for bravery. As far as we knew there was nothing higher to win in this war. Late the same night arrived the confirmation from the Führer's headquarters: ". . . I present you as the first officer of the German forces with the oak leaves with swords to Knight's Cross-of-the-Iron Cross. Adolph Hitler."

8

The Eastern Front

Early next day, June 22, 1941, after a terrific bombardment, the German offensive against the Soviet Union started on a front of about 2200 miles, running from Lake Ladoga down to the Black Sea. Three German army groups took part. One spearhead was directed toward Leningrad under von Leeb: it consisted of the Busch and von Küchler armies, the Höppner armored corps, and the Keller air force group. In the Warsaw sector was assembled the von Bock army group, with the von Kluge and von Weichs armies, the Guderian and Hoth armored corps and the Kesselring air force group. This was the strongest army and its objective was Moscow. From South Poland and Galicia, von Rundstedt pushed toward the Ukraine with the armies of von Reichenau and von Stulpnagel, von Kleist's armored corps, the Lohr air force group, together with the Hungarian and Slovakian units. On the flanks of this great front fought the allies of Germany. The Finns under Marshal Mannerheim with the army led by Dietl attacked the Karelian Isthmus between Lake Onega and Lake Ladoga. The Romanians under Marshal Antonescu with the German army of von Schoberth were out to liberate the eastern provinces which the Soviet had taken from them. They advanced over the Pruth River toward Odessa.

An operation of a dimension unheard of in the history of warfare had started. The size of the country and the hosts of troops, from European standards, did nothing to stop the run of the operation according to plan. The wedges driven by the German armored columns bit deeper and deeper into enemy territory, breaking all resistance. In the first days of the campaign gigantic battles of annihilation, using pincer movements, were fought. These brought in an unbelievable number of prisoners and huge amounts of war material.

From the first morning of the campaign onward German bombers, Stukas, fighters, and combat squadrons roared over the blazing front in continuous action, attacking airfields and depots of the enemy air force, troop concentrations and reserves, and supporting the army units in the manner that had proved so successful in Poland and on the Western front. The Stukas and combat fighters in particular proved their value during the closest collaboration with the army. The fighters quickly ran up a high score of kills. The fighting ability and the standard of training of the Soviet pilots was, in the early days of the campaign, inferior to ours. Soon after me, Mölders was decorated with the swords and a few weeks later received the jewels to the oak leaves, as the first soldier of the Wehrmacht for his one hundredth kill.

Complete elimination of the Soviet air force was never achieved, at least not in the sense of Douhet's conception. Our superiority was undeniable and lasted much longer than the anticipated length of the campaign. Yet in order to annihilate the enemy's air force we should have needed a much larger strategical air force with a considerably longer range. This did not exist. The immense size of the operational area and the countless tasks divided the strength of the Luftwaffe. The air force lost more and more the character of an independent arm; and as a result of the demands made on it by the extent and toughness of the struggle and by force of circumstances, it became more like an addition to the army. Like the navy the German Luftwaffe had been constructed and planned, in accord with its character, as an independent service of the main forces, obeying its own laws of development. Although its importance had been recognized, there had not been enough time to give it the required depth and breadth. Now we were forced to abandon the original conception of its character. The air force played the role of a sort of "fire brigade," its strength was frittered away, and it became more and more under the dictatorship of ground tactical ideas.

Involuntarily we had almost taken over the ideas of our Soviet enemy. The Red air force was never an independent force but always an integral part of the Red army. As such it was perhaps better organized and suited to its purpose and better employed in action than the German Luftwaffe. Right from the start the Russian air force had not been intended to fulfill any strategic purpose: it concentrated entirely on supporting the army. The accent lay on flying in battles. Any soldier from the Eastern front can tell how the Ratas, J-12s, Migs, and Lags made their lives difficult. The Russians had a primitive conception of their strategical possibilities.

The technical equipment and standard of flying were not very good, but they fulfilled their limited task of giving exclusive support to the army. We never managed to prevent the Red air force from doing this despite our superiority. Although the number of planes we shot down reached an astronomical figure, it gave us only a temporary and local relief, because most of their centers of aircraft production lay far beyond our range. It was as if one tried to exterminate a nest of ants by killing them one by one without being able to get to their heap.

The primitiveness of the country, the long distances, and the difficulties of supply caused serious difficulties. An air force is technically such an intricate and complicated apparatus that it is particularly dependent on supplies and repair organization. The factor that soon reduced the fighting ability of the Luftwaffe in Russia was not the Russian air defense, but the total absence of all prerequisites for the functioning of such a highly developed and therefore sensitive instrument of war.

One of the guiding principles of fighting with an air force is the assembling of weight by numbers, of a numerical concentration at decisive spots. It was impossible to adhere to this principle because of the continuous expansion of the Eastern front and because of the urgent demands made by the army. In spite of superiority and relatively small losses it was possible in the east to visualize a point in the future where the offensive strength of the Luftwaffe would diminish through a continuous exertion. The campaign had to be brought to a victorious end before this moment arose. The initial successes seemed to justify such a hope.

Special bulletins from the front chased each other home. Near Uman two entire Soviet armies and a part of a third had been encircled and annihilated. Leningrad and Odessa were surrounded. In the central sector, Timoshenko's armies, protecting Moscow, were decimated in fierce battles at Smolensk, Gomel, Mogilev, Bryansk, and Vyazma. East of Kiev and along the Dnieper, Budenny's armies were encircled by armored divisions and annihilated. A chain of brilliant feats followed. By the end of September the Germans and their allies had penetrated about 600 miles into enemy territory. The front ran approximately from Lake Ladoga and Lake Ilmen via Smolensk-Poltava down to the Sea of Azov.

The whole German nation received the war reports from the east with amazement. At the same time there was something oppressive about it, like somebody who is exposed to great danger without being aware of it. Even the greatest pessimists had not thought it possible that the Soviet Union possessed such colossal strength in personnel, material, and morale as she had revealed during these last months. Dared we think of her as already conquered? Or were there still greater surprises in store for us?

As was understandable, the entire interest of the German public as well as that of the leaders was turned toward the east. In the beginning of July the British had signed a mutual-assistance pact with the Soviet Union and now tried to assist their new ally in the best way possible. They increased the nonstop offensive. The only thing we heard about this were a few presumptuous and ironical remarks from some very complacent radio announcer. These remarks were sparsely scattered between special announcements of fantastic successes on the Eastern front. It would have been better had this fellow not mentioned the west! We knew quite well that the east was for the time being the decisive sector of the war. We too marveled at the successes which had been achieved there and we knew their importance. But it was simply intolerable that our fight in the west, waged on a forlorn outpost against an enemy which grew daily in strength, should be treated in this way. Each time we went into battle it was a fight for life or death. I am not ashamed to admit that before each sortie I was in a state approaching terror. As soon as I got up to a few thousand feet my fears vanished.

After my seventieth kill I was grounded by strict orders. This did not matter at first, as I could not move about for some days. But as soon as I could walk on a stick, I got myself two new aircraft and started to fly and to do some gun testing. I took it for granted that the grounding order only applied to combat flying.

Without my knowledge my leading rigger, Unteroffizier Meyer, had fitted an additional armor plating inside the roof of the cockpit. It was done with good intentions but on closing the lid I received a wretched bump on the head. I swore at him, but I was to regret it a few minutes later, because on this July 2 this test flight turned out to be nearly my last flight in action. A bombing raid was in progress on Saint-Omer with a fighter escort. I flew with my entire wing against them. We reached a favorable position for attacking. I gave the order for the attack and I was the first to dive down through the English fighter escort on to the bombers. Flying in a shallow right bank I fired from a distance of about 200 yards right down to ramming distance at one of the Blenheims in the first row of the formation. Pieces of metal and other parts broke away from the fuselage and from the right engine. Then she went up in flames and smoke. The remnants of her were found later. I could not observe the crash, because I got into a hot fight with the escorting Spitfires. While I was chasing one, a second got me. Everything rattled inside my crate. My cockpit was shattered. But what is more, my head got it again. Warm blood was running down my face. I was afraid of a blackout. I must not lose consciousness! With a great effort I succeeded in shaking off my pursuer and landing safely. My aircraft was a bit shot up: a 2-cm. cannon shell had exploded on the new armor plating on top of the cockpit. At the hospital Dr. Heim had to sew me up again. Without the armor plating nothing would have remained of this indispensable part of my body. Unteroffizier Meyer got special leave and 100 marks. I valued my head that much.

There was a spot of trouble because of my offense against the grounding order. From a strictly military point of view I had of course committed a breach of discipline. In a military organization orders—and my grounding was an order—are there to be obeyed. Therefore I did not feel so happy when I was ordered to East Prussia to fetch my swords from the Führer. I flew to Rastenberg and was driven to the Wolf's Redoubt, the code name for Hitler's headquarters. Here in the middle of a dark pine-tree forest behind barriers of barbed wire, new bunkers and barracks were being built all the time. Among guards, orderlies, and laborers of the *Todt Organisation* in their olive-colored uniforms, one could see the gleam of gold and red from the uniforms of generals and officers of the General Staff. Fantastic, unfamiliar uniforms of diplomats, high party members, and officials completed the strange picture.

Hitler did not mention my offense against the grounding order, but he wanted to know all about the new armor plating over the cockpit. He asked me to take more "care in action." I had expected that he would talk about the incredible successes of his army in the east. For the occasion I had already thought out some biting remarks about our forlornness in the west.

He did nothing of the kind. With the greatest of interest and with the fullest understanding of our situation he asked for details of our fighting on the Channel front. He had only words of appreciation for the action of these few fighter pilots who carried for the time being the full burden of the daily fight against the growing strength of the R.A.F. He understood quite well that the first deliveries of American aid to England had made themselves felt and that these deliveries would constantly increase. But he believed that this handicap could be overcome by us. The Soviet had already suffered terrible blows. The operations were going according to plan. The Red Army would be destroyed before the winter. Till then we had to grit our teeth. He had already been able to reduce the production of ammunition. The ammunition stores were full. Soon he would be in a position to relieve 50 army divisions. The conquered Russian territory was to be patrolled by a few fast-moving armored divisions. The air force would benefit from the relieved divisions and from the capacity of war industries which would be freed. The British position in the Near East was going to be attacked by a pincer movement from Egypt and the Caucasus. After clearing the Near East and the Mediterranean and with a speeded up aircraft and U-boat production, we should be in a position to deal England the final blow.

Thoughtfully, but with renewed hope, I returned to my base on the Channel coast. We certainly had to grit our teeth. But if the picture of the future that Hitler had outlined to me in bold strokes were to materialize, then the day would come when we could again confront our old enemy as an equal. But I must admit that what I had heard at the Wolf's Redoubt sounded a bit fantastic. But was not the whole war fantastic? Was it not incredible that this little Germany had leaped at the throat of the Bolshevist colossus, who was obviously getting short of breath? But woe to us if the deadly grip should be released for some reason or other. The end had to come quickly. If the fight against Russia were to be drawn out, there would be no chance for the Luftwaffe to regain the superiority she had temporarily lost in the west. A long fight in the east would wear down the air force.

I put such thoughts right at the back of my mind. There was no room here for them. The daily action needed all our physical and moral strength. He who wanted to live had to concentrate entirely on the enemy.

9

"War Is No Game of Cricket"

The British pressed us very hard and drove us round the ring with deadly punches. But we hit back whenever we could. In the late summer and autumn months I shot down 21 Spitfires, three Blenheims, and one Hurricane. I am pleased to say that tough as the fight was, it did not for a moment violate the unwritten laws of chivalry. Far removed from all humanitarian sentimentality and fully aware that our conflict with the enemy was a life and death struggle, we kept to the rules of a fair fight, the foremost of which is to spare a defenseless opponent. The German Air Sea Rescue Service therefore looked after any Johnny they found swimming in the Channel as well as after the German airmen. To shoot at a pilot parachuting down would have seemed to us then an act of unspeakable barbarism. I remember quite well the particular circumstances when Göring mentioned this subject during the Battle of Britain. Only Mölders was present when this conversation took place outside the Reichsmarshal's special train in France.

Experience had proved, he told us, that especially with technically highly developed arms such as tanks and fighter aircraft, the men who controlled these machines were more important than the machines themselves. The aircraft which we shot down could easily be replaced by the English. Not so the pilots. As in our own case it was very difficult, particularly as the war drew on. Successful fighter pilots who could survive this war safe and sound would be worth their weight in gold not only because of their experiences and knowledge but also because of their rarity!

There was a short pause. Göring wanted to know if we ever had thought about this subject.

"*Jawohl*, Herr Reichsmarshal!"

"Well?"

I was silent.

Göring looked me straight in the eyes and said, "What

would you think of an order directing you to shoot down pilots who were bailing out?"

"I should regard it as murder, Herr Reichsmarshal," I replied, "and I should do everything in my power to disobey such an order."

Göring put both his hands on my shoulders and said, "That is just the reply I had expected from you, Galland." In World War I similar thoughts had cropped up, but were equally strongly rejected by the fighter pilots.

I do not know what lay behind this conversation or if such an order had been suggested in any particular quarter. But had such a suggestion been made seriously, then it could only have come from someone who knew nothing of soldiery and the nature of chivalrous fighting. However it is possible that with this question, Göring wanted to get our backing in case he had to reject such a request, were it to be made or had really been made. In any case the subject was never mentioned again in the Luftwaffe, not even later when aerial warfare became so gruesome.

This question of chivalry was demonstrated very clearly by an episode that took place in the summer of 1941 on our side of the Channel. One of the most successful and famous fighter pilots of the R.A.F., Wing Commander Douglas Bader, was shot down in a dogfight over the Pas de Calais. It was never confirmed who actually shot him down. When Bader was captured, he particularly wanted to know who had shot him down, and wanted if possible to meet his master in the air. He said that for him it was an intolerable idea that possibly he had been shot down by a German NCO. It was not an NCO, but probably one of our able young officers, among whom there were some outstanding pilots. I had shot down that day two Spitfires out of Bader's formation. In order not to offend Bader we chose from among the successful pilots who had taken part in this fight a fair-haired, good-looking flying officer and introduced him to Bader as his victorious opponent. Bader was pleasantly surprised and shook his hand warmly.

He described his crash like this: "I saw pieces flying off my crate. The nose dipped. I looked round—the tail unit had practically gone . . . nothing else to be done but to get out as quickly as possible. That was easier said than done, especially as the plane dove vertically and began to spin. I pulled myself up with my hands. I had already got one leg outside. The other one, the right one, was wedged inside. I tugged and the plane tugged too. Then I was shooting through the air minus my right leg. That was going down with the aircraft. . . !"

The parachute opened. The impact with the ground was particularly painful because his leg was pushed up into his chest. It was an artificial leg, like the right one. He was taken to Saint-Omer Hospital in a pretty bad state. His first question was about his artificial limbs. One was standing beside his bed, and on his request a search was made for the other one under the wreckage of his Spitfire. It was found, very badly bent of course, but my mechanics soon straightened it out. Bader was delighted. The moment the doctors allowed him to get out of bed, he started his first attempts at walking. This man had terrific will power. He refused to stay in the single room which had been allocated to him. He wanted to be together in one room with the other British pilots in the hospital. He set the tone and upheld the spirit and the comradeship.

For Bader flying was a passion. He was not discouraged when he lost both his legs in a flying accident as a young man in 1931. In spite of all this he still flew. Through effort and skill he managed to join the R.A.F. at the beginning of World War II. He must certainly have been the only operational pilot with two artificial legs. British common sense had prevailed over all rules and regulations. He was soon making a career for himself. He became one of those leaders who saved their country during the Battle of Britain because of their inflexible tenacity.

One day the commander of the 1st Squadron came to tell me of the kind of "eagle" we had caught. He was full of enthusiasm. "You must come and meet him." Bader's ribs were more or less healed. I sent my large staff car, a Horch, which I rarely used myself, to the hospital in Saint-Omer. An officer, a sergeant-major, and the driver fetched Bader in style. Some of our commanders and several other officers were having tea with their British guest at the Group Staff headquarters. He was obviously surprised and impressed by the lavishness of the reception. Only after some time did he overcome the distrust he could not hide, in spite of his charming and winning manners.

Bader was on his guard against giving the slightest hint of any military information. Anyhow, we were strictly forbidden to interrogate prisoners: this was left entirely to specialists at the interrogation centers. Nevertheless I had given instructions that nothing should be said which could even resemble a question. He did not even admit how many enemy planes he had to his credit.

"Oh, not many," he said. He did not know how many had been recognized, and confirmations were still outstanding.

"Well, you must know approximately how many," I urged him.

"No," he replied, avoiding the issue defensively. "Compared with Mölders' and your bag, they are so few that it's hardly worth talking about them." Actually he had some 20 to his credit. Perhaps it really was only modesty that he did not want to talk about it with us.

Bader loosened up during the course of the free and easy conversation, so I proposed a little tour of our installations. He accepted with pleasure and obvious interest. The leg which had been salvaged from the wreckage squeaked and rattled like a small armored car. Bader asked me if we could not drop a message over England to tell his boys and his wife that he was well and to get him his spare legs, a better uniform than his battle dress, tobacco, and a new pipe to replace the one he had broken and was stuck together with adhesive tape. His wife would know what to do. The spare legs were on the left in the wardrobe. I offered him some tobacco and one of my pipes, but he refused. Naturally it was outside my province to give him a definite promise to fulfill this request which was certainly of considerable originality. But I promised I would do my best.

Our masterly camouflaged field attracted his attention as an expert. A long conversation about technical details followed, during which he praised the better points of the ME while we praised the Spitfire. Would I not allow him to sit in the cockpit of my plane? "Why not!" Everything had to be explained to him in the smallest detail. I enjoyed the interest and understanding this great pilot showed. He would have fitted splendidly into our "club."

Bader bent down to me from the cockpit of my plane in which he still sat and said. "Will you do me a great favor?"

"With pleasure, if it is in my power," I answered.

"At least once in my life I would like to fly a Messerschmitt. Let me do just one circle over the airfield." He said it with a smile and looked me straight in the eyes. I nearly weakened.

But I said, "If I grant your wish, I'm afraid you'll escape and I should be forced to chase after you. Now we have met we don't want to shoot at each other again, do we!" He laughed and we changed the subject. After a hearty good-by he went back to the hospital.

I immediately got in touch with Göring and reported my admiration for the legless commander and asked permission to have the spare legs sent. Göring agreed at once. He maintained that Bader's was the same spirit that had reigned among the air force during World War I. They had extended any possible service they could to their shot down opponents, even though they had been enemies. We were to make radio contact with the R.A.F. on international SOS wave lengths, offering free conduct to a British plane, which could land on an airfield near the coast and unload all the things Bader wanted.

Radio contact was made. Our message about Bader's capture and his wishes were confirmed by the English. I was pleased that here, in the middle of the war, an action was about to be performed which would rise above the national bitterness of the fighting on both sides.

Some time later Bader vanished. During the night he had let himself down from a top window of the hospital by sheets knotted together and had escaped. This was very unpleasant for me and the persons responsible. The Group Staff made a most embarrassing inquiry about his escape. Even his visit to our air base, for which I had not asked permission, came up during the stern investigations.

The whole affair became even more unpleasant on account of Bader's spare legs. The British did not wait for our detailed suggestions. Soon our aerodrome and other targets around Saint-Omer were heavily raided. We received a radio message over the same wave length; it had not been only bombs they dropped but also the requested spare legs for Bader. A large box was duly found with a large red cross painted on it and the words in German: "This box contains artificial legs for Wing Commander Bader, Prisoner of War."

This was not a very friendly reply to our well-meant proposal. To our minds bombs and charity did not go together. The critics held that this showed what the English thought of such fair play from our side.

Bader was soon recaptured and came under stricter observation in various prisoner-of-war camps. He made several more abortive attempts to escape, each one a further proof of his mettle. We fighter pilots on this side of the Channel do not associate ourselves with what Bader actually said to a German journalist after the war: ". . . I am not one of those who regard war as a game of cricket—first to shoot at each other and then to shake hands. Please emphasize this to your readers . . ." Even today we are still of the opinion that at the time we acted correctly, humanely, and fairly toward Bader.

I saw him again four years later. In 1945, after the war, I was taken to the Air Force Interrogation Camp 7, Latimer in North London, as a prisoner of war. I was then driven to Tangmere aerodrome near Southampton where R.A.F. group leaders were in conference. Wing Commander Bader, who had returned to England, was among them. This time I stood in front of him as a prisoner and he offered me his box of cigars. Our roles were changed. Bader concerned himself in the most charming manner about my personal comforts, but next morning he suddenly vanished again, as he had done once before. In 1945 the war went on despite unconditional surrender.

War is no game of cricket. Should this have surprised the German reporter?

10

A Somber Chapter

Late in the year 1941 a string of events happened of a kind that suited the general mood of cold fogs, leafless trees, and other depressing signs of autumn. On November 17 we heard over the radio an announcement from General Forces Headquarters: "The Generalluftzeugmeister of the Luftwaffe, Generaloberst Ernst Udet had a fatal crash this morning while testing a new type of plane. The Führer has ordered a state funeral." A little later I received orders to go immediately to Berlin.

Recently I had been with Udet at Elchwald in East Prussia, one of Göring's hunting lodges. The memory of what was discussed during our conversation there made me guess things which very soon came to light. Udet did not die in a crash; it was no accident. He shot himself at his home.

Udet was, of course, very much liked by the young fighter pilots. He was popular everywhere. With 62 kills to his credit from World War I he was an example to us, and also an experienced friend and comrade. His outstanding flying skill combined with a happy disposition, an incomparable charm, and the urge to get the best out of life, made it impossible to dislike him. He was a real person with a warm heart, talented and with a natural sense of humor. As a stunt pilot he traveled around the world, made films in Greenland with Leni Riefenstahl, went on expeditions to Africa, was feted in North and South America.

In 1933 he returned to Germany. His old comrade from World War I and his last wing commander, Hermann Göring, persuaded him after some resistance to join in the reconstruction of the Luftwaffe. He made a successful career of it. He became first an inspector of the fighter force and after that, in 1936, Chief of the Technical Department of the Air Ministry. In 1938 he was promoted to lieutenant colonel and a year later took over the responsibility for rearming the German Aircraft Industry as Generalluftzeugmeister. Udet certainly never strove for military power and influence. But once he was in this position he backed up all his colleagues and co-workers whether they deserved it or not. With all his human greatness and his sympathies he lacked a gift for organization and the severity that the job demanded. And if he proved unable to meet the demands of those who set him this task, they should bear the blame.

When I saw him for the last time I hardly recognized him: his spontaneous *joie de vivre*, his gay humor, and attractive warmth had all disappeared. He was in the depths of depression. The course of the war so far proved to him that the Luftwaffe was on the wrong track. "Fighters, fighters, fighters, that's what we need! Thousands of them." That was his often-repeated demand. Yet the production figures of the German fighter industry under his supervision were not enough even to replace the losses sustained on the Eastern front, to say nothing about holding or regaining air superiority in the west. He had a very good idea of what was coming to us, and said that the Western front was becoming a "Verdun of the air." Finally he lost his way in the political maze of the German leadership and collapsed under the task given to him.

His death touched me very deeply, especially when I learned that he had committed suicide. We had spent many happy hours together. Sometimes he had said jokingly, "Don't you come too close to my record with your number of planes shot down. Before you reach my figure I hope the war will be over."

I shall never forget the evening he took Mölders and me back to his bachelor flat, after we had discussed and dissected the war in the air. "Now we will shoot," said Udet, and he produced pistols, rifles, target disks, and a thick slab of lead as a butt. He was not going to admit that we were the better shots. "It's all because I'm thirsty," he said. With each new bottle of champagne we got worse. At the end of the evening Ernst Udet was the best shot.

Serious thoughts and happy memories passed through my mind as six of us fighter pilots, all wearing Germany's highest award for bravery, formed the guard of honor at Udet's coffin which had lain in state at the Air Ministry. We were in steel helmets and full-dress uniform carrying the outsized air force sword. Mölders should have been with us. After his hundredth kill he was released from the front and made General of the Fighter Arm. For some time he had been with fighter units in the Crimea. On account of bad weather he could not arrive in time for the state funeral at Berlin.

The funeral procession was very impressive. Göring walked behind the coffin all the way to the Invaliden Cemetery in the north of Berlin.

I traveled back to the Channel with Oesau, the commander of JG 2. Our train stopped at a tiny station in Lippe. The station master ran excitedly along the train calling my name, "Oberstleutnant Galland wanted on the phone!" I got out of the train. The man with the red cap was all confused. It had probably never happened in the history of this little station that an express train had stopped because of an urgent governmental call. I picked up the receiver. General Bodenschatz was at the other end of the line. He first asked me if I were sitting down. When I said no, he begged me to do so. Then he said, "Mölders has had a fatal crash. You must return immediately to Berlin; in fifty minutes a train will stop and bring you back here. This is an order from the Reischmarshal!" I fetched my suitcase and said good-by to Oesau. I was very upset.

The HE-111 in which Mölders had taken off from the Crimea had to make an emergency landing at Lemberg, because of bad weather. The following day, November 22, he gave the order to continue the flight, although his pilot was against it and the weather was appalling. On the trip one engine failed. They decided to land at Breslau. They went down through clouds and fog to make a blind landing. But the pilot lost height too soon. When he tried to open the throttle again the second engine conked. He just managed to clear a cable railway on that side of the airfield but the plane stalled and crashed from a low height. Mölders and the head mechanic were killed instantly. The pilot Oberleutnant Kolbe, an experienced flier who had been already in Spain, died on the way to hospital. The survivors, Mölders' aide-de-camp and the radio operator, were able to reconstruct the accident in full details.

Of course the wildest rumors circulated about Mölders' death. The public had become suspicious because Udet's suicide had been reported as being an accident. It looked as though by hushing this up they had tempted fate because now, starting with Mölders, there followed a series of tragic flying accidents in which leading politicians and high-ranking members of the forces lost their lives. The legends attached to these accidents would fill a book.

Mölders had very strong religious convictions. He stood up

against the polemic the party used, especially with regard to the Catholic Church and her institutions. But it is not true that he got into difficulties because of this or that his death had any connection with it.

Eight days after Udet's state funeral we were standing once more beside an open grave. Once more members of the fighter arm wearing the Knight's Cross stood the last guard of honor. Once more Göring exhorted a comrade. "Arise to Valhalla." Mölders was also buried in the Invaliden Cemetery, not far from Richthofen and Udet.

After the coffin had been lowered into the ground and the salvoes and speeches were over, the officers selected as guard of honor remained at the grave. During the funeral ceremonies very serious thoughts crossed my mind. Mölders had come victoriously out of more than 100 aerial combats in Spain and on the West Wall, in the Battle of Britain, and on the Eastern front. Then he was taken out of action. He, too, had flown again despite his grounding orders; he had shot down a few more Soviet fighters. Yet before he was able fully to develop his abilities of leadership, tested in so many battles, he suffered an airman's death in the home country, which was still peaceful at the time.

I was awakened abruptly by Göring calling my name and beckoning to me with his marshal's baton. I was somewhat embarrassed. No regulation laid down how to leave one's post in a guard of honor. I had not the foggiest idea what to do with my drawn sword in such a position.

"Now it is your turn," said Göring. "I name you herewith as Mölders' successor, to be General of the Fighter Arm."

I had been afraid of this, but I had not really counted on it. I have no recollection of my immediate reaction. I was never in my life happy at a desk. My squadron meant everything to me. Everyone who shared those difficult but wonderful times on the Channel coast will sympathize with me when I declare that I was numbed by the thought of having to leave my squadron. I told Göring this during a later conversation, but he remained adamant. Everything had already been discussed with the Führer. I should have a field of action of far greater importance than my present one. No arguments! He promised to convey my farewell wishes to my squadron in a few days' time in person since he had to go to France. He would visit the grave of his nephew at Abbeville and would go via Audembert to Holland.

Peter Göring had fallen about a fortnight before this conversation after his first victorious dogfight over the Channel.

He was of the same age group as my youngest brother and they had been inseparables. I had taken them both under my wing and had them transferred to my *Schlageter* Squadron. Peter Göring was a talented fighter pilot and a nice, well-educated boy who was liked by everyone, not because of but rather in spite of his uncle, who had already lost a great deal of respect, authority, and sympathy among the fighter airmen.

On that fatal November 13, I flew with Peter Göring as his accompanying aircraft against a formation of Blenheim bombers which were heavily protected by fighters. On our climb we passed near this hellish "goods train." We were over-taking British fighters right and left. This was so incredibly impertinent that it succeeded. This young, enthusiastic pilot had never seen so many Spitfires at such close range. When we were about 200 yards from the bombers I called out to him, "Let them have it, Peter!"

He was flying about 50 yards to my left. After the first bursts of fire his plane suddenly dove vertically. No one was behind him. I followed him down and saw a flame shoot up, marking his crash. He died in the knowledge of his first victory, probably shot through the head.

We buried him in the Soldiers' Cemetery at Abbeville, where lay already many comrades of the *Schlageter* Squadron who had given their lives in the Battle of Britain, defending the Channel coast.

My ideas on the new duties and tasks, which awaited me in Berlin were extremely hazy. I was no General Staff officer. I hated everything to do with staff. From a position of leading men, I was now going to become one of those "brass hats" for whom we had always used the most derogatory terms. I knew of course that these terms were most unfair. But here my ambition stopped and my anger started: I wanted to fight and swear at the command. Nothing else! In any case I had the firm intention of never losing contact with the men or becoming just staff.

11

Forward or Backward?

On December 6, 1941, the offensive of von Bock's army came to a standstill in the northwestern suburbs of Moscow. The German soldiers could see the spires of the Russian capital with the naked eye. They had reached the terminus of the Moscow tramlines. The Luftwaffe had raided Moscow several times. Military objectives in the district were within the range of our heavy artillery. The Russian diplomatic corps had been evacuated to Kuibyshev. The government was ready to follow them. It is a fact that the strategic objectives of the German Command had nearly been reached at the beginning of winter, 1941—nearly, but not quite. In order to overcome the distance separating us from victory in the east, we needed only a few more days of favorable weather. Now every child knows that the Russian late autumn converts the roads into bogs, and since Napoleon's disaster that Russian winters are cruelly cold and that any operation on a large scale is impossible for a European army. Rain and mud had slowed down our advance but it was the barbarous cold which brought it to a halt. At the start the cold was not only particularly fierce, but it began at the beginning of December, whereas usually it does not start before the New Year.

The German offensive therefore stopped abruptly on December 6. The Soviet got the breathing space they needed to mobilize their immeasurable resources. The Western Allies assisted this process by sending steadily increasing supplies. While at the Führer's headquarters it was hoped that we could deliver in the spring the decisive blow we had just missed, and while the attention of the general public was occupied with Pearl Harbor and the first amazing successes of the Japanese in their war against the Western Powers in East Asia, the fact remained hidden from most people that the curve of the graph indicating the German victories had passed its peak and would descend from now on. It was moving toward its final end with almost mathematical precision at a constantly steepening angle.

In Africa, during the late summer and autumn, Auchinleck had drawn up the British Eighth Army against Rommel's Afrika Korps, which had advanced to Salum. Tobruk, which Rommel had encircled, was held by the British garrison until the Eighth Army started the counteroffensive on November 18, 1941. Rommel defended himself by very skillfully conducted counterthrusts, was finally able to extricate himself from the grip of the pincer movement, and led the bulk of the Afrika Korps back to the area of El Agheila, where he made preparations for a new offensive.

In the Far East Manila, Guam, and Wake Island, the Philippines and British Malaya, Singapore, Borneo, Celebes, and Sumatra were occupied by the Japanese. The German public followed with amazement and admiration the amphibious Blitz victories of her ally. The military leaders looked upon these successes with the hope that they might ease their strategic burden.

On the other hand, everyone was shocked by the news from the Eastern front. It was not so much the fact that the operations had come to a standstill (at Rostov, for the first time in this war, the German line had to fall back) which seriously shook the belief in the leaders, but the fact that our army of a million men in the east was exposed to the Russian winter without suitable equipment and clothing. Hitler met this crisis in two ways. First, he organized through Goebbels a woolen-garment collection which mobilized a feeling of solidarity among the Germans. Secondly, he personally took over the command of the army. Fieldmarshal von Brauchitsch was dismissed. The Führer must have overestimated his reputation with the German people if he believed that he could steady the dwindling trust by such measures.

Perhaps he was successful to a certain extent. Yet inside the army the von Brauchitsch crisis had grave consequences. It brought out tensions which may have been more or less latent up to that moment, but which now increased steadily and finally became too strong to be bridged. Hitler's assumption of supreme command of the army also had a serious and adverse effect on the air force. As Commander-in-Chief of the Forces and Commander of the Army, all in one person, he must often have been faced with situations in which the demands of a coordinated war leadership and especially those of the Luftwaffe had to take second place to the needs of the army. This circumstance hastened the process of wearing down the Luftwaffe in the service of the army, which had started at the beginning of the Russian campaign.

The unforeseen prolongation of the Eastern Campaign threatened to upset the entire strategy of the German Command. Hitler had accepted a war on two fronts only on condition that a quick and total victory over the enemy in the East could be achieved. When the German offensive came to a standstill it meant the end of Hitler's plan to resume the air offensive against England after a speedy termination of the Eastern Campaign. This failure could not be disguised by the grandiose and far-reaching plans in the direction of the Caucasus for the coming spring.

As supreme commander of the Luftwaffe, Göring of all people should have realized clearly that he could never regain the temporary loss of air superiority in the west with a force, which, already in the Eastern Campaign, had been strained far beyond the limits of its capacity. Everything beyond this point could only be termed as "burning the substance." The German air industry was not equal to a war of such dimensions, nor was the ability to replace personnel. Even if immediate attempts were now made to adapt the Luftwaffe to the increased demands, it was impossible to foresee whether the effect of such changes would make itself felt early enough to prevent a total collapse.

This was the situation when I took up my new post as General of the Fighter Arm at the close of 1941. At that time I was not conscious of the way these things were connected. I was simply a fighter pilot, a wing commander with burning enthusiasm. Especially through my meetings with Hitler, Göring, and other political and military personalities of the Reich I had formed my own conclusions about the war and its continuation. But these thoughts had only hovered on the fringe of events. I had been totally preoccupied by the daily fight against the R.A.F.

Now my thoughts took definite shape and form and had to be substantiated by experience and knowledge. From one day to the next I had been given an extremely new task. No wonder I felt unsure of myself at first and very depressed.

The Berlin Office of the General of the Fighter Arm was in the Lindenstrasse, and was formerly the *Vorwärts* building. An apt name for the office of the military commander of so young and aggressive an arm. I am afraid the name had no suggestive effect on me.

During his short term of office Mölders had spent little time in Berlin. He had usually been at the front with the different units and had therefore left little trace of his activity. The department had existed since 1935 as the Office for Inspection of Fighter and Combat Aircraft and was held in turn by Udet, von Greim, Lörzer, Raithel, Junck, von Massow, and von Döring. When Göring promoted the head of this department to General of the Fighter Arm he extended the field of action and the powers of this office considerably. This expressed itself also in a new and extraordinary hierarchy. The General of the Fighter Arm was directly under the Chief of the Luftwaffe General Staff as regards flying matters, and in disciplinary matters he was under the Supreme Commander of All Forces: thus he had only two superiors, Göring and Hitler.

No wonder therefore that a new man in this post was distrusted by all the higher commands including the Air Ministry. Already on my inaugural visit in Berlin, this made itself felt. It was the same when I visited "Robinson," the H.Q. of the Luftwaffe at Goldap. I was received kindly, but there was no disguising the fact that I was considered superfluous and out of place. This was also my own impression of my new post. After my first official visit to General Jeschonnek, Chief of General Staff, I felt helplessly homesick. I flew straight to the coast to spend Christmas with my old squadron.

Here I found myself again. I soon saw things more realistically and knew that it was senseless to take refuge in resentment. At the same time I realized the great possibilities my new job offered me. Now I could fight all the inadequacies and mistakes which had made our lives so difficult at the front. It was doubtful whether I could succeed in achieving my object, but I had to try with all my strength.

In order to do justice to my task and to overcome the difficulties of distance and time which the terrific extent of the front had created, I got hold of two experienced veterans to serve as inspectors, Oberleutnant Weiss for the combat fighters and Oberleutnant Lützow for the fighter units. Slowly the Berlin department took on a definite shape. I made Goldap my headquarters. A coach was attached for me to the "Robinson" special train, in which I could live and work. Here I was not too close to and not too far from the three points at which the decisions about the fighter arm were made: the Staff Headquarters, Rominten, where Göring often stayed, and the Führer's H.Q. at Rastenberg.

Here I soon had some important conferences with Jeschonnek which left their mark on the further course of the war. Early in 1942 the spring offensive in the east was prepared, and we expected all that by a very small margin did not come off the previous year. For this purpose Jeschonnek had received orders from Hitler to mobilize as much of the Luftwaffe as he could possibly find. Since the fighter strength in the west could not be depleted any more, and since Rommel needed Stukas and fighters for the success of his new offensive against Egypt, which had opened in January with good initial results, there remained nothing else to do but to dig into the substance of the Luftwaffe. The fact that Jeschonnek was no magician, as was thought at the Führer's H.Q., but an able and lively Chief of General Staff, made no difference in this matter. He even decided to dig temporarily into the training reserves in order to produce the units so urgently needed. The priority demand was for combat fighters.

These were steps which showed clearly the tactical importance of the air force, but they jeopardized the basic training of the fighter force. As General of the Fighter Arm I had serious objections to these steps. I told Jeschonnek so and pleaded with him, pointing out that the Luftwaffe could not afford to look so exclusively to the east. The only enemy in the air to be taken seriously was in the west. At the moment we could still face up to him despite a growing numerical inferiority. But in England the vanguard of the U. S. air force had already appeared. In the future we had to take into account that it would be continuously strengthened and would increase its activity. This danger could only be averted by strengthening the air force to the very limit of our ability. This was not only a question of industrial production, which had taken an encouraging turn for the better, particularly in the line of fighter aircraft, since Milch had become the Chief of Aircraft Production, but it was above all a question of training and stepping up recruitment. I said to Jeschonnek, "If you reduce them now instead of forcing them up, you are sawing off the branch on which we are sitting."

Jeschonnek listened to me quietly and attentively. He did not dispute the validity of my argument and to a certain extent he even agreed with me, but he thought that the fundamental problem of the war was a different one. The campaign against the Soviet Union had been halted for known reasons, but the rapid annihilation of this enemy was now an essential prerequisite for the successful continuation of the war. All forces, including the Luftwaffe, now had to be concentrated on this aim. As before, the Führer was convinced that victory, already as good as achieved, was assured. The imminent spring offensive was to bring it about finally. Should this misfire and place a victorious end of the war in doubt, he would reproach himself deeply for not having contributed everything with regard to the air force to the success of this offensive and final victory. Anything we kept back now or saved as a result of some apparently justified reason would be lost anyhow. But everything we now surrendered voluntarily would be relatively easy to replace once the victory in the east was ours, and could then be successfully employed in the west against the main enemy in the air, according to the ideas I had propounded.

Jeschonnek spoke without vehemence, presumption, or demagogy. Yet he was far from taking things lightly. He was fully aware of the deathly crisis in which the Luftwaffe stood because of the war in the east. Nor did he close his eyes to the potential of the Western Powers. But—and this was the crux of his argument—now that we were in this fatal struggle with the Soviet Union, we had to see it through. There was no need to regard anything as lost yet. But we had to do everything possible in order to achieve the goal at stake.

The Chief of the General Staff had not weakened my argument. He had not even tried to do so. He had given me an insight into the problems of the war. I could not deny the logic of his reasoning. Only much later did I realize that in spite of his high intelligence and his absolute integrity he became more and more unconditionally under the spell of Hitler. I can record this fact only as a phenomenon and I refrain from criticism. Jeschonnek went straight and erect along the path which was indicated to him to his tragic end.

On January 28, I received, as second soldier of the forces, the jewels to the Knight's Cross. This came as a surprise. Mölders had received them after his hundredth kill. I was six short of a hundred. But Hitler did not want me to feel badly about my new job by thinking that it had prevented me from earning the highest German reward for bravery. Besides, he thought, all my 94 air victories were achieved exclusively against the western enemy and were therefore to be valued more highly. In any case when my bag was nearing the 100 mark I had taken the precaution to be more sparing with my reports because I did not want to be recalled from the front at that point, as had happened to Mölders.

12

Operation Thunderbolt Begins

Soon after I started my new activity as General of the Fighter Arm, on January 1, 1942, I received an order of extraordinary importance. Jeschonnek explained the task to me: Since March and June, 1941, the following battleships were lying in the French port of Brest: the two battle cruisers *Gneisenau* and *Scharnhorst* (each of 26,000 tons, armed with nine 28-cm. and 12 15-cm. guns) as well as the cruiser *Prinz Eugen* (10,000 tons, armed with eight guns of 20.3-cm. and 12 guns of 10.5-cm. caliber). These ships, partly as lone raiders and partly in squadron in a series of important and successful operations, had sunk more than 1,000,000 tons of British shipping since the war began, including the aircraft carrier *Glorious,* sunk by *Scharnhorst* and *Gneisenau* at Narvik in June, 1940, the battleship *Hood* by the *Prinz Eugen* and the *Bismarck* in May, 1941, and numerous enemy units and supply ships.

In Brest this German unit acted as "fleet in being" by tying down a considerable part of the British navy without stirring from port. The Royal Navy had not only to keep heavy sea forces on the alert in order to protect her convoys in the Channel but also had to suspend the use of the so-called Force H, intended to operate in the Mediterranean against German and Italian supply ships for the African war theater. The Royal Navy therefore had to keep this force, composed of battleships and aircraft carriers, in Gibraltar, for use in the operational sector east of the Strait. Thus indirectly the German warships in Brest for some time relieved Rommel, whose supply question in North Africa was a difficult one.

At the same time these ships acted as a sort of flytrap for the R.A.F. by absorbing a great deal of their attacking strength and diverting them away from the Reich. All told, the R.A.F. made 299 attacks on the warships in Brest harbor. The British during these actions lost 43 planes and 247 airmen. The

Gneisenau was hit twice and the *Scharnhorst* once very heavily. Yet both could be fully repaired.

With the increasing strength of these attacks we had to expect that the German warships might one day be put out of action or even become a total loss. In that event all the positive effect of this "fleet in being" would have ended and so would any hope of the German navy resuming operations in the Atlantic, based on Brest.

Hitler's decision to take the German warships out from Brest, however, was determined by considerations concerning the Eastern front. While the new offensive was being prepared against the Soviet Union, the latter urgently demanded from her Anglo-American Allies not more supplies but the opening of a new front to assist her in her desperate struggle with Germany.

Hitler rightly suspected that Scandinavia would be the most suitable territory for the Allies to open a new front. His suspicion was strengthened by reports from his information service of actions by British commandos in Norway and by doubts as to the neutrality of Sweden. He was in possession of reports, which seemed to him reliable, that a British-Soviet-Scandinavian offensive against the northern flank of Germany was planned for the spring. As a price for entering the war Sweden was promised Narvik and some territory around Pechenga. Hitler regarded this threat as very serious and saw the success of his own coming offensive against the Soviet endangered. Another reason for regarding Scandinavia as especially important was the fact that experiments with heavy water for utilizing atomic energy were being carried out in Norway.

In view of the preparations on the Eastern front there were no armies available for the defense of the northern territories. For the time being the Luftwaffe had to be satisfied with building airfields, preparing ground organizations, and storing supplies, without being able to send any considerable forces there. There remained the fleet in the northern seas.

Neither the navy nor the chief of staff had any enthusiasm for this plan. They thought that the threat was not an acute one, considered that the risk was too big, and pointed out that the crews were in no fit state for action after their long period in port. What is more, they did not want to miss a chance of taking up active operations again in the Atlantic. They now saw some prospects of this, because the British and American fleets were busy in the Pacific, thanks to the Japanese. Their reaction may have been caused by unwillingness to

85

relinquish the freedom of action of their own arm to assist in operations conceived by the Supreme Commander, whose concepts were of a military nature and therefore landbound. I myself, as a member of the air force, knew this feeling of opposition.

The air force also had its doubts. But at the headquarters of the Führer, in contrast to the army and navy, the reply was, "The Luftwaffe can do anything." Jeschonnek, who was explaining to me the details of the planned operation before the final conference at the Führer's H.Q., pointed out that the navy would burden the Luftwaffe with the main responsibility, for a very good reason.

For the transfer of the German units from Brest to Norway only two routes could be envisaged: one led around Scotland whereby an encounter with the Home Fleet, stationed at Scapa Flow, would have been unavoidable. The superiority of the Home Fleet (at least three battleships and two aircraft carriers) made the northern route impossible right from the start. The southern route through the Channel was bound to attract the whole R.A.F. to the German units, in addition to attacks from naval craft and concentrated fire from the British coastal batteries. Despite this it seemed to be the lesser risk if the German fighter force operating on the Channel could be effectively employed.

Jeschonnek understood the situation quite correctly when he predicted that the navy would not even discuss the northern route seriously but would vote for a Channel dash, demanding "close and continuous escort, with full air cover by a sufficient strength of fighters." He thought that in no circumstances should we allow ourselves to be nailed down to such a demand considering there were only two wings and a few training units totaling not more than 250 fighters stationed on the Channel coast. Göring sent Jeschonnek and me to the conference. He was not going to attend because he knew he could not say no to the Führer, although he was well aware that the available fighter strength on the Channel coast was quite inadequate for such a task. The Chief of the General Staff was to propose that I, as the commander of the available fighter force, should assume responsibility for the planned operation.

On January 12, Jeschonnek and I drove to the Wolf's Redoubt. Besides Hitler, Keitel, aides-de-camp, and stenographers we found Raeder, chief in command of the navy, and vice-Admiral Ciliax and Commodore Ruge, the commanders of the battleships, who had come to the Führer's bunker for this important conference. Raeder declared at the start that the preparations and plans for the Channel dash of the units at Brest had been undertaken without any bias. "But" he continued, "I do not think I'm the person to recommend this operation. If the order for this operation should be given, all the plans are ready, and Ciliax and Ruge will report in detail about this. In order to make your decision easier, my Führer."

Hitler gave a résumé of the fundamental principles which had brought him to the decision to transfer practically the entire German Fleet to Norwegian waters. Then Ciliax explained the plans which the Admiralty Staff had so far evolved. In doing so he stressed three points in particular:

1. The movements of the ships must be reduced to a minimum before the start of the operation.

2. The ships must leave the port of Brest by night, so that when passihg through the Channel they could use the daylight for the most effective defense.

3. The ships must be escorted from early dawn to twilight by the strongest possible fighter force.

At this point Hitler interrupted. He stressed the decisive importance of the Luftwaffe in the execution of this operation. Jeschonnek answered guardedly. It would be difficult to provide a permanent escort with 250 fighter planes. However he would use additional night fighters for cover during the early hours of the morning and at dusk. Raeder also demanded once more a strong fighter protection and raids on the British torpedo aircraft bases. The Chief of the General Staff spoke even more plainly. It was impossible at the moment to strengthen the air force in the west. The fighters would therefore be numerically greatly inferior to the British, at least during the afternoon. During the further course of the conference Raeder declared emphatically the success or the failure of the operation would depend solely on the efforts of the Luftwaffe. He begged the Führer to give the necessary orders. Hitler fell in with his wishes and ordered the Luftwaffe to do everything possible to insure the safety of the warships. But Jeschonnek stood firm and repeated that he could not guarantee continuous protection with the forces available.

Closing the conference, Hitler summarized: departure by night, the greatest use of the surprise factor, passing between Dover and Calais by day. He did not believe that the English would take lightning decisions. He regarded the fear expressed by the Admiralty Staff of a possible transfer of large R.A.F. forces to the southeast of England as having no foundation. The situation of the ships at Brest could be compared with that of a person afflicted by cancer. His life could only be saved by a major operation. The performance of the operation gave the chance of saving the patient, a refusal to operate meant certain death.

The minutes of the conference closed with the words: "Therefore the Führer decided in agreement with the opinion of the naval C.-in-C., that the operation should be prepared as suggested."

During the conference Hitler expressly demanded absolute secrecy as an essential prerequisite for a success. A special document in the form of a pledge was drawn up and all those present had to sign. Meanwhile the Führer took me aside and said, "You have heard that everything depends on the air umbrella with which you have to cover the naval units. Do you believe that this operation can succeed?"

What I replied was not only my honest opinion but turned out to be correct after the event. "It all depends," I said, "on how much time the English have to mobilize the R.A.F. against the ships. We need complete surprise, and a bit of luck in the bargain. My fighter pilots will give their very best when they know what is at stake."

I had carefully considered what I said, since I was aware of both the risks of the undertaking and the insufficiency of our forces. This point had been made quite clear to Hitler. He had ordered the operation nevertheless. As a fighter pilot I knew from my own experiences how decisive surprise and luck can be for a success, which in the long run only comes to the one who combines daring with cool thinking.

"Most of my decisions," Hitler said, "are daring. Only those deserve luck who accept the hazards of their venture." If the coup failed he would have the consolation of the knowledge that by having chosen the Channel route the bulk of the men could be saved by the proximity of the coast.

The preparations began immediately with the greatest intensity and under strictest secrecy. No one, besides those present at the conference, was allowed to be taken into confidence without special permission from the Commanders-in-Chief of the navy and the air force. By a special "Order of the Führer" I was made responsible for all questions connected with preparations and execution of the fighter protection for this undertaking. Under pretense of an imminent large-scale offensive against England, I prepared everything for Operation Thunderbolt, which was its official code name. The navy used the code word Cerberus in order to disguise their preparations for the common task. They pretended that the units would soon be sailing into the Atlantic, possibly even to the Pacific.

The camouflaging of the purpose of all these preparations which could not remain unknown to the enemy secret service in occupied France was assisted by a profusion of blinds and misleading radio messages, all for the consumption of the English monitor. Hitler had jokingly mentioned that he would disclose under greatest secrecy to his Italian partner that the naval units at Brest were soon to depart for the Pacific to assist the Japanese. This, he said, would be the quickest and safest way of getting such a piece of information to the British Admiralty. The channels through which the British Admiralty now received intelligence of the moves of destroyers and E-boats, of activities in the mine fields as well as the moves of fighter units were manifold. French Vice-Admiral R. de Bellot, for example, states in his publication, *La guerre aeronaval dans l'Atlantique,* that there existed a secret wireless link to the British Admiralty, conducted by the French naval officer Philippon. He alleges that Philippon sent to England all noteworthy details about the preparation of our undertaking.

The technical coordination of this typical combined operation was planned in such a way that the Luftwaffe was not under the navy but had to rely on teamwork. I must say here in advance that this coordination worked without friction.

The Naval High Command gave the basic instructions for operations. The operative command fell on the naval command groups in whose sector the ships were at the time, i.e., between Brest and the Scheldt Estuary. The West Naval Command group with H.Q. in Paris, and from the Scheldt up to the home ports on the Northern Naval Command group with H.Q. in Kiel.

Vice-Admiral Ciliax, commander of the battleships, came under their command for the duration of the operation. To him fell the duty of the tactical command from his flagship at sea. The commanders of the participating ships were Captain Hoffman (*Scharnhorst*), Captain Fein (*Gneisenau*), and Captain Brinkmann (*Prinz Eugen*).

Between the different naval centers of command and the air force, liaison officers were exchanged during the preparations in order to give the best chance of teamwork. My most important liaison with the naval C.-in-C. was established by Oberst Ibel as "fighter command afloat." With him was a No. Ia and fighter pilot with first and second fighter officers, as well as Oberst Elle in charge of the necessary wireless personnel. This staff was to be on board the flagship during the operation. In the *Gneisenau* and *Prinz Eugen* there were a pilot officer and a wireless operator.

During the trial runs we provided fighter escorts. These trial runs were absolutely essential for testing engines, radio communication, and guns. Naturally they were reduced to a minimum. Staffs and liaisons were working into shape. Between January 22 and February 10, 1942, on eight different days, single trial runs were made, and 450 sorties were flown, providing the escort for the trials. Several British planes were shot down. The R.A.F. came over almost every night to raid Brest, but the German warships were not damaged.

Other air force units including the necessary ground crews and the liaison personnel attached to them were added to my command for the duration of the planned operation.

These units came from the 3rd and the Reich Air Force Groups. No commander likes such interference, but bringing these additional units under my absolute jurisdiction proved an excellent idea and was justified as a means of concentrating our strength. Further, I gained the impression that the commanders were pleased to be relieved in this way of the direct responsibility for such an unheard-of and daring undertaking.

In order to reduce the distance between base and the objects to be protected, the ships were expected to be between Cherbourg and le Havre at dawn according to plan—the fighter units were standing by ready for action in the sector Abbeville-Lille-Calais. The headquarters for this sector (No. I) was at Le Touquet. At the same time we had to be prepared in case the progress of the ships was delayed by some reason or other, so that their position at dawn might well be much further west. For this emergency a second sector of bases had to be established in the area Le Havre-Caen-Cherbourg with headquarters (No. Ia) at Caen. A third sector lay between the mouth of the Scheldt, the Rhine, and the Zuider Zee, with its headquarters (No. II) at Schiphol. If everything went according to plan the fighters returning from action after 15:00 hours would land in this sector, reservice, and take off again as soon as possible to rejoin the ships. Finally there was a fourth sector to serve as base for the fighter escort, which would cover the ships on the following day, when they reached the German Bight. This sector reached from Jever to Wilhelmshaven and had its headquarters at Jever.

These elaborate preparations made a great demand on all the participants, particularly since they had to be accomplished unobtrusively. The secret had to be kept up to the last moment.

A lot depended on the preparations of communications. The airfields of each sector had to be linked up with the respective headquarters by a multitude of cross-connections. Besides an ultrashort wave I had at my disposal a long-wave radio line direct to the C.-in-C. of the flotilla and to the leader of the Fighter Command on board. A speed code was used on this line, and all intelligence was given according to a fighter signal chart. The leader of the Fighter Command on board was in direct communication with the fighter liaison officers on the other two ships by ultrashort wave.

Without going further into these technical preparations, which were elaborate and complicated, I only want to mention the following. The technical chief of communication and intelligence of the Luftwaffe, General Martini, was preparing new and strictly secret means of interference and deception against the enemy's radar system. The effectiveness of these were still unknown. The actual importance of such a deception and confusion of the enemy's command could not yet be judged.

Of decisive importance to the navy were the preparations for navigation and mine sweeping. The course of the naval units through the Channel was fixed not too close to the French coast despite the disadvantage which this entailed. Because of a greater safety from ground mines and the ability to reach a greater speed in deeper waters, it was decided to plot the course roughly in the middle of the Channel, with a depth of not less than 15 fathoms. To aid navigation the route was staked out by marking boats. Eighty mine-sweepers cleared 98 anchor mines and 21 ground mines on the route. Three mine barriers were detected and removed. During this operation we lost one mine-sweeper and one destroyer. All these actions had to be performed under absolute secrecy and could therefore only be carried out by night.

After my experience as commander of fighter squadrons which only the previous year had given protection to the ships at Brest, and especially after the experience gathered during the eight days of trials, I drew up a rigid battle order: "Rules for the execution of protective escorts to merchant convoys and naval flotillas."

I made a compromise between the logical demands of the navy which could be fulfilled, and the limited possibilities conditioned by the number of fighter units. A continuous escort at high altitude and low level could not be carried out by more thain 16 fighter planes. Each single wave of 16 aircraft remained approximately 35 minutes over the protected object. This varied according to distance from base to object. If they made no contact or only a slight one with the enemy during this time they had to stay for another ten minutes. The relieving wave arrived according to a precisely fixed schedule ten minutes before the time was up for the first escort to return. The number of aircraft over the ships increased therefore to 32 for a period of at least ten minutes and at the most 20 minutes.

Reservicing time had been reduced to half an hour, which was only possible by the greatest efforts on the part of ground and air crews.

The briefing orders demanded attacking enemy aircraft without loss of time from any position. If any enemy should penetrate to deliver a direct attack on the ships, the orders were to put these out of action by all available means—and if necessary, to ram them. Fights with enemy aircraft leaving the combat zone were to be avoided. The result of the fighter action would not be expressed in numbers of enemy aircraft shot down, but solely by the successful protection extended to the warships.

The essential feature of the planned actions and sorties was that in spite of the permanent numerically small, direct air cover of an exclusively defensive nature, there were at all times sufficient forces fully alert to undertake an offensive action against approaching enemy aircraft formations.

The two remaining fighter wings on the Channel coast, the 2nd and the 26th, took part in Operation Thunderbolt. Each was increased to 90 serviceable aircraft, ME-109s and FW-190s. In addition to this there were 12 ME-109s from the fighter training school of Paris. These were transferred to Le Havre for the duration of the operation. Finally the 1st Fighter Wing stationed in northwest Germany was available for the morning of X Day. They could not be counted on for the afternoon, because this wing had the task of escorting the flotilla next morning on its way through the German Bight, once it had succeeded in breaking through the Channel. It had 60 ME-109s ready for action. At best, therefore, I could count temporarily on 252 aircraft. This figure was bound to decrease considerably in the course of the operation. Of course there were no reserves. I had 30 ME-110 night fighters available for the early morning and evening periods.

In fixing X Day many factors had to be taken into account. The operation was specified as urgent. A later date than February was out of question because the short nights would have robbed us of the surprise element. Until the middle of February darkness would last from 20:30 until 8:30 hours. On February 15, there would be a new moon, which meant that there would be complete darkness, giving the greatest security for night action. Between the seventh and the fifteenth the water and tide conditions in the Channel were most favorable for the operation. The time between these dates was therefore considered. The Commander-in-Chief of Navy Group Command, West, was responsible for fixing the date.

Now the weather god had to be consulted. He played an important if not decisive part. The difficulties our meterologists had in giving a weather forecast so far in advance lay in the fact that with prevailing western weather conditions over the Channel, they needed data from the far Atlantic which was not available. They were dependent on the reports brought back by long-distance reconnaissance planes which took off from the western coasts of Europe. Three U-boats were now stationed in the eastern Atlantic and in the important weather area round Ireland, to observe conditions. On February 7 the weather became very uncertain, with a depression over the Continent. The meteorologists gave the following weather forecast for February 12:

"A depression has formed south of Ireland. Strong winds with the barometer falling north of Scotland make it highly possible that the depression will travel south with a speed of about 25 mph and will reach the eastern approaches of the Channel February 12, between six and ten o'clock. From there it will move further south. Therefore the weather in the Channel area will deteriorate rapidly during the morning, and after crossing the front (duration two-three hours) it will clear up again." The weather over the English take-off bases would therefore be favorable, while over our own air bases it would become worse in the same degree as it improved over the battle area in the Channel. In the afternoon our own bases, too, should have better weather.

This did not sound so good for us fighter pilots. By the way, the weather actually occurred as forecast, even if it was about six to eight hours late. But it saved us!

Despite the rather unfavorable forecast General-Admiral Saalwachter, at that time C.-in-C. of Navy Group Command, West, decided on February 11, 1942, as the date on which the ships were to leave port on Operation Thunderbolt-Cerberus at 20:00 hours. This was after a last operational conference held at the Palais Luxembourg in Paris on the same day. The fact that the navy, according to an old mariner's superstition, regarded the thirteenth as an unfavorable day for the operation, especially when it fell on a Friday, was not entirely without influence on the decision of the date.

From Paris I went to the Pas de Calais, where I assembled the chiefs of all flying units, right down to the squadron leaders, for a briefing, which took place during the night. When I revealed the purpose and aim of all the secret preparations that had fully occupied them during the past weeks, the surprise hit them like a bomb. Their enthusiasm for taking part in such a daring and important venture was equally great. On return to their units they were to open the detailed orders for action which I had previously handed them in sealed envelopes.

English reports show that on the night of February 11-12, the R.A.F. was also in a state of alert. The Vice-Admiral commanding the Dover station had received additional MTBs, and swordfish-torpedo carriers. During the previous days British aircraft dropped 1100 magnetic mines between the Frisian Islands and Brest.

Therefore it cannot be said that the British Command was completely taken by surprise by the German operation. The preparations, made so to speak on the doorstep of the British house, could not possibly have gone unnoticed. The countermeasures which were taken point out that they envisaged the possibility of a Channel dash by the German warships. However they did not expect a breakthrough in daylight, and all preparations against the passage of the narrow strait between Dover and Calais had been made with nighttime in mind.

With the fall of darkness on the evening of February 11, seven German destroyers assembled at the harbor entrance of Brest. These were to form a safety belt for the capital ships. At 20:00 hours as arranged, the *Scharnhorst, Gneisenau,* and *Prinz Eugen* left their berths. But they did not get very far. Air-raid warning alarm! The ships returned to their berths and tied up again. A smoke screen was thrown over the harbor. Flak guns of all calibers barked. That was a good start! Searchlights traversed the sky. About 20 to 25 Britnsh bombers made a routine raid from 6000 to 9000 feet. The men of the ships' AA guns were at action stations and joined in the fireworks which greeted the intruders. Bombs whistled and exploded in the harbor area. Luckily there was no damage to the ships. After the All Clear the ships were ordered to put to sea. The time was 22:00 hours. Two hours' delay! A few minutes before 23:00 hours the capital ships left the harbor of Brest. The flotilla started on its night journey. Operation Thunderbolt-Cerberus had begun.

13

The Channel Dash

During that night not one of us thought about sleep. Once the warships had left port two questions occupied us principally: Would the unit succeed in making up the time lost through the air raid? And had the attacking British bombers discovered that the expected German operation was about to begin? Its conclusion would largely depend on the answer to these two questions.

It was planned that the squadron should keep an average speed of 26 knots. In the beginning, with favorable tides, they were actually making about 30 knots. After rounding Ushant to the west of Brittany the formation set course for the Channel at 00:13 o'clock. A total radio silence was observed. Reports of position came therefore only from our radar stations along the French coast, which picked up the warships at intervals. Each time this was a pleasant surprise. After the loss of two valuable hours I was fairly certain that at dawn I should have to transfer the fighter forces standing by from the Pas de Calais down to the Le Havre-Caen-Cherbourg sector. Allowance had been made in the plan for such a change, but it would have meant an additional strain on everyone concerned. Each new report showed that the warships were catching up on their initial delay until, early in the morning, it was clear that they would make up their time and, with the first light of day, would be in the prearranged position exactly to the minute.

The second question, too—that of a possible discovery by the English of the preparations to leave port—seemed to have received a positive and highly gratifying answer for us. Nothing stirred on the enemy side. The ships were still out of reach for the radar station on the British coast.

At 6:30 hours decks were cleared for action on board the battleships, which were traveling at high speed through the darkness toward the Channel. Off Cherbourg, a flotilla of torpedo boats joined the unit to strengthen the outer safety belt, which so far had only been formed by destroyers. The whole unit consisted now of the two battleships, the cruiser, seven destroyers, and eight to fifteen E-boats. The latter were relieved from sector to sector.

The weather was cloudy with a 1500-foot ceiling and relatively good visibility. At 8:14 hours the first night fighters took off in complete darkness. They were over the fleet at 8:50 hours. From now on, during the whole day, fighter forces kept in continuous and direct contact with the ships.

The air umbrella, a small one, of course, was opened. Our destroyer fighters were flying only a few feet above the water in order not to be detected by the English radar stations. All radio communications were of course silenced. At 8:54 hours the dawn broke. The units were off the Cotentin peninsula.

The first dramatic note crept into the operation when naval security forces discovered a previously unnoticed mine field off Dieppe only a few hours before the ships were due. By an all-out effort of four mine sweepers a channel was swiftly cleared. Nevertheless the decision to pass through this barely cleared path was a very risky one. But there was no alternative except returning and calling the whole operation off. The unit passed through without incident.

The night fighters, which flew mainly on the port side of the warships, the side toward the enemy, had been joined in the meantime by day fighters. The operation ran according to plan. Discovery by the enemy, which luckily had not yet occurred, had to be avoided for as long as possible. In briefing the pilots, each commander had therefore stressed to the utmost the orders: *fly at lowest possible level and maintain radio silence.* Those who knew the general lack of radio discipline in the Luftwaffe, and particularly among fighter pilots, can imagine how worried I was about this now. Yet during this operation my boys were equal to the navy, whose wireless discipline is traditionally famous and unequaled. Only later, after the naval formations had been detected and under the pressure of the heavy air fights in the afternoon did the well-known radio chaos of the Luftwaffe break out again.

In addition to the escorting fighters flying in relays, we had in reserve for immediate action about 25 to 30 aircraft standing by on the different bases. The pilots sat in their machines, belts fastened, and aircraft ready to take off. This fighter force which was not tied to an inflexible defense task fought particularly well later in this action and thus proved again that the fighter, even when tackling a purely defensive task, must never lose the initiative to his opponent, in accordance with the fundamental principles of the fighter arm.

About 11:00 hours the night fighters were taken out of action. They landed on airfields in the Dutch sector ready to continue the escort in the evening. At this hour the naval units were just off the mouth of the Somme. Thus they were only 40 miles from the narrowest point of the Channel between Dover and Calais. For two hours in full daylight German warships had been passing along the English coast, following a route which in the history of British sea supremacy no enemy has dared to take since the seventeenth century. The silence was almost sinister.

At 11:00 Middle European Time (ten o'clock English time) an alerting radio message from a British fighter was intercepted by our listening service. It said nothing except that a large German naval formation consisting of three capital ships and about 20 warships was steaming at high speed toward the Strait of Dover, present position about 50 miles off the mouth of the Somme. The secret was out.

At least we had to accept this as a fact according to the intercepted radio message. The decision for giving the cue to drop all attempts at disguising our operation lay with me. The fact that the first countermeasures by the British Command were not taken for about another hour proved the wisdom of my decision not to be driven to rash measures by this alarming message, but to continue to observe all the measures intended to keep the operation hidden from the enemy. The English give 11:05 o'clock British time as the time of discovery, that is 12:05 o'clock German time. Yet the first report of the British fighter was a whole hour earlier. It appears that they gave no credence to the report; they simply sent up another reconnaissance plane and ordered a full alert. An hour later the reconnaissance brought them the confirmation of the report which had been regarded as impossible. Churchill states that the British Admiralty did not receive this information before 11:25 (12:25 o'clock German time).

By then the German warships had nearly reached the narrowest point of the Channel. The cloud ceiling had descended to 600 to 900 feet. It was raining slightly, but the English coast was faintly visible. Off Boulogne an additional 15 E-boats joined the formation, screening it on the enemy's side. So far we had had incredible luck. Considerable fighter forces had been saved. If the discovery had happened earlier, perhaps during the night or even on leaving port, the fighters would have by now been tired or completely exhausted. As it was, the air crews were still fresh at the time the ships were passing the most dangerous part of the route. Under normal conditions this would have been the climax of the battle. Now the crews were looking forward with confidence to the air battle which was bound to start shortly.

The German high-frequency experts took a large share in creating the obvious confusion of the British Command. Usually we gave little heed to these contraptions, which always remain a mystery to the uninitiated. There were quite a few of these laymen in the High Command of the German Luftwaffe, including its commander, who once said to me that his understanding of these things was overtaxed when operating a radio set. One should value all the more the activities of these experts who often have to struggle against stupidity, unintelligence, and even ill will! They had created strong interference with the British radar stations by a series of installations and other methods. They had also directed interference transmissions against the British fighter intercoms. By special instruments in bombers they had simulated radar signals giving false reports of approaching large formations, against which the English actually sent strong fighter forces. The confusion created in this way continued even after the German warships had been clearly located and when practical deception was no longer possible.

The first enemy action was recorded at 13:16 hours. British coastal artillery fired on the *Prinz Eugen*. Simultaneously a scrap started between German and British MTBs. The German destroyer *Hermann Schömann* interfered and closed the action. *Scharnhorst* reported being under artillery fire from 300 to 400 yards to port. The first air encounter took place at 13:34 hours. Our fighters were now operating at closest range from their bases. I could therefore increase the fighter cover. The first British attack was by six Swordfish torpedo carriers with Spitfire fighter escort making a low-level attack. Our fighters flung themselves on the attackers. The fighter radio control on board the ships was the first to break the wireless silence in order to direct the fighters according to sight. While a part of our escort involved the Spitfires in a series of dogfights, the torpedo attack was foiled by cooperative action of the ships, AA guns and fighters. Not one of the Swordfish escaped. They were all shot down.

Thus the first English attack performed with death-defying courage was repulsed. I gave the cue word "Open Visor." This canceled the order for radio silence and disguise, and the regulations for low-level flying. The fighter cover was now graded at different altitudes. We could disregard the enemy radar location.

A lull occurred in the fighting, during which the British and ours kept in contact with each other. I did not always have a clear picture of the following events in my Fighter Command H.Q. Nor was it possible to survey the air battles from aboard ship, because they extended over large areas. The German radar stations on the coast had to concentrate their attention on newly approaching British forces rather than devote themselves entirely to a continuous report of the fighting, even had they been in a position to understand the events. I will therefore quote here only the essential data from the fighter command logbook on board the flagship *Scharnhorst*, which relates a lively section of the heavy fighting as far as it happened in sight of the warships. It must not be forgotten that the majority of the dogfights took place outside the range of observation. The logbook of Fighter Command on board the flagship reads:

14:37 hours	Drifting mine 100 yards to port quarter of *Scharnhorst*.
14:55 hours	Dogfight between German fighters and five Whirlwinds (twin-engined bombers) which attacked *Gneisenau*.
14:58 hours	*Prinz Eugen* reports fight between five German fighters and two four-engined bombers. One bomber shot down, confirmed.
15:03 hours	22 of our fighters overhead.
15:04 hours	Weather over the Channel has deteriorated, but still permits low-level flying of our fighters. French coast visible.
15:13 hours	Dogfights between English and German fighters close to the flotilla.
15:15 hours	"Fighter Command on board" gives warning of approaching bombers. They came in under or just in the cloud ceiling. Single small formations of English fighters all over the place.
15:20 hours	Two Whirlwinds attacking *Gneisenau*, they approached from port quarter, one bomber was shot down by German fighters.
15:22 hours	*Gneisenau* observed the shooting down of a further English aircraft by German fighters.

15:24 hours	Near *Scharnhorst* one Whirlwind shot down by one of our fighters. A dogfight with another one, chased by several fighters. Thick smoke poured from one of the engines of the Whirlwind. Near *Gneisenau,* heavy fights.
15:26 hours	Near *Prinz Eugen,* English aircraft shot down by our fighters.
15:27 hours	More bombers near the naval formation, partly in the clouds. Weather: Cloud ceiling 900 to 1200 feet, three to five miles.
15:29 hours	*Prinz Eugen* fired at several English twin-engined aircraft. Ceased fire as a formation of our fighters reached a favorable position for attack.

At this moment the flagship *Scharnhorst* was heavily shaken. The lights failed. The wireless went dead. She had struck a mine. She left a trail of oil behind her. Now she was standing still. The leading ship of the destroyers, Z-29, was ordered alongside to take aboard the commander and the fighter liaison. At the same time the weather was deteriorating rapidly. Cloud ceiling 500 to 600 feet, visibility one-half to one mile, rain. The naval formation proceeded with *Prinz Eugen* and *Gneisenau* as well as the bulk of destroyers and torpedo boats. The enemy concentrated on the *Scharnhorst* and the destroyer Z-29. It was 15:50 hours. Near *Prinz Eugen* an MTB approached. Change of course, detonation of the torpedo 1000 yards aft. With the stopping of the *Scharnhorst* the naval formation split up. *Prinz Eugen* and *Gneisenau* proceeded with the main destroyer and torpedo boat force, while *Scharnhorst* stayed behind.

15:50 hours	Destroyer Z-29 has come alongside the *Scharnhorst.* The commander of the flotilla and the fighter liaison transferred. It is expected that the *Scharnhorst* cannot proceed to her destination but has to be towed to the nearest Dutch port. Destroyer Z-29 is alone, she has lost contact with the other ships because visibility has become worse.
15:55 hours	Twin-engined bombers approaching destroyer Z-29. They are attacked and pursued by a swarm of German fighters. They vanish from sight.

101

16:01 hours	A bomber attacks the *Scharnhorst*. A stick of bombs falls 80 to 100 yards to port.
16:05 hours	*Scharnhorst* under way again.
16:05 hours	Three bombers attack destroyer Z-29. Aircraft beaten off AA fire.
16:12 hours	Two English aircraft approaching *Prinz Eugen*. Weather: Cloud ceiling 900 to 1200 feet, visibility very bad.
16:14 hours	Several Blenheim Mark IV's attack *Gneisenau* from starboard.
16:17 hours	Two Blenheims attack *Prinz Eugen*. One aircraft hit by AA fire.
16:22 until 16:25 hours	*Gneisenau* reports gunfire to port. (English destroyer units from Harwich.)
16:30 until 16:40 hours	Torpedo-carrying aircraft attack *Gneisenau* and *Prinz Eugen*. Ships change course. Two bombers attack destroyer Z-29 from astern. Beaten off by AA fire. Low-level attack by enemy bombers on *Prinz Eugen*.
16·40 hours	Weather: Cloud ceiling 450 feet, visibility 1 to 1½ miles, rain. The extraordinarily bad weather conditions hamper the fighters. The low clouds offer a welcome cover for the attacking bombers. The ensuing combats cannot be observed.
16:44 until 16:55 hours	*Prinz Eugen* observes one of our fighters shooting down a bomber. A bomber approaches destroyer Z-29. *Gneisenau* gives orders to destroyers to attack enemy destroyers. She herself has opened fire with medium and heavy guns. Near *Prinz Eugen* sticks of bombs and near-misses from the English destroyers. *Prinz Eugen* fires heavy guns at enemy destroyers. One destroyer on fire. (The destroyer HMS *Worcester* was set on fire, but managed to reach an English port.)
16:56 until 17:00 hours	Single Handley-Page Hereford's attacking *Prinz Eugen*, *Gneisenau*, and destroyer Z-29. One aircraft crashes in flames

In the meantime German bombers were attacking the English destroyers. German reconnaissance aircraft were ordered to keep an eye on the Home Fleet.

Because of low clouds and bad visibility, both the R.A.F.

and the Luftwaffe could only fly singly or in small formations. The flotilla was far drawn out. It was unavoidable that our own fighters and bombers occasionally attacked German naval units. A great chaos reigned over the whole battle area, lasting, except for a few intervals, until nightfall.

17:00 hours A German bomber, type DO-217, dropped two bombs on the destroyer *Hermann Schömann*. Further attacks of single English Hampden bombers. *Gneisenau* reports one aircraft shot down. Parts of shot-down aircraft float by.

17:10 hours Bomber attacks and contact planes. Weather: Cloud ceiling 600 feet, visibility ½ to 1 mile, rain.

17:14 until *Prinz Eugen, Gneisenau,* and destroyer Z-29 are
17:39 hours approached and attacked respectively by English bombers. The following types are recognized: Bristol Blenheim, Bristol Beaufort, Wellington, and Handley-Page Hereford.

17:42 hours The commander-in-chief battleships requests renewed and stronger fighter protection, despite the bad weather, against the running attacks and the many contact aircraft. Besides the fighters, night fighters are now in action, taking off from Dutch airfields.

17:55 hours German fighters pursue a bomber, flying straight over the *Prinz Eugen,* and shoot him down in flames.

17:57 hours A contact plane (Hampden) shot down in flames by AA fire from destroyer Z-29.

18:06 hours Low-flying torpedo carrier, flying through AA barrage, dropped torpedo against *Gneisenau*. Surface runner, ship avoided it by changing course. Further attacks on *Prinz Eugen*.

18:20 hours *Prinz Eugen* to *Gneisenau:* "Hanging on to you 5620 yards starboard astern."

Short lull in activities.

18:31 hours *Gneisenau* has temporarily to reduce revolutions on starboard shaft for technical reasons. This causes her to fall back in speed and position.

The weather position developed almost dramatically for fighter action. In the Pas de Calais (No. I) take-off and

103

landing were still unaffected. The approach to the flotilla in the Channel could only now be made in low-level flight. But the distance of 120 miles was now so far that after 30 minutes' escort flight, a return to the starting base was out of the question. The fighters therefore had to land on Dutch territory (No. II). But there the weather was at its worst. Over large stretches the clouds were at ground level. It was no easy decision for me to send the fighters into the bad-weather zone to land after their fourth sortie on this day of a major battle, but I had no alternative. In fact there were quite a few emergency landings outside the airfields, some of which ended in crashes. But most of the pilots landed safely. On their own initiative, without waiting for orders, a few determined flight lieutenants and squadron leaders took off again with small formations before darkness fell after rapid servicing and refueling. They were conscious that everything was at stake here. No scruples about safety existed on that day. The fighter pilots had done more than their duty. They were carried away by the grandeur of the operation and showed an enthusiasm I did not think would have been possible any more after the long and hard struggle the squadrons had waged on the Channel, after the heavy losses they had sustained, and after so many bitter disappointments.

Meanwhile the commander-in-chief of the battleships had renewed misfortunes. Since his flagship had received the damage from the mine he had been aboard the destroyer Z-29 which now developed engine trouble in the port engine. Again the commander-in-chief and the fighter liaison with a limited staff had to be transferred. The destroyer *Hermann Schömann* was ordered to stand by. Under continuous attacks by British aircraft and in a rough sea the transfer was effected by means of a cutter. At 18:45 hours, while the admiral was still bobbing up and down in the cutter, the *Scharnhorst,* which had been brought under way again, went off at full speed, trying to catch up with the flotilla. This must have been a great personal disappointment, which however was mitigated by the satisfaction that the *Scharnhorst* was now able to continue toward her destination.

Toward 19:00 hours it was getting dark. Day and night fighters were battling with the last Wellington bombers which attacked incessantly and with tenacity. *Gneisenau, Prinz Eugen,* and *Hermann Schömann* reported kills by fighters and AA fire. At 19:35 hours total darkness reigned. Fighter action was ended for the day. Successes and losses could not yet be assessed. One thing was clear: we had completed our task to form and maintain an air umbrella over the German warships while they were breaking through. I transferred my action station to Jever on the German Bight.

During the night the R.A.F. was very active. Besides intensive air reconnaissance they were mainly busy with mine-laying operations, in order to mine the while route right up to the German Bight and the Elbe Estuary. Our night fighters kept in contact with the enemy, but there were no major actions.

The British mines still did some damage that night. Shortly after 21:00 hours the *Gneisenau* shook under an explosion. All engines stopped. She had hit a mine! Yet the damage was only superficial. After a short time she was under way again making 25 knots. An hour and a half later the *Scharnhorst* hit another mine. She too could soon continue, although only at first with ten, later with 15 knots.

Still during darkness the *Gneisenau* and *Prinz Eugen* reached the mouth of the Elbe and cast anchor. At that time the German Bight was still outside the range of British fighters. After their heavy defeat in their attack on Wilhelmshaven on September 4 and December 18, 1939, the British bombers did not venture any more during daytime into this area which was well covered by radar stations.

Next morning, February 13, the *Gneisenau* and the *Prinz Eugen* continued their journey to Kiel in daylight through the Kaiser-Wilhelm Canal. At dawn the *Scharnhorst* had taken aboard again the commander-in-chief and the fighter liaison while she was in the estuary of the Weser. At 10:30 hours she arrived together with the *Hermann Schömann* at Wilhelmshaven. The German High Command made the following announcement:

"During the air and sea battle in the Channel area on February 12, one English destroyer was hit and set on fire. The full complement of a German naval force under the command of Vice-Admiral Ciliax, after breaking through the Channel between Calais and Dover, reached their ports of destination, sustaining the loss of only one E-boat. Forty-nine British aircraft were shot down. Generalfeldmarshal Sperre's fighter units under the command of General Coeler (bomber and reconnaissance) and Oberst Galland (fighter and night fighter) especially distinguished themselves."

This communiqué was extraordinarily reserved and did not express anything near the actual success of the operation. The reason for this was that the operation was not regarded as complete until the ships had reached their Norwegian port of destination.

Shortly after the *Scharnhorst* had anchored at Wilhelmshaven there was a conference on board the flagship. Present were the commanders of the navy and air force who had taken part in the combined operation. The findings were:

1. The operation was a complete success.

2. The British destroyer *Worcester* was set on fire. According to first reports 49 English aircraft, bombers, torpedo-bombers, and fighters were shot down by fighters and naval AA guns. (This figure later rose to over 60.)

3. Our own losses had been small. Our advance boat (a fishing vessel) had been lost in an air attack; eight other ships were damaged.

The damage by mines to the capital ships had been unavoidable but was not irreparable.

The navy lost 13 men killed and 68 wounded; the air force lost 11 men and 17 aircraft.

The Channel dash had been a great shock to the enemy. Churchill, giving this event considerable space in his history of World War II, admits frankly that the British public was shocked by the news and that there was nation-wide indignation. "In order to calm down the heated minds" an official inquiry was held which came to the amazing conclusion that after all the Channel dash "had been of extreme advantage to us." It is not known if, at least in England, this assertion was found to be very convincing. It is more important what Churchill has to say about the run of the operation itself. He blames the failure of the British defense on the fact that the British Command had been forced, at the time, to send nearly all its torpedo bombers to Egypt. Nevertheless the forces employed by the British were considerable according to Vice-Admiral R. de Bellot: "About 250 aircraft of the Fleet Air Arm, Coastal Command, and the Strategic Bomber Command, assisted and escorted by about 15 fighter squadrons, took part in the attack. Only 39 aircraft managed to launch attacks on the German naval formation, but without success."

The remarkable thing about Churchill's description is that it shows that Hitler in his planning judged the suspected reaction of the British Command. Faced with the German surprise they showed amazingly little ability to improvise. This was the only possible explanation which all those who took part in the venture could find for the unbelievable fact that the formation was not attacked before noon when it had already nearly reached the narrowest point of the Channel. This was the key to the success. Churchill says that the British Admiralty was of the opinion the Germans would favor the cover of night for such an operation. "The German admiral" preferred to use the darkness for slipping out of Brest and facing the risk of passing through the Channel by day. "Without being hit either by the coastal batteries of Dover or by the torpedo attacks, the German flotilla continued on its way, and on the morning of the thirteenth of February all ships had reached their base."

The British Prime Minister describes in detail the failure of the radar organization during the operation. Until after the war one was of the opinion in England that it had been an unaccountable episode, a national misfortune. Only after the war was it discovered that the reason for the unaccountable failure was no less than a clever trick of the chief of the German radio communication, Martini. Unfortunately the German Command did not draw the necessary conclusions from this victory in the radar war and did not start a rapid development of this weapon. The English learned from their defeat and developed radar interference to a perfection which later on during the bombing war became fatal for the Reich.

The weather during the battle was considerably worse than had been expected. It is a matter of opinion if this circumstance was more favorable to the attacker or the defender. Experienced pilots rather think that during bad weather bombers can find cover in the clouds from enemy fighters and AA fire and that navigation and flying in clouds entails no difficulty for them. Single-seat fighters on the other hand are much more allergic to weather conditions, therefore the assertion seemed to be justified that in this case the R.A.F. was much more favored by the weather than the Luftwaffe. For the navy the worsening of the weather was from a tactical point of view very welcome.

The pilots of the R.A.F. fought bravely, tenaciously, and untiringly, but had been sent into action with insufficient planning, without a clear concept of the attack, without a center of gravity, and without systematic tactics.

It was a military sensation of the first order considering that this operation was accomplished within range of the Home Fleet and in an operational area that is one of the narrowest and most difficult natural straits in the world. Moreover, despite the fact that the bulk of the German air force was at the time engaged in Russia and more of its forces were tied in the Mediterranean and in North Africa, it managed to maintain a decisive superiority over the R.A.F.

No wonder that the Channel dash of the German battle-cruiser group under the protection of the Luftwaffe caused amazement, alarm, even horror, in England. Since Tourville and his victory over the English-Dutch fleet off the Isle of Wight in the year 1690, England had never seen strong enemy naval forces passing through her Channel.

14

Between Norway and Africa

The Channel dash had come off, but the German warships had not yet reached their Norwegian port of destination. It was obvious that the enemy would make every effort to hunt down the prey which had escaped once, and if he could not do it off his own coast he must try it off the enemy's coast. The R.A.F. harried the ships in their camouflaged anchorages and on their further journey.

After the necessary repairs, preparations, and discussions, the naval units reformed and sailed from Wilhelmshaven and Kiel in a northerly direction. The *Scharnhorst* and *Gneisenau* remained in German ports for the time being because of the damage sustained. Their place was taken by two older cruisers. I was again entrusted with the fighter protection. I made my H.Q. first at Jever on the German Bight, then at Esbjerg in Denmark, and finally at Stavanger in Norway. The difficulties of communication in these territories, and especially the spanning of the Skagerrak, caused the operation to run less smoothly than on the Channel front, where our means of communication were excellent. Besides the fighter forces from the operational area we again used destroyer aircraft and night fighters. After further heavy engagements with the R.A.F., I was very glad when the ships under our care sailed unscathed into the fjords. These were protected by flak batteries and also afforded natural cover.

Hitler's orders had now been carried out. A year later, January, 1943, Hitler came to a conclusion which caused a great deal of surprise and not a few objections. He considered that it would be best to break up the capital ships of the navy. He was convinced they were outmoded and no longer suited for fast-moving wars. This brought about the last difference of opinion between the Führer and the Commander-in-Chief of the Navy, and resulted in the resignation of Raeder in January, 1943. The U-boat specialist Admiral Dönitz became his successor. He still had confidence in surface vessels, and Hitler was finally persuaded to change his mind.

The Battle of the Atlantic, which had been highly successful during the first years of the war, now reached a critical turning point. During the month in which Dönitz became Commander-in-Chief of the Navy, 19 U-boats did not return from their hunting grounds. The next month, March, 1943, a further 15 did not return; in April, 16; and the loss of 37 U-boats in May convinced the German Command that in the Atlantic—as before in Africa and on the Eastern front—the luck of war had turned against Germany. Of 1160 German U-boats put into service up to the end of the war, 700 were lost. Of the 39,000 men who went out on missions. 33,000 did not return!

From the beginning of the war until the end of 1941 the Allied navies and the neutrals serving with them, lost altogether 2,432 ships with a total of 8,938,828 tons: 562 of these ships with a total of 1,553,440 tons were sunk by the Luftwaffe. This figure does not include the relatively high figure the Luftwaffe claimed in sinkings by mines (388 ships with a total of 1,002,424 tons). The air raids too on ports and harbor and supply installations increased the British supply difficulties. This gave rise to Churchill's remark, "Had the enemy continued with these raids the situation of the Battle of the Atlantic, which was anyhow critical, would have grown worse."

The Bay of Biscay had been particularly strongly mined by the British against the operations of the German U-boats. Only narrow channels could be cleared through the extensive mine fields. In these fixed routes the U-boats were exposed to strong air attacks. The demand of the navy for fighter protection could not be fulfilled either in the coastal waters or out at sea. For a long time the U-boats suffered their heaviest losses on approaching or leaving the vicinity of their bases.

But it was radar that brought about the turn of the Battle of the Atlantic. Enemy ships and aircraft were speedily equipped with this electric eye. The German Naval Command was forced to remove the operational area of the U-boats away from the west coast of England into the North and South Atlantic and even further westward, finally as far as the Gulf of Mexico, the Caribbean Sea, and the east coast of South America. Yet our losses increased at the same rate as the enemy's ability to replace theirs by new ships and finally even topped their figures. New German inventions such as the schnorkel, the Walter turbine drive, and the extraction of oxygen from sea water, came too late and were not available in sufficient quantities at the critical moment. Air supremacy and radar finally decided the fate of the strongest German weapon in the war against the west.

These developments could not yet be assessed in the first month of the year 1942. The huge gaps that our U-boats and aircraft tore in the chain of the enemy's supply ships darkened the panorama of the war for the British. The Channel dash had hurt their pride as much as the loss of Singapore.

The British war leaders thought that even the Near East was endangered, and gave this as a reason for their reticent attitude toward the American plan of opening a second front in Europe immediately. Roosevelt wanted to assist Stalin as quickly and effectively as possible. At the end of March, 1942, the U. S. General Staff completed its operational plan for northwest Europe, known as Operation Roundup. According to this plan the invasion of France was to take place in the autumn of 1942 or the spring of 1943. It was to be prepared by large strategic bomber raids. Twenty-one squadrons of the USAF were to assist the R.A.F.

Early in April, 1942, the American Chief of General Staff, General George Marshall, and Harry Hopkins, Roosevelt's personal adviser, flew with this plan to London on the President's orders. Marshall tried to convince Churchill of the necessity of an early attack against Western Europe in order to give some relief to the Red Army.

Churchill wanted to restrict the Anglo-American activities in Western Europe to slowly increasing strategic bomber attacks. Agreement was reached that until the middle of September, 1942, one American armored division, two and a half infantry divisions, together with about 400 fighters, 300 bombers, and 200 transport planes were to be sent from the U.S.A. to England.

The Allied bomber offensive against the Reich originated therefore not as an independent strategic operation, like the German air raids against England in the summer of 1940, but rather as a part of a general invasion plan.

On July 4, 1942, the first six American crews dropped bombs on the European mainland. General Eisenhower drove to the air bases and personally addressed the pilots. Their targets were German airfields in Holland. Only two of the six Bostons reached the target area. Two planes were shot down the others heavily damaged.

The first daylight raid on August 17, 1942, by the 87th Bomber Squadron on the Eighth AAF which had arrived in England in the meantime, was more successful. Eighteen

Flying Fortresses, led by General Eaker, returned without loss after completing their mission—an attack on Rouen-St. Otterville. They were received by C.-in-C. General Spaatz, many American and English officers of the General Staff, and some 30 journalists. General Eaker had already come to the conclusion that low-level flights into German occupied territories were impossible without fighter escort.

Churchill would have preferred to see the American bombers go into action in Africa. Only after Rommel threatened Egypt for the second time in the summer of 1942 were the Americans persuaded to divert 20 Bostons, destined for Stalin, to the British fighting at the Halfaya Pass.

On May 26 the Afrika Korps broke out of the El Gazala position to which they had retired in the autumn of 1941 under the pressure of Auchinleck. Tobruk fell on June 20. On June 29, after an advance of 1450 miles, Rommel stood before El Alamein: two hours by car from Alexandria. The British fleet left the harbor.

On July 1, Rommel tried the final breakthrough with the remaining strength of his Afrika Korps. British resistance stiffened as they fell back on their starting point and supply base. An encircling move misfired. The offensive failed. It was a repetition of Moscow: With victory already in sight the German advance flagged and stopped. At the gates of Moscow an early and bitter winter halted the German offensive, but here lack of supplies and British air superiority defeated Rommel. Without air supremacy over the central Mediterranean Rommel's supply problem could not be solved.

The successes on the African war front had dropped into Hitler's lap. It was a fallacy if the enemy thought that the German operations in the direction of the Suez Canal and the oil fields was a strategical move of global dimension, aimed at the most sensitive spot on the periphery of the British Empire, planned in coordination with the Japanese. Rommel himself wrote on the African campaign that he simply "slithered" into it. German units were sent to Africa as a kind of fire brigade when the Italian colonies went up in flames and were in danger of being burned out. Hitler explicitly called the hastily formed Afrika Korps "a barricade unit" and stressed that he did not want to pin down any strong armored forces in a war theater so far away. The successes Rommel achieved therefore were quite unexpected, and the strategical possibilities they opened lay outside Hitler's original plans and aims.

When it was decided to strengthen the German forces in Africa it was too late. In December, 1941, the 2nd Flying Corps was transferred from the Eastern front to Sicily and North Africa. In addition to supporting the ground troops, who put up a resistance with clever delaying tactics, the main task of this force was to paralyze the British air and sea base of Malta, in order to insure the bringing up of supplies and reserves for Rommel's new offensive in 1942.

After my return from Norway I was preoccupied with the problem of Malta. This little rocky island of 150 square miles was favored by nature to control the sea lane between Italy and the African coast which at this point is about 320 miles wide. When the war broke out and Italy had to strengthen her position in the Mediterranean and in Africa, she should, before any other action in Africa, have made an effort to take Malta. That this was possible was exemplified by the taking of Crete by German parachutists and landing troops. The need to take Malta was repeatedly impressed upon Mussolini by the Germans. But he could not make up his mind to do so, and even rejected our offer to take the island with German forces as being incompatible with the Italian national conscience.

So we tried to put Malta out of action from the air. At the outset the air defenses of the island were absolutely inadequate. In the winter of 1941-42 the Luftwaffe ruled the central Mediterranean. A hail of German bombs rained down on Malta. Units of the British fleet lying in Valletta harbor suffered great losses and damage.

This was the last propitious moment to take the island by a raid. But the Italian fleet, which should have played the leading part in such an action, did not leave port. It lay idle.

During the time the English had to fall back on Egypt, they concentrated all their efforts to hit Rommel at his most vulnerable point. All the skill and bravura of the Afrika Korps were in vain if its supply line could be cut. Malta, the key to air superiority over the central Mediterranean, was still in British hands. Considerable R.A.F. reinforcements arrived. Soon there would be no more talk of German-Italian air supremacy in this sector. The struggle grew more and more intense. Our two fighter wings, the 27th and the 53rd, no longer sufficed. Our air force was less and less able to protect the supply routes across the Mediterranean against the British sea and air forces operating from Malta and Egypt. Daily our fighter units were weakened because of escort duty for the convoys. The more urgently the Afrika Korps, exhausted by their whirlwind advance through the desert, needed supplies the sparser they became.

When Rommel was halted at El Alamein, Göring started the

so-called Malta Blitz. The island was to be annihilated by a concentration of all available forces of the Luftwaffe in the southern theater of war. A new trial of absolute air warfare on the Douhet principle was going to be staged. Wave after wave of our bombers with fighter escort attacked important war installations on Malta. Heavy damage was caused. The British had built a skillful labyrinth of semisubterranean hangars and aircraft pens on their airfields; they repaired the crater-dotted runways so quickly that the effect of a heavy raid had been wiped out after a few days. The Malta raids resembled more and more the heartbreaking task of Sisyphus. Thanks to continuous reinforcement of fighter and AA defense our losses increased from raid to raid. Nothing is more demoralizing for a soldier than to see no results from his actions, however great his effort. We had already experienced this over England. Actually the Malta Blitz was a repeat performance on a smaller scale . . . with similar disappointments, similar losses, similar failure.

At this time I received orders to report to Göring at Naples. The commodores and commanders from the units engaged in the Malta operation went with me. Göring criticized their actions sharply. As he had done once before on the Channel front, he had laid the blame mainly on the fighters for the loss of the bombers, which they had failed to protect. I had a passage of words with Göring because I refused to accept the premise that the failure of the Malta offensive was due to the inefficiency of the German fighters. It was always easy to find fault with the execution of escort duties, but our weak fighter units had done their best. There was no lack of skill and fighting spirit. They were splendidly led. Nevertheless at no time did we achieve the required degree of air superiority or satisfactory bombing results. The Malta radar and fighter service seriously impeded our units. Once more the English fought gallantly with their backs to the wall. I flew to Sicily in order to survey once more on the spot the execution of our fighter missions.

Again it was the fault of the over-all strategical concept in our conduct of the war that made the task of the Luftwaffe and in particular that of our fighters so difficult and exhausting. In the summer of 1940 we had quickly and unexpectedly come into possession of the west European Atlantic coast, a position which imperatively made England the strategic target. In the summer of 1942 we stood equally unexpectedly on the Egyptian border, from where it suddenly seemed possible to cut one of the essential British lifelines. In both cases we hoped to achieve our goal with insufficient forces and with quick improvisations. Both attempts were just as unsuccessful.

The air offensive against Malta was called off after heavy losses and unsatisfactory results. Attacks continued on a small scale, and occasional raids with strong forces were made. Transports of supply and reserves for Rommel became more and more problematical. Montgomery amassed in Egypt more than double the amount of tanks and troops that were available to the Axis. Still more overwhelming was the British preeminence in the air. Aerial reconnaissance confirmed more than 800 planes on airfields near the front. Opposing these were not more than about 60 serviceable aircraft of the well-tested 27th Desert Fighter Wing. The toughness and the results are reflected in the fate of the "Pilot of Africa," the youngest officer in the German forces, who fell over Tobruk on September 30, 1942, after 158 victories: Hans Joachim Marseille.

Marseille was the unrivaled virtuoso among the fighter pilots of World War II. His achievements had previously been regarded as impossible and they were never excelled by anyone after his death. In the short span of little more than a year his life as a pilot completed itself. During this period he flew in 388 actions, shot down 158 enemy planes, 151 of them in Africa.

I saw Marseille for the last time when I flew from Sicily to Africa to visit our fighting units, to get a firsthand picture of the conditions in which they fought. Difficult as they were, and hopeless as their struggle seemed to be, there was none of the defeatism which had been mentioned at Naples. They merely realized, as we had done on the Channel, that they had been given a task which was beyond their strength.

The report I made of my experiences and impressions in Africa was therefore unlikely to be well received by the Reichsmarshal and his staff. My report described the conditions with disconcerting frankness, since this seemed to me best in view of the seriousness of the situation. I pointed out the inevitable debacle that had to come if no immediate and decisive improvement could be achieved in strength, supply, and reserve of our fighter units. I departed from the style and mode of expression etiquette demanded. I believed I was best serving the front line and the command if I passed on my impressions fresh and direct. This was a fallacy. The only result my report had was a "rocket" for the tone in which it was couched. Otherwise nothing happened.

On October 23, the British Eighth Army, led by Montgomery, opened the counteroffensive at El Alamein. During the previous weeks the R.A.F. blitzed the only supply route to Rommel's position with everything they had. After a tremendous artillery barrage, the British tanks thundered forward against the German-Italian positions. The resistance was desperate. For eight days the artillery pounded, combat and battle fighters dropped their bombs, motorized units of the Eighth Army attacked, without achieving substantial results. The El Alamein position held out. But on November 2 Rommel reported that his troops were exhausted and were doomed in spite of their heroic resistance. The answer from the Führer's headquarters was: "Victory or death!"

The identical order from the Führer concluded the Battle of Stalingrad, which also started on the first days of November, 1942. During the summer the German armies had penetrated deeply into the Caucasus and had reached the Volga in an attempt to hit at the major Russian bottleneck of supplies and oil by taking the Maikop oil fields and by cutting the link with the oil fields of Baku. This gave the southern flank of the Eastern front the shape of a widely drawn arc, which absorbed more and more forces, including the Luftwaffe. On my inspection flights I established the fact that our fighter force suffered mainly from a shortage of planes. The units had rarely more than ten to 12 serviceable aircraft at their disposal. With terrifying clarity I saw the workings of the process of attrition to which the air force was doomed by the opening of the Eastern Campaign.

This second large-scale offensive on the Eastern front also came to a standstill. The swastika was flying on Mount Elburz, but the army never got further than their positions at Terek and Tuapse. On the Volga the Sixth Army penetrated the western suburbs of Stalingrad, where for weeks on end bitter street and house to house fighting raged. On November 8 the Soviet opened her counteroffensive which led to rapid successes and the encirclement of the Sixth Army. During the next three months the eyes of the German people, full of anguish for their sons, were directed on Stalingrad. When Generalfeldmarshal Paulus capitulated on February 3, 1943, with the remnants of his army, decimated by lack of supplies, hunger, and cold, Germany had a grim presentiment of the approaching horror.

15

A Glance at the Other Side

I celebrated Christmas with my squadron, as I had done the year before. These days were for me a kind of rest from the whirl of events during those years. In 1940 I was in command of the 26th JG and we were in the last phases of the Battle of Britain. The next Christmas, 1941, was already overshadowed by events on the Eastern front. I had just taken over my new post as General of the Fighter Arm, so actually I did not belong to the unit any more. This year I arrived as a major general. My promotion dated from November 19, 1942. At 30 I was the youngest general in the German forces. Responsibilities and duties, rank and work, robbed me of the best years of my military career. I felt this very strongly and that is perhaps the reason why I was constantly drawn to my old squadron, which had become a second home for me. This Christmas was mainly spent in serious discussions. The responsibility for the defense against the Anglo-American air raids rested with the few German fighters in the west. These raids grew daily in weight and intensity as the combination of the two forces improved. Only four fighter groups in the west were protecting the Reich. Five groups were fighting in the east from Murmansk to the Caucasus and three in Sicily and Africa. On none of these fronts was their strength sufficient to cope with the demanded task. The blanket was simply too short.

The German High Command employed more and more makeshifts and improvisations. If at any particular spot a hole was torn in the overextended fronts, it was mended by forces from another spot, which one hoped could be spared until here, too, the threadbare blanket tore and again needed repair. This may temporarily succeed. It may even be the only correct thing to do, provided there are justified hopes of a fundamental change in the general situation of the war. What worried me most was to see that our war leader and to an extent our Luftwaffe Command closed their eyes to undeniable facts and

117

certain developing signs regarding aerial warfare against the west, which it was the duty of any responsible command to investigate.

This applied particularly to a study and evaluation of the enemy's positions, especially with regard to the imminent bombing offensive against the Reich. This was only in its beginnings, but it already showed clearly the outlines of its later dimensions. I considered it my duty to give this question special attention. Of course at the time I had not all the sources available on which the following description of the developments on the enemy's side are based. But the main trend was as obvious to me as it should have been to anyone in a responsible position in the Luftwaffe Command.

We had known for a long time that important moves were in preparation by the Western Allies in the field of aerial warfare. From the sources of information available to Luftwaffe Command, the following facts emerged. The Americans had the B-17 Flying Fortress and the B-24 Liberator, four-engined long-range bombers with an extraordinary performance and powerful armament. Their production capacity was able to turn them out in sufficient quantities. The Americans were planning to send across the Atlantic large formations of these bombers, obviously intended for day raids. Yet the German Command did not take this available and true information seriously. They took it to be so much bluff.

But it was also known that General Spaatz, who was in charge of the preparation and organization of dispatching USAF units to England and was later chosen to be their commander-in-chief, had already sent an advanced detachment under General Eaker to England in February.

The total success of the Anglo-American air offensive against the Reich was finally achieved by the mass of American war material, superior in quantity. It was sufficient to form a gigantic air force within a few years for the different U. S. theaters of war and to satisfy the demand of the Allies with thousands of aircraft. Those who during the last phases of the war saw the American air fleets of hundreds of planes in close formation, flying in daylight, smothering the defenders by weight of numbers, those who saw the terrible effects of their concentrated bombing, are inclined to see in them the actual victors of the Battle of Germany. However this would be misjudging the British share in the success.

England was the first military power in the world to create an air force as an independent arm. The R.A.F. came into being during World War I. Already in 1918 both England

118

and Germany had strategic bombers, but neither side used them in any outstanding action. But while in Germany the development of the technique and tactics of aerial warfare was interrupted for many years after 1918, England had correctly followed up the idea of strategic bombing.

The bomber must have appeared as the ideal instrument of war against the potential major enemy, Germany, which has a much larger population than England. The bloody battles of Flanders which destroyed the flower of English youth during World War I must have been a terrible warning to the English war leaders. They must not confront Germany like that a second time. But with strategical bombers based on the island itself they could hit at the very heart of the enemy.

Churchill summed up the bombing war in the following words, in a speech in the House of Commons on August 20, 1940, while the Battle of Britain was still raging:

"There is every reason to assume that this new type of warfare is in conformity with the spirit of the British nation and with the resources of the Empire. If once we have the necessary armament and once we get a move on, it will be more advantageous for us than the somber masses of Paschendaele and at the Somme."

And British Air Minister Sir Archibald Sinclair was right when he said, "Our mightiest weapons are the Red army and the Royal Air Force."

While the German Luftwaffe in its reconstruction neglected the production of long-range bombers, England had pressed on energetically with the development of such types since 1935. The four-engined Stirling and Halifax bombers were produced, and from the two-engined Manchester was developed the Lancaster, the best night bomber of the last war.

Up to the beginning of World War II the number of strategic bombers remained very small. This was in accordance with the British peacetime principle of only keeping the fleet up in strength and ready for action. But as regards planning and industrial capacity, all prerequisites were ready for building up the bomber arm in the shortest time into the powerful instrument the war leaders demanded, should the occasion arise. This occasion of course arose with the English declaration of war on September 3, 1939. In *The Royal Air Force Manual* it says, "The bomb is the most important weapon of airpower and the bomber the effective carrier to bring it to the target. An offensive weapon consisting of bombers is the most important factor to give a nation air power."

The German air offensive of 1940 forced England to concentrate all her strength on defense. The fighters had absolute priority over the bombers. On top of this came our interference with the aircraft industry, so that the British bomber program was very much delayed.

In Allied reports on the war in the air, one can find the statement that the R.A.F. during the first two years of the war, i.e., until the middle of 1941, only dropped leaflets over Germany. This is incorrect. Although one could not talk of strategic bombing raids during this period, up to the end of 1940 a total of 155 raids on the Reich's territory were recorded, 22 of them on Berlin. The strength of the raiding forces was small and the results insignificant.

The year 1941 passed relatively peacefully from the point of view of the English bombing offensive against the Reich. The few larger-scale raids, like the day raid on the Ruhr on August 12, and the night raid on Berlin on November 7, had more political than military significance. These raids, like the "Nonstop Offensive" against the occupied Western territories, were supposed to give the Soviet ally a feeling that they were not alone in their fight against the German forces.

All this changed fundamentally at the beginning of 1942. England had recovered from the German Blitz. She had quietly built up her bomber force and was determined to make the best of the opening given to it by denuding the Western front of fighter and AA defenses, all of which were required in the east and the south. One could hardly imagine more favorable conditions for an opening of the bomber offensive against the Reich with a minimum of losses. Moreover in February, 1942, Air Marshal Sir Arthur Harris, an able and energetic officer, took over the R.A.F. Bomber Command.

The first strategic raid with strong forces took place during the night of March 3, 1942, against a target in France: the Renault works at Paris. A large part of the bombs fell on the neighboring working-class district, causing 250 casualties. The unfavorable effect of this raid on the French attitude toward her former ally was even heeded in England.

The failure of the Paris raid caused a heated argument in the Allied camp as to the way a strategical raid should be carried out. Even before Pearl Harbor the Americans had decided to adopt the principle of hitting the enemy decisively by paralyzing single important and specially selected targets in Germany. These were essentially power stations, centers of communication, factories of the aircraft and light metal industries, as well as refineries and synthetic fuel installations.

Reichsmarshal Göring (center) and Galland (facing Göring) talk at an advance fighter base during the Battle of Britain. (*Photo by Herbert Rost*)

Pilots scramble at fighter base. Messerschmitt ME-109 was work horse of the Luftwaffe Fighter Command in first years of war. (*Photo by Herbert Rost*)

B-24 Liberator mortally struck by a German ME-109 over oil refineries at Vienna, Austria. Note crew member coming out of escape hatch. (*Air Force Photo*)

The Focke-Wulf 190 Fighter replaced the ME-109 in 1943 and shortly became the favorite of the German Fighter Arm. (*Air Force Photo*)

ME-410 was employed as a destroyer for ground-support aircraft. It was also used as a light bomber. (*Air Force Photo*)

Despite badly damaged right wing, this Consolidated B-24 "Liberator" maintained formation on the bomb run over Toulon, France. (*Air Force Photo*)

Captured photograph shows "Viper," one of many new and lethal weapons in development at war's end. A piloted, rocket-propelled missile, "Viper" was designed to attack aircraft with cannon, rockets, or by ramming. (*Air Force Photo*)

A four-jet airplane with a speed of 670 mph, the Arado AR-234 was designated as a fighter! It carried a two-ton bomb in its concave underside. (*Air Force Photo*)

The Dornier DO-335 utilized the pusher-puller principle. A fast, hot aircraft (top speed 500 mph), the DO-335 never got into mass-production. (*Air Force Photo*)

Called "The People's Fighter" the Heinkel HE-162 was largely constructed of nonstrategic materials, did not reach mass-production until Germany's fate had been sealed. Here is one of the rare flying pictures of this craft. (*Air Force Photo*)

Twin-jet ME-262, with top speed in excess of 540 mph, could have been in large-scale production by 1943. Hitler, however, insisted on committing this revolutionary aircraft piecemeal as a fighter-bomber. (*Air Force Photo*)

Jet planes at the Obertraubling jet assembly plant in Germany, abandoned for lack of vital parts. (*Air Force Photo*)

Enormous defensive power of the B-17 plus overwhelming U. S. fighter support proved too much for German fighters. (*Air Force Photo*)

Smashed and gutted buildings in Hamburg bear witness to Allied supremacy in the skies. (*Official R.A.F. Photo*)

A P-47 Thunderbolt flies over the bomb-gutted ruin of Hitler's retreat at Berchtesgaden, Germany. (*Air Force Photo*)

The eventual American raids on the German ballbearing industry was a classical example of the U. S. planning of attack.

The Americans seemed to regard daylight raids with strong formations from high altitudes as an ideal compromise between results and losses of such precision raids. To this end they had developed the B-17 Flying Fortress and the B-24 Liberator with performance, armament, armor, navigational aids, and bombsights most suited to this special task. The first Flying Fortresses were tried out in action by the British. As a result of Lend Lease the R.A.F. in the spring of 1941 had already received 20 bombers of this type. Among other targets they raided Brest and Wilhelmshaven without results. Six months later, September, 1941, we took stock. During this period only 39 missions were flown with the 20 B-17s. It was thought that at the most only two of 1000-pound bombs dropped found their intended target. All other missions were partially successful. Not a single fighter was shot down during these raids. On the other hand eight Flying Fortresses were lost. This was stated by the Americans in their publication, *The Army Air Forces in World War II*.

German propaganda once more used this failure and the ensuing English-American controversy very cleverly by exchanging the psychologically effective and suggestive name Flying Fortress to Flying Coffin. It used this expression over all the English-speaking radio talks transmitted to America and England. The German fighters, however, held quite a different opinion.

After the discouraging first experience with the Flying Fortresses, the British suggested converting the B-17 into a night bomber. The R.A.F. saw their theory and experience upheld. Daylight precision raids brought less success and more losses than night area bombing. Even if night raids sometimes missed their actual targets, each bomb produced some sort of effect and was therefore not wasted, according to English opinion. Bombs which fell short or wide of the industrial target were absorbed by the surrounding residential districts and therefore added indirectly to the planned weakening of the enemy's war potential. The most important feature was that the losses during the night were so much smaller than by day. This was the decisive argument which overruled everything and made the British decide to stick to night bombing.

But the Americans were equally faithful to their theory of daylight precision raids. They refused to be impressed by the failure of the British B-17 experiment. They were absolutely convinced of the quality of their Flying Fortresses and of the effectiveness of their mode of attack. They were correct, as was soon to be proved. They did not accept the British argument and pointed out two major mistakes the R.A.F. had committed. They had been used at an altitude of at least 30,000 feet, but for the most part over 39,000 feet. Yet the B-17 was constructed to give its best performance between 24,000 and 27,000 feet. At a higher altitude technical interference occurred which the British crews could not cope with. The second mistake was that the B-17 had been used in far too small formations and sometimes they had even been sent up singly. In this way the heavy firing power of the B-17 did not achieve that terrific concentration which made any attack on a larger formation of them so suicidal. Had the English sent up the available 20 B-17s in close formation they would have achieved the same results as the Americans did later.

The Yankees stuck as stubbornly to their conviction as the British. This was going to prove most advantageous at a later date for both of them, because obviously each theory had its good points. A soldier who is familiar with his weapon can only achieve a maximum effect with it when he believes in the way it is tactically employed. In this way the English and Americans complemented each other in a most fortuitous manner. From a combination of the English night bombing and the American daylight raids originated the practice of 24-hour attacks, round-the-clock bombing.

These joint ideas were already formulated in principle at the conference at the White House in Washington, to which Churchill flew, on December 20, 1941, a fortnight after Pearl Harbor. This conference, known under the code name Arcadia, lasted until January 14, 1942. Together with a large staff of political and military advisers Roosevelt and Churchill laid down the fundamental principles for the combined Anglo-American conduct of the war. It was mutually agreed that Germany was the major enemy. A strategic bombing offensive was to be the overture to her final annihilation. On the last day of the Arcadia Conference the Allied Chiefs of Staff decided to transfer for this purpose large units of the U. S. air forces as quickly as possible to England.

For the time being of course the East Asiatic front was closer to the Americans than Europe. On the priority list for sending U. S. forces overseas which was drawn up as soon as the British guests had left, England figured only in third place after Australia and the South Pacific. On January 27,

General Spaatz, later Commander of the Eighth AAF operating from England, was appointed to prepare, organize, formulate, and effect the transfer of the required air force. In February, 1942, the formation of the first units of the Eighth AAF started in air fields in North and South Carolina. Spaatz had a large program in mind. Within a few weeks he wanted to create 23 squadrons of B-17s and five squadrons of light bombers, four squadrons of dive-bombers and 13 squadrons of fighters.

He completed his program on April 27, 1942. The first advance troops of the Eighth AAF, a total of 1800 men, disembarked at Liverpool. At the beginning of June a further troop transport left an American port. The bulk of the Eighth AAF followed on June 10 on the *Queen Elizabeth*. The planes were flown across. But while the personnel were either already at sea or in the process of embarking, a very critical situation arose because the Japanese were threatening Midway Island. All available American aircraft were ordered to the west coast, including those of the Eighth AAF. The latter did not cross to Europe until the end of June.

The American plan was a gigantic undertaking. Many hundreds of aircraft were to cross the 3500 miles from America to England for the first time in formation. The route was: Canada (Labrador), Greenland, Ireland, Scotland. Airfields for intermediate landings were prepared and a huge ground organization stood by. The greatest distance to be covered nonstop was 1250 miles. The flights were not ferried across by transport command but were flown by their actual crews. On June 23 the first 18 Flying Fortresses took off. By the end of 1942, 920 planes were sent, and 882 arrived safely in Scotland. From then until the end of the war the stream of planes across the Atlantic never stopped. When this gigantic operation started, it was nearly 15 years to the day since Charles Lindbergh had flown across the Atlantic from west to east.

In December, 1942, Roosevelt announced that U. S. aircraft production per month was 5500 planes. Those who knew these figures and the extent of the organization which was soon to turn these aircraft into a realistic military power could well be worried. But the Luftwaffe Command decided that these figures were fabulous, just as they had done with the information of our secret service. This information tallied in every respect with what we heard, of course for propaganda purposes, from Roosevelt.

Göring said in his speech at the Harvest thanksgiving on

October 4, 1942: "Some astronomical figures are expected from the American war industry. Now I am the last to underrate this industry. Obviously the Americans do very well in some technical fields. We know they produce a colossal amount of fast cars. And the development of radio is one of their special achievements, and so is the razor blade. . . . But you must not forget, there is one word in their language that is written with a capital B and this word is Bluff."

Propaganda *may* be horrible, but bombs *certainly* are. Yet both are used in war. It was propaganda when Roosevelt quoted imposing production figures to quiet the Soviet or his own people who one year after the U.S.A. had entered the war could see only little progress and were getting restless because the second front had not yet been opened up. It was also propaganda when Göring denied or ridiculed the same imposing production figures in order not to upset his people, whom he hoped he would be able to protect from Allied raids by throwing the concentrated strength of his Luftwaffe against the West after the end of the Eastern Campaign. If Göring not only denied these figures and facts publicly but simply closed his eyes to them, then this was no longer propaganda but an irresponsibility of such magnitude that it can only be measured by the consequences it had for the Reich and for all those people entrusted to his care and protection. Göring expressly forbade the Luftwaffe to count on the "alleged American production figures"; he forbade even a mention of them.

While the Americans were mobilizing their air force potential against Germany in 1942, the British Bomber Command did not remain idle. Harris prepared the first big blow against a German city. Lübeck was attacked on the night of March 28-29, 1942, by 200 to 300 bombers with a total load of 500 tons of high-explosive bombs and incendiaries. The damage was considerable. The casualties among the civil population for the first time reached four figures, with 300 killed. A month later Rostock was raided during the nights of April 24 and 27 by a similar force with a similar result. The losses of the attackers in these raids were insignificant. The formation flew in a wide arc and came in from the sea. The first two large-scale raids were a great shock to the German public, although it never learned the full extent of the losses, the strength of the attackers, nor the extent of the damage. I now hoped for some positive reaction on the part of the war leaders, at last concentrating with all energy on the defense of the Reich, especially by pushing through the fighter-construction program as presented by Fieldmarshal Milch, Chief of Aircraft Production. Hitler reacted in quite a contrary manner. He ordered an immediate retaliation raid which was carried out against the English town of Exeter, with insufficient strength, heavy losses, and a vast propaganda campaign. The motto was now more bombers for retaliation and no more fighters for defense. This motto was adhered to right up to the collapse.

When Cologne suffered the first 1000-bomber raid on the night of May 30-31, 1942, it showed clearly enough the extent of the coming extermination raids. At that time Harris had scraped together everything available in the R.A.F. All squadrons with all staff, reserve, and training planes loaded to capacity with bombs were sent out that night. Within 90 minutes the center of the city lay in rubble and ruins, with 460 dead, 45,000 homeless, 3300 houses and 36 industrial buildings totally destroyed, and 20 per cent of all buildings in the town damaged. That was the score. The following night Essen was raided in nearly the same strength.

The German countermeasure was a retaliation raid on Canterbury. The material effect of this raid bore no comparison to the British raids. It was totally erroneous to expect such a strong effect on public morale that the English Command would be moved to stop their bombing offensive. In mitigation, however, one can perhaps take into account that, like the German people, Hitler, who initiated these retaliation raids, was also kept in ignorance of the actual strength of the attacker. Moreover, our own strength may have been given to him in exaggerated figures. During one of these raids, on October 31, I lost my youngest brother Paul. He had 17 kills to his credit.

Not a month had passed before the third large-scale raid was carried out against a German city. Nine hundred and sixty bombers raided Bremen on the night of June 25-26. Raids of similar strength followed on Wilhelmshaven, Mainz, Kassel, and Düsseldorf. Until September more than 25 different German cities were raided, each time with more than 1000 British bombers.

From now on Germany had to count upon continuous night raids on her towns and centers of war industries. An increase in the attacking force and the bomb load could now be expected with the same certainty as one could expect deeper penetration and less possibility of saving the war industries by transferring them feverishly to central, east, and south Germany. The armament industry, already overtaxed by the gigantic extension of the fronts, was now exposed to direct annihilation attacks. Those who knew the developments in the enemy's camp should have seen clearly that the complementing of the British night raids by American day raids was only a matter of time. Nothing could change the fact that the war was going to be lost unless the air raids against the Reich could be stopped—not even the marvelous spirit with which the civilian population of the bombed areas bore the raids, nor the tirelessness of those who created and worked, not even the surprising ability of the bombed industries to repair the damage and restart production. Whatever the shape of the total strategical concept of the German leadership at the time, however it intended to carry on the war, whether in the east, south, or west or on all fronts together, whether offensive or defensive, was it not high time to put air armament and active air defense as a top priority?

16

The Hour Has Struck

I can be accused of many things, but no one can say that I was ever a "yes man" to Göring. In this respect I was considered the *enfant terrible* of the Luftwaffe. In the following chapters I shall have to mention many more clashes, which went far beyond what can be judged as permissible between the C.-in-C. and his subordinate, even in the most liberal army.

One of the scenes of such arguments was Castle Veltenstein near Nürnberg. Göring loved staying in this medieval castle set in the most attractive surroundings. Later we had many more briefings and discussions of the situation there. In autumn, 1941, Kammhuber, Mölders, and I were ordered to go there. The British night raids were becoming more than just nuisance raids and were taking on alarming dimensions. The German night fighters were still under development and Göring wanted to enforce his idea that the day fighters should also do night fighting. We had to reject this. On the one hand our two fighter wings in the west were fully employed in the defense against the British Nonstop Offensive, and on the other hand they lacked all technical and training requisites for night flying. Göring's intentions were typical of many measures taken by the Luftwaffe Command. Our Supreme Commander constantly conjured them up under the pressure of necessities.

I took this opportunity of pointing out what I had seen of our untenable position at the front against the R.A.F., which had been caused by sending almost all our fighter forces to the east. There was no mistaking how welcome this theme was! Although I fully realized that nothing could be changed for the moment in the allocation of the fighter forces, I suggested that we should start preparations at once for a capable defense against the west. Göring brushed me aside. "This whole phony business," he said, "won't be necessary any more once I get my squadrons back to the west."

When the Battle of Britain petered out and the march to the east began, the time had come to prepare with the fullest energy the defense of the Reich. Denuding the air front in the west of fighter aircraft was almost like begging the enemy to stage an air offensive. Because of her central geographical position, Germany was exposed to air raids and was on several other scores particularly vulnerable from the air. Dense populations, concentration of industry, overloaded power supplies, a centralized network of transport, and many other factors presented excellent conditions for an attack from the air and therefore demanded timely and elaborate countermeasures. The leaders of the Luftwaffe certainly had enough hints, suggestions, and warnings in this direction.

The hour for the defense of the Reich had struck. But no one wanted to admit that, at least in the west, we had lost the initiative, that we had been driven out of the role of attacker and into that of defender.

An air force is, according to its intrinsic laws, by nature an offensive weapon. Air supremacy is of course essential for this. If this has been lost then the fighter force has to be strengthened first of all. Because only the fighter force can achieve this essential supremacy so that the bomber and with it the entire air force can go over to the offensive once more. England had just given us a practical demonstration of this. It is amazing and shocking that this thought never occurred to either Hitler or Göring.

In actual fact a sort of defense of the Reich had existed since early 1941, but what did it look like! The post of Air Force Central Commander was created. Under him were all home stations and their ground organization, the flak batteries in the homeland, air intelligence, and later also the night fighters. He was an AA gunner. That was understandable because the active defense of the Reich consisted mainly of AA forces. It is characteristic that at the beginning of the war antiaircraft guns were highly overrated. As a result of experience gained on maneuvers and in the Spanish civil war, fighters were only regarded in air defense as an extension to the AA guns. They were thought of as a luxury weapon, and one did not quite know how, when, and where to use them.

The idea of defending an objective therefore prevailed. In the same way we used our squadrons to protect the Kroll Opera House, fighters were now attached in front of flak zones in vulnerable sectors. This dispersed the few fighters available for the protection of the Reich. "He who wants to protect everything, protects nothing." is one of the fundamental rules of defense. The Luftwaffe Command never complied strictly with this rule. When near the end of the war even the Gauleiters in

128

their capacity as Reich defense commissars were allowed to an ever-increasing degree to interfere in purely military matters, the idea of objective defense celebrated its final triumphs. More and more fighter squadrons and flights were demanded for the defense of specific objectives, which the gentlemen in question thought to be of national importance. The development of the war in the air already demanded a centrally controlled defense of the Reich, conducted from an air strategical point of view of large-scale air battles.

A ray of light in the sad landscape, which the defense of the Reich represented, was the night fighter. When the English large-scale raids started in spring, 1942, the German night fighters had reached a high standard of performance. By a systematic increase of the defensive successes of the German night fighters and flak batteries, the hope was justified that the nightly large-scale raids might be stopped or at least become rare operations. In the raid on Cologne 36 British planes were shot down. The German night fighters had registered their six hundredth kill. This figure rose to one thousand by September and reached two thousand by March, 1943.

Eighty per cent of these kills were multi-engined bombers.

These are remarkable figures when one considers that at the beginning of the war German night fighters were practically nonexistent. How was this possible? Had we forgotten the German and British night raids of World War I? Did international air travel stop with the fall of darkness? Had the technical and navigational methods not been sufficiently perfected to warrant the expectation of heavy night raids? German air superiority at the start was bound to force the English to shift their offensive to nighttime! This was Göring's opinion on the subject at the beginning of the war: "Night action?—that will never happen!" And why should it not happen? Perhaps because large-scale air activities at night, either offensive or defensive, required tremendous preparations and needed a long initial period before it could work, and because we thought to make both these contingencies superfluous by a quick victory. Here, too, instead of thorough consideration of all possibilities and their inclusion in planning—as was the habit of all German generals before now—there was now childish and intense wishful thinking: "It cannot be because it must not be!"

At the beginning of the war only a single squadron of ME-109s was experimenting with night flying for fighters, the so-called Moonlight Squadron. It operated independently with searchlight batteries, more or less following the rules of daylight fighting. The results were most unsatisfactory because they were too dependent upon the weather. Early in 1940 these experiments were discontinued. When in July, 1940, General Kammhuber was ordered to organize night fighters on a large scale, all that existed was a night-fighting research squadron, which had been formed in the meantime, consisting of DO-17s and ME-110s. He attacked his task with systematic energy. To him must be given the credit of having created the German night fighters.

Twin-engined night fighters also started as moonlight squadrons. The fighters attacked from waiting positions after their prey had been caught in the searchlights. Dark but clear nights were therefore particularly suitable. The main approach routes, the Ruhr and the German Bight, were therefore fitted out with so-called "light strips." These were areas about 15 miles deep in which searchlight batteries were stationed. The next step was the development of the radar strips lying ahead of the light strips. This however was only possible after suitable sets were available in sufficient numbers. In October, 1940, the delivery of the first Würzburg A-radar sets started, soon to be followed by the Würzburg Giant with a range of 40 miles. The radar or wireless gauge stations for night-fighter direction were equipped with these, and later complemented by Freya sets and additional directive instruments. These enabled a very precise location of the target inside the range of the stations and accurate attacks by the fighters standing by in the waiting areas. This method was called the *Himmelbett*. Thus was born the first successful·directing system of "dark night fighters." It was based on a series of many hunting grounds covered by radar in which one or later several fighters lay in ambush for incoming or outgoing bombers, which flew either in single file or side by side. Once located, target and pursuer were relayed from one station to the next. As long as the English flew in open formation on a broad front, this method brought good results on bright nights. But the limitations and weaknesses of this method were obvious as long as the number of radar instruments available allowed only the establishing of strips instead of wide zones, finally covering the whole territory over which enemy planes approached their targets. I shall explain later when and how this weakness was utilized by the R.A.F. Four or six of these night-fighter stations using the *Himmelbett* method were now united into a night-fighter area. The command of a night-fighter area was, if possible, joined with the local command of the searchlight units and the flak batteries. At the end of 1940 the 1st Night Fighter Division was at last formed in Holland. At the outset they consisted of three squadrons of night fighters, mainly the late destroyers. The commander was General Kammhuber. Until June, 1941, he enlarged the sphere of the night fighters so extensively that out of this 1st Night Fighter Division grew the 12th Fighter Corps (Night). By the beginning of 1943 it had grown to six night fighter wings, far below the strength that was really required.

In the meantime Kammhuber on orders from the Führer was responsible for the further building up of the total night-fighter force with exception of the Eastern front. The Area Command of the 3rd Air Force Group, France, was wrongly neglected.

One of the most important requirements for an active air defense is air intelligence. This had already been created in 1933, but up to the beginning of the war it was under the jurisdiction of the police. Only then did it come under the Air-*Gau* Commander. It was purely an eye-and-ear observation service. The highest technical equipment was a pair of binoculars. The personnel consisted of some old reservists of the intelligence battalions, pensioned policemen, unfit men, or overaged civil servants from the local authorities, and a horde of female assistants. Whatever air activity was observed by the individual observation posts traveled by telegraph to the air-report collecting centers and from there to the air observation commanders. These in turn informed the sections concerned: fighters, AA batteries, air-raid warning chiefs, railway officials, important industrial works, and an ever-increasing number of political offices. Up to the year 1944, the air intelligence service of the Reich worked without radar equipment.

In addition to this, there was the front-line air intelligence service run inside the operational area of the army by air intelligence troops. The army and navy had their own services. As a further organization of this type the radar service for the night-fighter division was created toward the end of 1943 from all these and at last formed one unified organization designed to coordinate all observation; radar-eye-and-ear intelligence. The purpose was to give a total picture of the air situation as a basis for fighter action and for all the other active or passive air defenses. The radar industry had progressed sufficiently by 1942 to warrant large-scale production. It would take too long to go into the field of radar and communication with its endless and ever-new possibilities, so I prefer to describe one of the newly created central combat stations of a fighter division, which the men ironically called "Battle Opera Houses."

Five of these giant bunkers were built in succession at Arnheim-Deelen, Döberitz, Stade, Metz, and Schleissheim. On entering, one was immediately infected by the nervous atmosphere reigning there. The artificial light made faces appear even more haggard than they really were. Bad air, cigarette smoke, the hum of ventilators, the ticking of the teletyper, and the subdued murmur of countless telephone operators gave one a headache. The magic center of attraction in this room was a huge frosted-glass panel on which was projected by light spots and illuminated writing the position, altitude, strength, and course of the enemy as well as of our own formation. The whole was reminiscent of a huge aquarium lit up, with a multitude of water fleas scuttling madly behind the glass walls. Each single dot and each change to be seen here were the result of reports and observations from radar sets, aircraft spotters, listening posts, reconnaissance and contact planes, or from units in action. They all merged together by telephone or wireless in this center, to be received, sorted, and within a few minutes transposed into transmittable messages. What was represented here on a giant map was a picture of the air situation in the sector of a fighter division, with about one-minute delay.

In front of the "stage," i.e., the sparkling map, in the proscenium box, on rising steps like an amphitheater, were seated several rows deep the fighter-directing officers, who gave the necessary orders to their night fighters or airborne units, based on the dispositions of the battle in progress. The battle was conducted from the balcony. This part of the theater was connected with all command posts and outside posts by a network of telephone lines, a real work of art. In addition, there were hosts of visible and invisible battle-disposition personnel. It was a technical sight which would impress not only the layman. No wonder that each Gauleiter who saw it once felt an urgent ambition to have a combat station of his own.

These control centers were undoubtedly of the greatest value despite the great expenditure of manpower and material and despite the servile dependency to which they forced the Command. One must realize that the situation projected here was after all only a representation of the actual events in the air. The fighting men often regarded the expenditure on these centers critically and wished that their demands and suggestions could have found more understanding, but it must not be forgotten that here the fundamental instrument to lead the entire defense of the Reich had been created.

From autumn, 1942, on, the day fighters in their air defense actions also profited from the lead the night fighters had undoubtedly achieved because Hitler had given them priority for radar, means of communication, and personnel. The unification of command and organization of the day and night fighters, which any intelligent person would have demanded, was at last achieved.

My influence on such decisions was limited by my position as General of the Fighter Arm, in which capacity I had not power of command. On the other hand my advice was sought on all important questions concerning the fighter arm by the Commanders-in-Chief of the Luftwaffe, the Chief of General Staff, the Staff Command, the Quartermaster General, the General Chief of Aircraft, the personnel and other offices of the Luftwaffe. I gave my ideas and suggestions, and occasionally they were even put into practice.

The unification of the day and night Fighter Command in autumn, 1942, was one of them. The fighter division became the leading unit, under whose command the day and night fighters as well as all communication personnel were united. The mammoth control stations received a double staff. We spoke of "day and night porters" in order that from now on the day and night fighters could have a 24-hour service. By autumn, 1943, there existed five such fighter divisions: Berlin-Central Germany No. 1 Fighter Division; German Bight No. 2 Fighter Division; Holland-Ruhr No. 3 Fighter Division; South Germany No. 7 Fighter Division, and the Eastern Marches No. 8 Fighter Division.

The 3rd Air Force Group in the west had no night fighters. Yet in air defense it had to fulfill a double task: first, to protect France with her objectives of military importance, and second, the defense of the advance zones of the approach routes into the Reich. Territorially the area of this Group was divided into wing leader zones, each with a control center. The means and organization at their disposal corresponded in comparison with the Battle Opera Houses to the outfit of a provincial amateur theater.

The position in the east was quite different. Jeschonnek asked me in the autumn of 1942 to make here some real improvisations in the field of night-fighter action. The idea was to prevent the landing and provisioning of Russian partisans and to stop the nuisance raids. In addition to the fact that there were no radar sets, a great difficulty arose because the ancient planes used by the Russians flew at only from 60 to 100 mph. The primitive can also be a weapon. The planes, for which bomber, reconnaissance, and "destroyer" units had voluntarily parted with their crews, were only put into action on bright nights, in conjunction with searchlights. In the northern parts of the Eastern front the nights were sometimes so bright that searchlights were unnecessary. Later, on the Eastern front, we loaded radar and fighter control stations on railway trucks, the so-called "dark-night trains"; and one night fighter wing was formed (NJG 6).

I have tried to give a concrete yet naturally incomplete picture of the situation as I saw it between the years 1942-43. At that time any sober and responsible person could see that we were facing an attempt to smash the German war potential from the air. I repeat that up to this time all my attempts to explain to the High Command the seriousness of our position miscarried. After the failure of our air offensive on England they embarked upon a path of criminal carelessness. They did not want to see the danger, because they would have had to admit their many omissions and neglects. Unpleasant reminders were regarded as a great nuisance.

17

Following the Latest Bomb Crater

On August 11, 1942, General Spaatz, Commander-in-Chief of the Eighth AAF, stationed in England, reported to General Arnold, C.-in-C. of the USAF: "We must have air supremacy over Germany before a satisfactory end of the war can be achieved." This was the clearly formulated conclusion of the first probing by American bombers against the European coast defended by the Luftwaffe. Spaatz also knew from his British colleague Harris that the first large-scale night raids on the territory of the Reich, convincing though they may have been, were by no means body blows. Although the greater part of the German air force and many AA batteries were tied down on the Eastern front, flying in from the west was far from being a pleasure trip. The American bombers made their raids on the French-Belgian coastal areas only with strong fighter protection. After the 36 aircraft lost in their first 1000-bomber raid on Cologne, the British had to pay again with 52 bombers in their raid on Bremen which was made in similar strength. According to British statements the R.A.F. made a total of 1000 major attacks during 1942, 17 being heavy raids during each of which more than 500 tons of bombs were dropped. They had to pay with one aircraft for every 40 tons of bombs dropped. Such a relatively favorable ratio was never again achieved by the German air defenses on an average over a longer period. The following year it cost the British only one aircraft for 80 tons of bombs dropped.

The percentage of losses is in direct ratio to the number of planes participating in a raid. We had already learned in our raids on England that as long as we attacked with a force of about 200 aircraft a loss of 20 planes constituted only ten per cent. But when the strength of the raiding forces decreased, and the raids were nevertheless continued, then it was not rare that of 20 bombers sent out in a night six were shot down. This was a 30 per cent loss which was unbearable in

135

the long run. The situation during the British night raids on Germany was analogous but reversed. The constantly growing strength of their raiding forces reduced the percentage of their losses. This favorable development was assisted by a series of other factors: higher bomb load, higher ceiling of the bombers employed, new methods of approach, attack, and interference. The above-mentioned axiom, that percentage losses rise in inverse proportion to the strength of the attacking force, applies not only to the success of the fighter and night fighter in air defense but also to the losses they sustain in action.

The system of approach used by the British at the outset for their large-scale night raids, i.e., loose formation on a broad front, flying at large intervals, offered the German night fighter the greatest chance. The radio and radar sets directing them worked without interference up to the summer of 1943. The defensive fire from the bombers at night had only a relatively small effective radius. British long-distance night fighters were rarely encountered at that time. Our losses in night fighters were therefore considerably smaller than those of the day fighters. The majority of these losses were caused by the weather, by technical faults, or by our own flak. Exceptional demands were made on the flying ability of the night-fighter pilots. Some night-fighter aces achieved a remarkable number of kills. A stock of unusually gifted, experienced, and successful experts was produced. Some of the leaders of flights, squadrons, or wings achieved more personal success than the entire unit they commanded. Success became altogether too individual. We neglected to make the high standard of performance of the individual night fighter more general by intensive training and advancement of recruits. But to do this we should have had to use experienced night-fighter pilots as trainers, and these could of course not be spared from active service.

Night fighting came into the foreground of public interest. It is quite understandable that the German population was excited by the successes of these men who night after night hurled themselves against the British bombers. The Luftwaffe Command exaggerated the percentage successes of the night fighters by understating the strength of the raiding forces. This may have been understandable and very effective from a propaganda standpoint, but it led once more to a very dangerous self-deception.

Because of the encouraging results of the night fighters we forgot at times the limits of night fighting set by present procedure. In the main we regarded a complementing and concentrating of the existing organization as a means of intensifying and consolidating its possible effectiveness. The gaps still existing in the radar network were to be closed, and the action of the night fighters was to be increased accordingly. Yet the use of new tactical methods such as pursuit, target, and long-distance night fighting were neglected despite urgent demands. The successes of the German night fighters in 1942 could have been more formidable, and they could also have been more lasting. Our Command allowed the enemy to dictate the necessary defense measures instead of countering actively with original measures, planned with foresight.

One of these ideas was the long-distance "intruder," which Kammhuber had already tested in 1940. He organized four flights of DO-I7Z and JU-88C6 bombers which operated with great success over the British bomber bases. Great and promising possibilities were opened up here. Combating the bombers during their take-off and assembly, and pursuit on the outward and return journeys up to the time of their breaking formation and landing, would have been an effective extension of night-fighter action over the homeland. Yet the leaders, and Hitler first of all, could not get accustomed to the idea of long-distance night flying. They rejected the idea and in August, 1943, demanded its cessation. Hitler was not interested in planes shot down at night over England. He needed more tangible evidence for the German people who were getting more and more worried about the nightly raids.

The reasons given for the cessation order were that new locating instruments in the aircraft must not fall into the hands of the enemy. The instrument in question was a *Bord-Radar,* an electric eye which showed up other aircraft in the dark in a limited sector ahead of the plane. At first it had a range of only one and a half to two miles. With this set it was no longer necessary to direct the pilot from the ground until he was in visual contact with the enemy. Now he only had to be directed until the wireless operator caught the enemy bomber on his radar screen. For the further approach the wireless operator directed the pilot. Under conditions of average visibility—about 200 yards—he could open fire. The *Himmelbett* method, directed from the ground, could have been extended to a limited pursuit tactic, beyond the range of the ground station. *Bord-Radar* sets were therefore demanded with appropriate urgency. The first instrument of this kind, Lichtenstein BC, was superseded in October, 1943, by the improved SN-2 which had a range of two and a half to four miles.

The introduction of a special type of night-fighter aircraft on the other hand remained debatable. The HE-219 was intended as such and was developed and tested accordingly. She was supposed to remove the essential weaknesses of the ME-110, which had been mainly used so far. These weaknesses were: small range and a crew of two. A long and bitter fight ensued over the HE-219 among the Luftwaffe Command, the General Chief of aircraft, and Kammhuber. The result was that the prototype went very late and in insufficient numbers into production. Only toward the end of 1943 did the HE-219 go into action. Never more than two squadrons were equipped with this type. In the meantime more and more night-fighter units were re-equipped with JU-88 bombers and with later developments of the same type, which generally served very well. I remained neutral in this debate because Milch's opinion seemed reasonable to me: He thought that the advantages of the HE-219 over the JU-88 bombers were not considerable enough to justify burdening our aircraft industry with still another type at this particular stage of the war.

Since the beginning of the Eastern Campaign the night fighters suffered most from the shortages which grew more severe in all branches of the Luftwaffe. There was a shortage of crews, of aircraft, of sundry radar instruments, of methods of communications, of personnel. Thus the south and middle German divisions existed only on paper. The development of its radar and communication network was only just beginning. Operational fighters were not available. Night-fighter schools therefore had to go into action with their instructors as a temporary solution. As the required units for covering the whole Reich simply did not exist, the calling of night fighters into action was changed at short notice according either to previous enemy reconnaissance activities, intelligence from listening posts, according to weather conditions, or perhaps only on assumptions. The "traveling circus" system occasionally produced surprising results, but more often useless expenditure of material and disheartening failures. Among the crews the saying was: "The defense of the Reich follows the latest bomb crater." It was very much to the point and was used more and more frequently and not only by the night fighters. Flak gunners, searchlight batteries, artificial fog units, and almost anything which could be moved about by the active air defense made the same observation.

During 1942 the day fighters were less in the public eye

than their night comrades. That was bound to occur as long as the bombing offensive against the Reich consisted mainly of British night raids. Nevertheless it was the day fighter that had to carry the main burden of the air defense in addition to his other tasks.

Besides the night raids the British made single, daring, and often successful daylight raids on targets in France, Italy, and often deep into the territory of the Reich. They were carried out by a specialized group of Lancasters. They raided selected single targets of importance in low-level attacks with small formations. This day activity of the R.A.F. ran parallel with the more and more established and improved area bombing technique of the night raids. Until October, 1942, 45 of these daylight raids were made, among others, on the U-boat shipyards at Lübeck, Danzig, and Godingen. One of the first raids of this kind was on April 17 on the MAN works in Augsburg (U-boat engines). According to English reports 12 four-engined Lancasters took part in the raid, eight reached their target, seven of these were shot down. The R.A.F. was not to be discouraged. In fact this success of the German defense was a mere chance, which could not be repeated. Yet it strengthened the opinion of the Luftwaffe leaders that the danger of daylight raids on Reich territory need not be taken seriously.

These English day raids remained single operations. Although they were continued in 1943, they were small and infrequent. Besides these, carefully selected objectives of special importance were raided in low-level attacks at night. In this way they managed to obliterate the Luftwaffe information center at Teltow. In this attack not one bomb fell outside the fencing of the site bombed. Of similar precision and lasting effect were the daylight raids of May 17 on the Eder, Möhne, and Sorpe dams. Large cylindrical bombs, especially made for this purpose, were used which on release were set in rotation by an additionally fitted mechanism. These special bombs could be released in low-level flight at an exactly calculated speed, height, and distance to hit the dam at a predetermined and most favorable point below water level. The Möhne and Eder dams, which respectively held 130 and 202 million cubic meters of water, were torn open in this manner. The Sorpe Dam was not hit. The damage was great. Besides the loss of life and material caused by floods, the water and power supply to the Ruhr was strongly affected. The English estimated the loss in production as high as 35 per cent. The Luftwaffe Command immediately ordered the transfer of balloon barrages and smoke-screen units, as well as light flak batteries to all important dams. Nineteen Lancasters made this raid, 11 of which returned to England. The examination of the aircraft shot down and the interrogation of the captured crews showed that the R.A.F. executed this raid only after extremely precise preparations from a technical, tactical, and training angle.

Despite the considerable success of these raids as regards their effect on the German war industry, Harris stuck to nightly saturation bombing of German cities, which, although of far less military importance, he held to be correct and justifiable. In many statements for the benefit of the German people he admitted openly that these raids were intended to have a political and psychological effect.

In the meantime in the west we had our first experience of attacking the American multiengined bombers in daylight raids. There was no doubt that our fighter pilots were insufficiently prepared for the fight against the formations of Flying Fortresses with their strong fighter escorts. In the beginning we overrated their firing power and invulnerability, which all the same were very considerable. An infantryman is paralyzed by "tank fright" when first confronted in battle by an enemy tank until he discovers that these monsters too have their vulnerable points. In the same way the fighter pilot has to overcome his shyness of the new enemy. But the defensive firing power of a formation of Fortresses as well as the invulnerability of each individual bomber were very real facts. One can reckon that a formation of 27 B-17s can bring to bear at least 200 heavy machine guns, with an effective range of 1000 yards to stern, i.e., in the direction from which fighters usually attack. On the other hand, according to experience, it took about 20 to 25 hits with 20-mm. shells to shoot down a Flying Fortress.

In the early winter of 1942 I was once more with my units in the west. This time I wanted to collect experiences and data in order to improve our combat methods against the American multiengined bombers. These methods were to receive many additions and changes during the course of the war.

Not only had our pilots to overcome the psychological barrier, but absolutely new tactics of attack had to be devised. Up to now we had only fought against the bombers singly. Although we approached the enemy in formation, the attack was made singly, or by a *Rotte,* a fighter aircraft with its accompanying plane. Now it was a case of confronting the

140

massed defensive fire of a four-engine bomber formation with a complete flight or squadron of our fighters. From the stern attack we had to change over to a frontal attack. This was something completely new. The 2nd Fighter Wing, Richthofen, under its commander, Egon Meyer, had already developed its own technique for a frontal attack, but the results in aircraft shot down were still very small. This was chiefly a question of armament. The ME-109 carried only one 20-mm. cannon and two normal machine guns. This could by no means be regarded as sufficient in the fight against multiengined bombers. This armament, too, constituted an incomprehensible regression in the new ME-109F compared with the E series, whose production had stopped in the previous year. The latter had two 20-mm. cannons mounted in the wings and two normal machine guns. The one cannon of the new ME-109F was of course more modern, had a quicker rate of fire, a better trajectory, and what is more was centrally mounted over the engine and fired through the hub of the propeller. Nevertheless there were conflicting opinions as to whether the new armament should be regarded as a step forward or backward. Mölders shared Udet's opinion that one centrally mounted cannon was better than two in the wings. I regarded one cannon as absolutely inadequate, particularly as I considered machine guns outdated for aerial combat, merely senseless fireworks. One could hardly impress an enemy fighter with them any more, to say nothing of multiengined bombers. Naturally I recognized the advantages of centrally mounted weapons. But if the armament consisted of one cannon only, then I preferred two decentral cannons, especially when I thought of the gradually declining standard in skill and training of the majority of our new pilots, which was unavoidable as the war dragged on. Not every pilot was as good a sharpshooter as Udet or Mölders.

This problem of the ME-109 armament was also brought to Hitler's notice, how and by whom I do not know. During a conversation he asked me for my opinion. Did I consider the better armament for the ME-109 a cannon in the central axis or two in the wings? I did not ponder long: "Better all three." Hitler was pleased. My answer corresponded with his ideas. He used the fact that later development proved him repeatedly correct as an argument in his attempts to put into practice odd ideas of his own in the field of armament and technics, against the advice of experts.

Immediately after this conversation came the order to increase the armament of the ME-109F. Two additional 20-mm.

cannons were mounted below the wings. These "gondolas," or "bathtubs" as we called them, naturally affected the performance of the plane badly. The aircraft defaced in this way was as good as useless for fighter combat. But at least with three cannons she had now a firing power with which one could achieve something in the battle with the Flying Fortresses.

Later on when the fighter escort of the Americans became more and more effective, the "bathtubs" had to be removed again. The escorting fighters became the primary target. Shooting down bombers took second place. Many favorable chances were missed by neglecting to provide stronger armament for our fighters. Much more suitable was the FW-190 first with two and later with four 20-mm. cannons and two machine guns. The air-cooled radial motor was less vulnerable and gave the pilot a natural cover during attacks. But the delivery of FW-190 was inadequate. Four fifths of the total fighter production still consisted of ME-109s. Not only the defense units of the Reich but all theaters of war clamored for FW-190s. One of its weaknesses was that above 21,000 feet its performance fell off rapidly. As the B-17 usually came in at that height, it was of course handicapped in combating the American fighter escort.

The question of armament and ammunition had already preoccupied me when I was in command of the JG 26. Aircraft with new types of armament or ammunition were brought to me as soon as their technical tests had been completed. In this way one day in early 1941 I got the first ME-109 with two heavy machine guns instead of the normal one. They were supposed to be synchronized to fire through the propeller disk. During my first flight in this kite over the Channel they refused to do so. Nearly everything went wrong. I flew alone, fairly low, direction England. I fired, and I was infuriated by the constant jamming of the guns. Further I was amazed by the remarkable flames from the muzzle. I had never seen anything like it: real fireworks in front of my cockpit. Again the guns jammed. I could not coax one more shot out of them. Halfway between the English and French coasts I turned back. Suddenly a shadow appeared under my left wing. I could almost have touched it, I saw the red white and blue circles on the wings. It was a Spitfire. The pilot drew closer. I was paralyzed. He laughed, I think, waved to me, and banked away, direction England. I never found an explanation for this mysterious encounter over the Channel. I suppose he was following me and luckily for me his guns must have jammed at the same time as mine.

When I landed my knees were shaking badly. I was not very impressed when I received the report that three quarters of the propeller had been cut through. That was the explanation of the fireworks. The synchronization had been wrongly adjusted or was faulty. I insisted on a detailed technical inquiry, but in the shape of a personal report from the man responsible. Each shot that had been fired a fraction of a second too late or too early had hit the propeller and exploded there. At the neck of each blade there was a piece as big as a fist missing.

The American daylight raid offensive against the Reich would certainly have been at its height at the end of 1942, or early 1943, had the development in North Africa not taken such a stormy course. On the day the first Flying Fortresses landed in Scotland after a flight of more than 3500 miles across the ocean, Rommel's troops mobilized for the attack on Alexandria. In the wadies of the El Alamein position the existence of the British Empire was at stake. No wonder therefore that the attention of the British Prime Minister was directed more toward checking Rommel's new attack than towards the airfields of Scotland where the planes of the Eighth AAF were landing from July 1 on. Therefore the greeting of the American troops by the British government did not turn out as enthusiastic as the ocean flyers had expected it to be. While the Eighth AAF was assembling in England, Churchill made lively efforts to get rid of them as quickly as possible. He turned to Roosevelt with the urgent request to postpone Operation Roundup in favor in Operation Torch, the landing in Africa, planned long before to trap the German Afrika Korps in a pincer movement.

Roosevelt acquiesced to the justified British wishes. In July, General Spaatz received the order to form the Twelfth AAF for North Africa out of the Eighth AAF which was still in its modest beginnings. As one unit after another was sent to Africa —up to the end of December, 1942, four fighter and two heavy bomber groups—he asked himself not without acrimony: "What is left of the Eighth AAF after the interference of Operation Torch?"

Not very much. But the Anglo-American landing in North Africa on November 7, 1942, was a complete success. Thanks to this operation the situation of the war for Germany had again fundamentally taken a turn for the worse. The war on two fronts had become a war on three fronts. Not from the west, nor the east, nor even the north, which we had thought

143

to be in danger, but from the south the enemy knocked on the doors of Europe for the first time. The occupation of the remaining part of France was the obvious reaction of Germany. This again drove many leading Frenchmen over to the side of the British and the Americans, among them Admiral Darlan, who was then Supreme Commander of all French Forces. I had met him a year before, when on December 1, 1941, I accompanied Göring in a special train to a meeting with French Chief of State Pétain at Saint-Florentin. Darlan and the old marshal were both equally willing for an understanding and cooperation with Germany, but both had the interests of France uppermost in their minds. I remember Göring saying lightly before the conference with Pétain, in which cooperation between the French and the German fleets was to be discussed, that the conversation would not last long. "In twenty minutes I shall have finished with the old gentleman." Göring and Pétain retired for their talks. The accompanying staff (I was among them) waited in the adjoining coach of the special train. We had ample opportunity to converse at length. The anticipated 20 minutes which Göring had mentioned passed. Half an hour passed, a whole hour, two hours. After about three hours the two at last emerged. Judging from the color of Göring's face, it was he who had been finished by the 80-year-old marshal.

When it was a question of French interests Darlan too showed a similar toughness toward the Anglo-Americans after he had gone over to them. He was no easy ally. On December 24, he was assassinated under mysterious circumstances in Algiers. De Gaulle had a free hand. The initial resistance of the garrisons in North Africa which had been true to Pétain flagged slowly. Eight days after the occupation of Vichy, France, the rest of the French fleet scuttled itself in the harbor of Toulon. The doom threatening the Axis troops in Africa could not be averted. Although Rommel had reported to Hitler the hopelessness of his situation and the certain destruction of the Afrika Korps, even before the landing in his rear, his heroic army still fought for more than six months on African soil.

In April, 1943, I flew to Tunis. The situation of the two German fighter wings which were fighting there was desperate. The superiority of the Anglo-Americans was overwhelming. Although all possible efforts were made at last on the German side to bring up sufficient supplies to the army and although the 2nd Air Fleet under Kesselring had in the meantime gone into action on the Southern front, and even though the Italian fleet had come out of hiding, nothing could stop the continuous advance of the enemy against the Axis forces which were now compressed into an ever-decreasing area. Here in Africa could already be seen what a year later was going to happen on a larger scale on the European battlefield: an army, however strong, determined to defend itself with the utmost bravery, can accomplish nothing without air cover. Relentlessly the ring closed in on Tunisia.

Supplying the encircled troops by air demanded catastrophic losses. The transport planes could not be adequately protected. Of the still available aircraft more and more fell out because of the shortage of spare parts. That is why 20 or more aircraft were shot down in a single supply mission, because of insufficient or nonexistent fighter cover. Despite this they continued to supply the troops in Tunis right to the last. The performance of the transport crews is beyond praise. Even though they had succeeded in getting their planes with the urgently required load safely into the caldron, while refueling, unloading, and reloading they were exposed to uninterrupted bombing and low-level attacks. If they survived these they had to face the return journey which was no less dangerous than the fly-in. Landing at last in Sicily, they were often raided on their airfields. The devastating decimation of the Luftwaffe on such forced missions was nothing new. But here, because of the extended duration, we used up the very substance of our air force.

On May 7, 1943, General von Arnim capitulated with the remnants of the Afrika Korps. Kesselring, as Commander-in-Chief, South, had since early 1943 also been commanding the army units in the southern theater of war. Richthofen took over the 2nd Air Fleet. The General of the Combat Fighters, Peltz, was ordered to lead the bombers, and I was put in charge of the fighters based on Sicily.

Up to the last hour Hitler strictly forbade an organized evacuation of Tunis: "Europe is being defended at Tunis." It is needless to describe here the losses of personnel and morale caused by this order and by many similar ones later on. Now the beaten Africa fighter planes were expected to prevent the bombing offensive which was the prelude to the imminent Allied landing. But first our pilots flew two or three times across the Mediterranean back into the witches' caldron in order to save the faithful ground crews from certain capture. We took up to three men on each flight. It is known that a large, powerful pilot has hardly room for himself in our single-seater fighters. It is still a mystery to me how three mechanics could have got inside the FW-190 in addition to the pilot. What happened here was another proof of the real tie which existed throughout the war between the ground staff and the flying personnel of the Luftwaffe.

Alternately commanding from west and east Sicily, I instigated almost anything that was still justifiable. But we could really do nothing against the overwhelming Anglo-American superiority. Our pilots were exhausted to a terrifying degree. From North Africa and from Malta the American and the British air fleets took us in a pincer move and the grip became tighter every day. Our ports in Sicily, our bases, the supply and repair stations in the south of Italy, all were subjected to the Anglo-American hail of bombs. Bari, the assembly station for the aircraft replacements from home, was hard hit several times. Hundreds of new fighter aircraft were lost. The Luftwaffe was burning up in the Southern theater of the war. On July 10, I flew to Berlin in order to report to Göring. He received me with these words, "You must return immediately. The Allies landed today in Sicily."

Hell had broken loose in Sicily. The British fleet dared to show itself off the east coast of the island. We were powerless. Under the screen of the Allied air superiority the guns of the navy controlled a broad strip of the coast. No sign of any counteraction by Italian naval forces. A British paratroop operation in the Catanian lowland had been frustrated. JU transport planes brought up German reinforcements from Italy. Hitler ordered, "Not one German soldier must leave the island. The Luftwaffe must put all available personnel at the disposal of the army. Europe and Germany are being defended in Sicily."

But neither such desperate orders nor the troops that were giving their all could in the long run prevent the victory of the powerful enemy forces on land, at sea, and in the air. At the last moment came the order to evacuate Sicily. The fact that anything at all reached the Italian mainland was solely due to the flak batteries. Their unique concentration protected the continuous ferry traffic so effectively that the hordes of Allied planes of all types could only half complete their mission from a great height.

The fighter units arrived in a lamentable condition at their new bases in south Italy. Almost all stocks and materials had to be left behind. Nearly all the remaining aircraft we had saved were destroyed by a murderous raid on Viterbo by the Fifteenth AAF. We had not even enough left to stage a makeshift action. On top of that there was the order waiting for us

146

to take up the defense immediately. "Yes, but with what?" we asked in desperation! The units were not only exhausted by a disastrous battle but, because of a belated evacuation that had been delayed beyond the last minute, they were crushed both as regards material and personnel.

Vieck took over the command of the remnants of fighter units that were left over from the African and Sicilian debacle. I was recalled to Staff H.Q. and I delivered my second report on the situation in the air at the Southern theater of war. It was couched in an even less considered tone than the first one, which had caused such an unpleasant stir the year before. I demanded in all seriousness and determination considerably greater effort in the fields of air armament production and training than had been hitherto made. Had they gone to work then with full energy, they might have been able to prevent many of the things which occurred later.

18

The House Without a Roof

The year 1943 saw Germany in retreat on all fronts. After the fall of Stalingrad the Red army went over to the attack at the Donets. In February they took Kursk, Voroshilovgrad, Rostov, and Kharkov. Manstein's Caucasus armies partly fought their way back over the Isthmus of Kerch into the Crimea. The Soviet advance toward the Dnieper was halted. In July the German troops at Kursk lined up for the last large-scale offensive. It was repulsed.

Badoglio's *coup d'état* followed the Allied landing in Sicily. The Italian resistance until the capitulation was only a token one. On September 9 the first Allied troops landed at Salerno on the European mainland. With the few German troops, and with those of the Duce who had been freed from the Gran Sasso by paratroops, Generalfeldmarshal Kesselring organized some tough and extremely able resistance.

Hitler had coined the idea of the European Fortress. This fortress was to be defended to the last breath. Roosevelt, in a message to Congress on September 17, 1943, doubted its invincibility, because "Hitler forgot to put a roof over this fortress."

This may well have been true at the time. If one understood by a roof the German Luftwaffe, then this had not been forgotten in the beginning. On the contrary, there had been a time when we had reason to fear nobody in the air. But instead of strengthening this roof once it was in existence, so that it could stand up to coming loads, it had been burned piecemeal since the opening of the Eastern Campaign. And now when the tempest of war raged over the German house, the roof offered insufficient protection to the inhabitants.

On January 27 Germany experienced the first American daylight raid. It was directed against Wilhelmshaven. The bombers of the Eighth AAF were escorted by P-38 Lightnings. This was a twin-engine long-distance fighter which had similar shortcomings in combat as our ME-110. Our fighters were clearly superior to it. The Americans achieved no particular results in their first operation against the Reich. But they had arrived. Their existence could not be denied. Nevertheless the German High Command did not take this event seriously enough. As before, they were of the opinion that the American multiengined bombers could not succeed in day raids. They thought that even numerically inferior German fighter forces would inflict such heavy losses on them that larger operations with greater penetration would prove too costly. Their own failure over England was still fresh in their minds, but they overlooked the new possibilities that were opened to the Americans by improved technics. The range of the American bombers covered all targets in Europe. They could allow themselves wide detours in order to circumnavigate the strongly defended areas. Their bomb load, cruising height, defensive fire power, and invulnerability assured the USAF right from the start better conditions than the Luftwaffe ever had. Notwithstanding all these, the Americans first had to solve the problem of fighter escort. So far they had flown among the borders of the Reich with an escort of Spitfires and Thunderbolts, from there to the objectives escorted by Lightnings only. Göring rejected as impossible a further penetration by fighter escort when I pointed out that this was a development obviously to be expected. The next problem for us was going to be the quantity, once the American production and training were running at full speed.

Göring hoped that the newly formed fighter wings, 1 and 2, which were stationed in the two major approach areas, Holland and the German Bight, would be sufficient to beat off the Americans in daytime. I did not agree. I thought this kind of peripheral defense basically wrong, not to mention that our group leaders and crews were unfamiliar with combating the new type of adversary. After the American daylight raids on Reich territory had become reality, although Göring had thought them to be impossible, he believed that he could counter them successfully by establishing defensive strips on the outer limits of the German defense area. This concept reflected the political-propagandist wish to keep enemy aircraft as far as possible out of sight of the German population. But in order to do this the fighter forces should have been much stronger. With only two fighter wings and the extent of the coastal front one could not dream of preventing a breakthrough.

I was of the opinion that with the existing shortage of fighter aircraft only a central defense rather than an outer defense ring could promise any success. Squadrons and wings of fighter planes in the inner circle was my idea, rather than a few flights in the outer circle. With my idea one had to accept the shortcoming that the American forces penetrated far into our territory in full daylight before they could be attacked by our fighters and that, according to circumstances, distant areas and targets remained outside the range of our now-concentrated fighter force and could not be covered at all. On April 17, 1943, the first heavy raid on Bremen was made by strong American multiengined bomber formations. They were escorted by Lightnings. It was the beginning of a series of similar U. S. daylight raids, which varied in strength and results. The defensive results were poor. Our widely drawn-out fighter forces could only get small groups of 20 to 25 aircraft to engage the enemy. They were much too weak to achieve anything decisive against the fighter-protected bomber force.

Göring complained to me several times about the "miserable failure" of the German fighters. He pointed out quite rightly the different faults in tactics and the insufficient training of the newly formed squadrons. He was still of the opinion that once these faults were remedied we could stop the American day raiders. Against this I pointed out that the Americans would shortly come with new and improved fighter escorts capable of penetrating deeper. We must look upon the present-day raids only as an overture, therefore we ought to be prepared for the coming events with quite different and additional measures.

I expressed the same opinion to Speer, the Minister of War Production, who asked me what I thought about the chances of day precision raids by American multiengined bombers on the Ruhr. He feared these much more than the British night raids, which had been going on since May 5 under the name of the Battle of the Happy Valley. Night after night towns on the Rhine and the Ruhr were receiving showers of incendiaries and high-explosive bombs. Cologne and Aachen were particularly heavily hit. Many other industrial centers like Essen, Dortmund, Duisburg, Bochum, Wuppertal, Krefeld, and Oberhausen were repeatedly and severely raided. Single large-scale raids were directed against Berlin, Hamburg, Kiel, Rostock, Stettin, Munich, Stuttgart, and Nürnberg. Despite considerable damage and losses these nightly area bombings did not produce a decrease in our war production. Speer therefore felt most apprehensive when I told him that I foresaw the early possibilities of American daylight raids on the Ruhr. He, in contrast to other responsible leaders, did not remain passive when faced with events. His indisputable successes were due for the most part to his ability to plan and organize. Therefore he did not want to be caught unprepared by unexpected events. I was able to explain to him in detail and with absolute frankness my point of view about the possible development.

A short while later I was called to see Hitler. He asked what had to be done to prevent the daylight raids. I told him that this was mainly a question of relationship of strength between the raiding force and the defending fighters. I said that three or four times the number of fighters compared with the U. S. bombers were needed in order to build up the required fighter concentrations all over the territory of the Reich. With such a strength we could disperse the enemy formations and could as good as annihilate them. But should the Americans increase their fighter escort, I would require in addition the same number of fighters as were accompanying the bomber formations. But the first and most important requisite for the destruction of the bombers was the achievement of air superiority against the American escort fighters. Hitler listened to me quietly. He seemed to accept the need for three- to fourfold superiority of the fighters over the bombers for the defense of the Reich. He rejected energetically my hint about a possible extension of penetration of the American fighter escort. Göring had told him that such a possibility was quite out of the question. On this note he dismissed me.

I received the news that my brother Wilhelm had fallen after 50 air victories in the west. He had been shot down by Thunderbolt escort fighters near the German frontier in the vicinity of Saint-Trond.

I knew quite well that with the terrific burden of the various fronts my demands for fighter reinforcements for the defense of the Reich must have been found very irksome. In the east and in Italy every aircraft was needed to assist the army in carrying out Hitler's orders that every inch of ground had to be defended. At this moment we should have transferred fighter aircraft from the front to the Reich. Giving ground at the fronts meant giving up foreign soil, but at home it was already a question of German survival. I had to look for support elsewhere. Milch had greatly increased air-arm production within the limited powers given to him. He met my worries with full understanding and agreed to do everything in his power to push the production of fighter aircraft. He drew up a fighter program providing for the production of 1000 aircraft a month. Neither Göring nor Hitler received this program with enthusiasm because they saw that it would lead to a reduction of the bomber production. Instead of giving Milch the full weight of their authority, they curbed his initiative by insisting that bomber production must take priority.

At the outset Milch fulfilled his program, and during the first eight months of 1943 he actually delivered 7600 fighter planes. That was a tremendous increase. But despite the acute danger which threatened the Reich from the air, fighter production still had no priority over bomber production, and aircraft production maintained its status in the general war industry. Unfortunately, of this wonderful increase in fighters, only a very small portion was allocated to the defense of the Reich.

The main reason for this was the disastrous developments at the fronts. In addition to high casualties, the strictly applied withdrawal tactics ordered by Hitler cost us enormous amounts of material. Retreating "according to plan," which had become a stock phrase, existed only in the terminology of war reports. In reality we fell back only when it was no longer possible to save equipment, reserves, repair outfits, and spare parts. On the Southern front the fighter units had to be re-equipped twice because our positions were evacuated too late. In this way a large part of Milch's fighter production went up into flames in these constant retreats which became more and more costly.

At this time, to crown everything, there was a universal demand for fighters. The battle squadrons discovered that the FW-190 was the ideal aircraft for them. Göring ordered re-equipment with FW-190. Of course we had plenty of them! Front-line reconnaissance realized that the ME-109 was best suited for their purpose. They got them too. In France two new units were formed, the so-called long-distance fighter-bombers (*Jabo-Rei*). An able flight lieutenant of the JG 2 achieved surprising successes against ships on the south coast of England with an FW-190 as a fighter-bomber. Now, with additional fuel tanks and bombs slung underneath, the *Jabo-Rei* was going to be used against strategical targets further afield, especially in the Bay of Biscay. All very well, had we not urgently needed every available fighter plane for the defense of the homeland.

Yet another wrong conclusion was at the back of this cry for fighter aircraft for these thousand and one uses. Air superiority was lost on all fronts. As a result losses in all units increased, and the special planes like reconnaissance, bombers, and battle fighters were of course too slow to stand up against enemy fighters. Instead of re-establishing air superiority with more fighters, we weakened it by taking away planes from the fighter arm and using them for other purposes. The importance of this interference is shown by the fact that in the year 1944 alone 13,000 ME-109s and 4500 FW-190s were diverted to reconnaissance and battle squadrons.

A special chapter was the fight against the Mosquito. England had developed an all-purpose aircraft with an extraordinary performance whose action over Germany caused a lot of trouble. The twin-engined De Havilland had a speed that none of our fighter planes could approach. By day it flew on reconnaissance flights at high altitude, but it also performed bombing missions. It had a very precise bombsight called "Oboe." It was also successful, at little cost, in nuisance raids at night. Until we were able to send up the ME-262 jet fighter planes, we were practically powerless against the Mosquitoes. Like their namesake they became a plague to our Command and the population. Our fighters could only catch up with them when we dived on them from a much greater height during an attack, temporarily achieving higher speed. But as the Mosquitoes already flew at a great height, this maneuver could only be performed when the approach of the aircraft was discovered early enough and if it could be passed on from one radar station to another. Here were the difficulties: First, our radar network was by no means without gaps, and second, the Mosquito was of wooden construction, so this little "bird" only gave a very faint signal in our sets. These were facts which one simply had to accept for the time being. Anyhow, with this aircraft alone the German war industry could not be hit decisively. There was no danger that we might lose the war on account of the Mosquito. It was for quite different reasons that Göring went mad about our inability to stop these raids. In daytime they flew without losses and went wherever their mission took them; at night they chased the population out of their beds. The latter who were justifiably annoyed at this started to grumble, "The Fat One can't even cope with a few silly Mosquitoes."

Ignoring me, Göring recalled two experienced group leaders from the east and ordered them to clear up this daily nuisance in one way or another. Two strengthened flights were formed specially for this purpose, bombastically christened 25th and 50th Fighter Wings. The aircraft were "souped up" by all sorts of tricks. Special methods of attack were worked out. Without avail! As far as I know neither of these units ever shot down a Mosquito! They were dissolved in autumn, 1943, and I was able to use the aircraft in the general defense of the Reich.

That summer, after Milch's fighter program had not fulfilled my hopes, I tried to scrape together forces from all sides for the defense of the Reich. We did not succeed in regaining air superiority in Italy despite desperate but belated efforts. Only when our Command finally realized this did I succeed in my attempts to get some exhausted groups transferred from the south to the defense of the Reich. The east, too, had to part with two squadrons. Further we were able to form two destroyer wings, ZG 26 and 76, from different units which had been in action in the east, the south, and the west. At considerable cost they helped to close the gap, as long as the Americans did not send a technically superior fighter escort. These destroyers were particularly valuable because of their wider range and their stronger armament.

Finally we drew on the night fighters and used them in daylight action against the American raiders. The readjustment of the crews did not proceed without difficulties. They had been used to flying as lone wolves and to attacking singly. Now they had to be restrained for formation flying and close mass attack. With day and night duty the limits of endurance of men and material were greatly exceeded, but the situation demanded extraordinary measures. When the new American fighter escorts appeared, the losses of the night fighters became too great in daytime: they had to be taken out of action or were used for screening on the Swedish and Swiss frontiers. It had come to light that more and more enemy stragglers or single damaged bombers took refuge in these neutral countries. At that time we were making all kinds of efforts in order to overcome the critical phase in the defense of the Reich, which had arisen through the appearance in daylight of the multiengined bomber. Our Command did nothing of importance in this direction. In certain ways the forces had to help themselves. The men and the fighter force were experimenting and constructing all the time. The front, only theoretically prepared, was facing an entirely new situation, with which it tried to cope by using its own initiative. This had its advantages and disadvantages. On the one hand it resulted in valuable ideas and suggestions for the improvement of tactics and equipment, armament and technics; on the other hand it was an impossible situation that flights, squadrons, and wings should experiment with the technique of the fighter arm. In order to get these activities under control I formed the 25th Experimental Commando, under my direction, to examine the suggestions that came from the front-line units, from the industry, or from the population.

If they looked promising, they were tried out in action. Of the multitude of novel methods of warfare I would like to mention only a few: rockets, increase in aircraft armament, aerial bombs on bomber formations, the trailing rope with or without bomb attached, rocket batteries and cluster bombs with automatic photocell ignition. Hundreds of suggestions were examined and scores of them were tried out, mostly in hot actions. The aim of all our trials was to find ways and means of breaking up the closed bomber formations. We had good results with the 21-cm. rockets, which could be fired from a distance of about 800 yards, i.e., at the limit of the effective range of defensive fire the bombers could put up. Undoubtedly we were on the way to absolutely new weapons for fighters against bomber formations. Then the American escort fighters created new problems.

One of our achievements at this period was the "Rosarius Traveling Circus." This was a flight comprised of all airworthy captured planes we could find. They traveled through the West from unit to unit in order to familiarize our pilots with enemy technique. The leaders could fly these enemy types themselves. In this way we found out that we had usually overrated their performance. The circus proved a great success.

All these midsummer weeks of 1943 were a bit easier, although we dared not hope that we had overcome the danger of the bombing war against the Reich. However the roof over the house had at least been patched up a bit. The night fighters had achieved remarkable results. The British proportion of losses had reached such a height that any further increase would become unbearable, as we knew only too well from our own experiences. As regards the American bombers we had so to speak weathered the first shock. The formations of the Eighth AAF in their raids on the territory of the Reich encountered a fighter defense which was already effective although numerically still weak.

Right into July the British bombers raided Germany almost nightly and the American daylight raids became heavier and more frequent. Then, in the middle of July, there occurred a sudden lull, a strange and absolutely unusual phenomenon: the Reich had been free of enemy raids for ten days and ten nights.

This boded no good.

19

The Fateful Hour for the Luftwaffe

In the technical field we got into a most difficult and em-
barrassing situation in 1943. Our fighter production had
fallen behind that of the Anglo-Americans in quantity as
well as in quality of performance. We needed more powerful
engines, longer range, more effective armaments, higher speed,
better rate of climb, an adjustment of the ceiling of our
planes to that of the enemy. There was no shortage of proj-
ects and plans to put all this into the building program. But
their execution, that is to say the readjustment of mass production to the new types, would have produced a momentary
stoppage, which was unbearable in the tense situation of the
war. Such a stoppage could only have been accepted had the
planned improvements promised a really convincing success.
To achieve only a limited technical advance on a par with the
Anglo-American standard would win nothing because of the
unavoidable temporary loss of production. We needed a great
jump forward to be able to encounter numerical superiority
with superior performance.

As long as this jump was not possible, our technicians simply used one makeshift after another. The ME-109, which
most of the squadrons were still flying, was nicknamed by
our pilots in the west "The bulge," and not without reason.
Numerous improvements to engine, armament, and equipment that each new series received were unsuited to the basic
design of the aircraft. They appeared as "bulges," maiming
the outer appearance that had once been sleek and streamlined, and affecting its characteristics and performance.

The new types ME-209 and ME-309, promised as part of
the armament program for 1943 and which I had flown on
trials, were not put into mass production on account of production losses, technical risks, and delivery delays. The T.A.-
152, which was supposed to be an engine of unusual power,
was postponed from one armament program to the next until

nearly the end of hostilities. For increased engine performance we had to be satisfied with makeshift arrangements.

In the spring of 1943 I nursed the greatest hope of a sensational technical jump ahead when I flew the first Messerschmitt jet fighter. This was the aircraft which could have given us, at one blow, the necessary technical superiority to offset the numerical strength of the Allies. But things turned out quite differently. This is a particularly sad chapter in the history of the German fighter force which I shall deal with later on. With this aircraft we could have made that big jump in our development so urgently needed in the air to make good our inferiority. All the capacity that now went into the mass production of the improved but not greatly superior types like the ME-209 and 309 would have been lost to get a jet fighter, which would soon have gone into mass production. This is why we went on producing mainly ME-109s and FW-190s. Of course on this score I can be considered jointly responsible.

That the enemy had also recognized the necessity to display his technical and tactical achievements was proved by the blow that the combined Eighth AAF and the R.A.F. delivered on Hamburg. This series of large-scale raids was a step by the enemy from gradually intensified area bombing of German cities to a planned war of extermination. To this end the enemy had not only gathered sufficient strength during the ominous pause with its strange and disquieting effect, but had also devised a series of tactical and technical innovations, which he now used together in one blow. The effect was indescribable.

On the night of July 24-25 about 800 heavy British bombers assembled over England. It was already after midnight. This mass formation approached Hamburg from the northeast, passing over Lübeck, the city with a million in population, on the Elbe, the German sea gate to the world. A narrow, restricted area, comprising the harbor and part of the inner city, was raided mainly with incendiaries and phosphorus canisters. The raid was carried out in close formation and with the greatest precision, unmolested by German defense. What had happened?

Not one radar instrument of our defense had worked. The British employed for the first time the so-called Laminetta method. It was as primitive as it was effective. The bomber units and all accompanying aircraft dropped bundles of tin foil in large quantities, of a length and width attuned to our radar wave length. Drifting in the wind, they dropped slowly to the ground, forming a wall which could not be penetrated by the radar rays. Instead of being reflected by the enemy's aircraft they were now reflected by this sort of fog bank, and the radar screen was simply blocked by their quantity. The air situation was veiled as in a fog. The system of fighter direction based on radar was out of action. Even the radar sets of our fighters were blinded. The flak could obtain no picture of the air situation. The radar target-finders were out of action. At one blow the night was again as impregnable as it had been before the radar eye was invented. Furthermore, during this dark night, dark also for the Reich's defense, the British used for the first time a new method of approach: the bomber stream. This was a compromise between the loose, stretched-out formation on a broad front, as was usual for the night approach, and the tightly packed formation, in which daylight raids were flown. The bombers flew in several waves on small fronts, each wave behind the other, as the single aircraft used to fly, with a synchronized course, altitude, speed, and time: the E.T.A. They formed no definite formation. Only occasionally two or more planes flew in visual contact. Out of many small raindrops, which used to unite over the target area into a cloudburst bombing effect, a stream had already formed during the approach that broke through our defenses in a bed five miles wide. Our already-insufficient peripheral defenses were powerless against this new method. With a breakthrough of a bomber stream in a narrow sector, naturally fewer enemy aircraft got caught in the thin, interrupted veil of defense than on an approach in open formation on a broad front.

During the first British large-scale raids it took one and a half hours to drop 1500 tons of bombs; with the new method of attack only 20 minutes were needed for the same performance. The number of aircraft required for the same bomb load had been halved through the use of improved types. Altitudes for the run-in and bomb-release were higher. To sum up: unchanged effect with less effort and risk for the attacker, reduced chances of success for the active defense, i.e., for flak and particularly for the night fighters. The effect and results of this first new type of raid were extraordinary. Numerous smaller and larger fires were started. The civil defense had difficulty in coping with these. While they were still working the Americans carried out a daylight raid on the following day, July 25. That night the British bombers returned to Hamburg. The attacking force and the corresponding effects were not on the same scale as the original blow, but the strength of the ARP (Air Raid Precautions) and the defense was growing lame. Large conflagrations raged in the center of Hamburg. From now onward the American daylight raids and the British night raids, in varying strength, alternated in uninterrupted sequence until on the nights of July 28-29 the R.A.F. rallied once more all their strength for two destructive blows.

Hamburg was an inferno. In his secret report the chief of the Hamburg police wrote: "Horror reveals itself in the howling and raging of the fire, in the hellish din of exploding bombs and in the death cries of the tormented people. Words fail before the extent of the terror which shook the population for ten days and ten nights. The marks left on the face of the town and of the people can never be erased."

For the first time in this war the Anglo-American idea of "round-the-clock bombing" was applied for the destruction of one of the large German cities. This concentration in time and bomb load on one target had a decisive result. The material effect combined with the effect on morale. Defense, shelters, and all manner of ARP organizations faced a task that was beyond them. A catastrophe had overtaken the city. The Allied Air Force Command could record a tremendous success.

After the last bombs of this series of raids had dropped on Hamburg during the night of August 2-3, we began to take stock. The amount of bombs dropped was approximately 80,000 high-explosive bombs, 80,000 incendiary bombs, and 5000 phosphorous canisters; 250,000 houses were destroyed, i.e., nearly half of the city; one million people were bombed out or fled. Shipping, industry, and supply suffered great damage. The death roll was only completed in 1951, six years after the war: it numbered 40,000; 5000 of these were children.

A wave of terror radiated from the suffering city and spread throughout Germany. Appalling details of the great fire were recounted. The glow of fires could be seen for days from a distance of 120 miles. A stream of haggard, terrified refugees flowed into the neighboring provinces. In every large town people said: "What happened to Hamburg yesterday can happen to us tomorrow." Berlin was evacuated with signs of panic. In spite of the strictest reticence in the official communiqués the terror of Hamburg spread rapidly to the remotest villages of the Reich.

Psychologically the war at that moment had perhaps reached its most critical point. Stalingrad had been worse, but

159

Hamburg was not hundreds of miles away on the Volga but on the Elbe, right in the heart of Germany.

From a military point of view sober conclusions had to be drawn from these events. The Allies had proved that extermination raids of strategical importance on the territory of the Reich were possible. The components of their success were:

1. Concentration of raiding forces on one target.

2. Combination of day and night raids.

3. Simultaneous application of new means and methods: radar interference, bomber-stream, etc.

After Hamburg in the wide circle of the political and the military command could be heard the words: "The war is lost." The run of events proved them correct. The war was lost. But not because of the catastrophe of Hamburg. That was only a result of a development which had started much earlier. It was inevitable. Those who had remonstrated and warned at the beginning of the Eastern Campaign had been told that the weakening of the Western front in the air, from where disaster had now appeared, was only temporary. This argument broke down when the operation in front of Moscow came to a standstill. The hope, which was nursed afterward, of overthrowing the Soviet colossus in the second onset was even less convincing. Nevertheless Jeschonnek, for example, did not consider the war lost as long as this hope existed. Only after this hope had been wrecked on the Volga did he see no way out and commit suicide. The reason was not despair about Stalingrad or that he blamed himself for our lack of planes, but because he believed in Hitler's genius and had subordinated his opinions and reason, and with them the fate of the Luftwaffe, to the arguments of the Führer. Hamburg only came as a surprise to those who had closed their eyes to the general development of the war in the air and had blindly followed their optimism, for some reason or purpose of their own. Now they collapsed. They regarded everything as lost. There had been enough reason for this in 1941 and 1942! Germany, in the summer of 1943, still had potentialities, with the occupied territories considerably larger than those with which she had achieved her strategic successes in the first years of the war. Her armies were still fighting hundreds of miles beyond her borders. But the offensive campaigns against Asia and Africa brought us no decisions as far as the great powers, Russia, America, and England, were concerned. The time factor working for the Allies had reached a point which forced us more and more onto the defensive. In the defense of the European Fortress the air was the most important, the most urgent, but also the weakest front. Hamburg illustrated this clearly to everyone.

None of the components of the Allied successes represented something that we were powerless to overcome. The German high-frequency branch was certainly in a position to counter the new methods of radar interference. They got busy and soon solved the problem satisfactorily; in general their initiative in research, development, production, and action can only be praised. Nor was the bomber stream a problem, provided we increased our defense methods. Highly effective weapons and successful methods of fighting the British night raids had been developed; if only they could have kept pace with the enemy's strength and methods of attack, they would have caused such high losses that the enemy would not have been able to endure them. Nor were we helpless against the American daylight raids, although we had to make up a lot of leeway, thanks to previous neglect and stupidity. The cooperation of Anglo-American day and night raids could only have catastrophic results if our inferiority in active defense continued. An immense increase of our aircraft production, as was achieved in 1944 under very much more adverse conditions, would to my mind, have re-established the security of the Reich against Allied large-scale air raids.

Radical reorganization of the defense, absolute priority for the air industry, and increase of fighter production were the demands of the hour. They were so to speak "in the air," when Göring called his closest associates to a conference at the Wolf's Redoubt in East Prussia. The reason was the catastrophe of Hamburg and its purpose: to prevent a second Hamburg. The ruins of the city were still smoldering. The last bombs of this series of attacks had not yet fallen. Göring did not show his face in Hamburg. He merely sent a telegram of condolence to the Gauleiter and the sorely tried population. Its text was never published. It would have created a riot. Bodenschatz went to Hamburg instead. He had just returned full of shattering impressions and had reported to Hitler. In Göring's office at the Führer's H.Q. he explained to us repeatedly that something drastic had to be done, such a disaster must never happen again. No objection was raised, nor were there any differences of opinion as to what was to be done now. Problems arising from the raids on Hamburg were discussed in the presence of Chief of the General Staff Korten, Jeschonnek's successor, the Chief of Aircraft Production (Milch), the Air Force Commander, Central, the chief of

Air Communication, the General of the Combat Fighters, (Peltz), the General of the Fighters, and many officers of the Luftwaffe General Staff. Göring summarized the result: the Luftwaffe, after its offensive phase, in which it had achieved outstanding success, must now change over to the defense against the west. It should be possible to stop the Allied raids against the Reich by concentrating all forces and their effects on this one aim. The most important task of the Luftwaffe now was not only to protect the lives and property of the German people who lived in the threatened cities, but also to preserve the potential of the war industry. Under the protection of the forces concentrated on air defense the Luftwaffe would soon recover the strength to attack once more. Then we would prepare for the counterblows. He was aware that he was making additional demands, but he was confident that his arm would not betray the trust he had in it.

Never before and never again did I witness such determination and agreement among the circle of those responsible for the leadership of the Luftwaffe. It was as though under the impact of the Hamburg catastrophe everyone had put aside either personal or departmental ambitions. There was no conflict between General Staff and war industry, no rivalry between bombers and fighters. Only the one common will to do everything in this critical hour for the defense of the Reich and to leave nothing undone to prevent a second national misfortune of this dimension. Göring seemed to be carried away by this general mood. He left us alone for a while and went into the Führer's bunker to get the go-ahead for the measures we had planned.

We remained behind, tense with expectation. In this hour the fate of the Luftwaffe was decided. The Supreme Commander himself realized that our air leadership against the west had taken a wrong course. Like us he appeared to be convinced and also determined to put the helm about. For two years we had been on this wrong track. After the Battle of Britain we should have switched over to defense in the west. We should have given the fighter priority over the bomber, as the British had done when they were threatened by the German raids, before they took the offensive again. Only the re-establishment of air superiority over our own territory would put us into the position, which one day would allow us to resume the offensive. But while we were obviously inferior because of the denuding of the west it was senseless and harmful to try and continue the fiction of offensive activity. Now at last the High Command had come to this conclusion. It would be a tough job to reorganize the Luftwaffe in so short a time from an apparently strategic-offensive arm into an effective defensive one. But none of us doubted that we could do it. Even the General of the Combat Fighters, to whom it must have been obvious that his bomber force would have to relinquish its priority, at least for some time, was convinced by the Hamburg facts. To regain and to insure air superiority over the Reich was our mutual decision. At this juncture of the war in the air it could only be achieved by fighter planes. The participants of the conference, fully conscious of their responsibility and seriously concerned about the air defense of the Reich, had sought a way to avoid certain disaster. They believed that they had found it. Everything now depended on the last word which Hitler would have to say. I myself was convinced that he would pass and support our findings with the whole weight of his authority.

Then the door opened and Göring followed by his chief aide-de-camp came in. He did not say a word, stared in front of him, walked past us, and went alone into his adjoining room. We looked at each other in amazement. What had happened? The aide-de-camp gave some long-winded explanation from which we understood that Hitler during the course of a heated discussion had rejected all our suggestions.

After a while Peltz and I were called in to Göring. We were met with a shattering picture; Göring had completely broken down. His head buried in his arm on the table he moaned some indistinguishable words. We stood there for some time in embarrassment. At last Göring pulled himself together and said we were witnessing his deepest moments of despair. The Führer had lost faith in him. All the suggestions from which he had expected a radical change in the situation of the war in the air had been rejected. The Führer had announced that the Luftwaffe had disappointed him too often. A changeover from offensive to defensive in the air against the west was out of the question. He would give the Luftwaffe a last chance to rehabilitate itself. This could be done by a resumption of air attacks against England, but this time on a bigger scale. Now as before the motto was still: Attack. Terror could only be smashed by counterterror. This was the way the Führer had dealt with his political enemies. Göring had realized his mistake. The Führer was always right. All our strength was now to be concentrated on dealing to the enemy in the west such mighty retaliation blows from the air that he would not risk a second Hamburg. As a first measure in the execution of his plan the Führer had ordered the creation of a leader of the attacks on England.

Göring rose. "Oberst Peltz," he cried, "I herewith appoint you assault leader against England!" Detailed discussions followed and extraordinary measures were taken for a speedy formation of an assault corps.

It is difficult to describe how I felt at that moment. Annoyance and revolt were mixed with a failure to understand and a wish to resign. What was left of the leaders' unanimity on the question of air defense? What could I do here now? Should I not have asked to be relieved of my post? The only reason I did not resign was because I was convinced that the Führer's decision was not irrevocable. I was mistaken. It remained irrevocable. In all my efforts to oppose a development which I regarded as disastrous, I came up against an invincible barrier: "the Führer's orders."

20

From One Crisis to Another

The "leader of the assault on England" threw himself with great energy into his task. With new methods and new aircraft (JU-188 and HE-177) he was able some time later to revive the attacks on England. According to the Führer's orders, all efforts of the Luftwaffe were to be subordinated to this aim. In spite of this the new offensive never achieved a strategical importance: it could not do so because all the necessary conditions were missing. Some English targets were again damaged, but our own losses were too big and finally became unbearable. In comparisan with the annihilation raids, which the Anglo-American bombers kept up continuously from then on, our raids must have appeared like pinpricks.

The effort of the Luftwaffe was not only wasted but indirectly proved a boomerang, because it was made at the expense of the home defense. The most urgent problem that arose after the raid on Hamburg was how to meet the British night raids without the help of the radar stations, which were put out of action by interferences. Night-fighter action, which hitherto had achieved remarkable results, now showed its weaknesses. It could not function without radar. A way out had to be found quickly. In contrast to our technically complicated and therefore highly sensitive method of night fighting, it was a very simple idea which brought a temporary solution. The "Wild Boar" was created—a method of night fighting using single-seater, single-engine planes, without electrical aid and not guided from the ground, but relying on direct sight.

During the nightly large-scale raids it had become obvious that because of the huge conflagrations almost daylight conditions reigned over the targets, and hunting British bombers was possible without fighter direction. Major Hermann, a bomber pilot, championed the idea of "bright-night" fighting over the targets and tried it himself successfully in daring actions. Of his own accord, but adapted to the emergency situation of the night fighters, Hitler ordered the immediate formation of a special fighter wing. The pilots, who were required to have had experience in blind flying, reported voluntarily for duty from various branches of the Luftwaffe. The aircraft had to be diverted from the day fighters. In a very short time three squadrons of single-engined planes were in action. Of course they created chaos in the well-organized system of the night-fighting command, the flak batteries, and confused the picture of the situation in the air, but they were an indisputable success. Hermann was vested with special powers and under his leadership the 30th Fighter Division (Wild Boar) was formed.

The conditions of illumination over the burning towns were improved by several methods. If the bombers were flying above a layer of thick cloud, the latter would look like frosted glass if lit up by magnesium flares and searchlights, and the silhouettes of the attackers could be clearly distinguished from above. If the clouds were too thick, so that the light from below could not penetrate them, parachute lights were dropped from above and the flak guns fired light shells and rockets. The civil air defense became very confused. Hitherto they saw to it that not the slightest ray of light broke the total blackout. To light a cigarette in the open had been regarded as a major offense. Now during the nightly raids one could read the paper in the street.

In autumn, 1943, Kammhuber left the command of the night fighters. He became commander of the 5th Air Fleet in Norway; Stumpf who had commanded it, was now put in charge of the newly formed Air Fleet, Reich (previously known as Air Arm Command, Central). The 12th Flying Corps was renamed 1st Fighter Corps. Beppo Schmid took over its command. He was now in charge of the 1st, 2nd, 3rd, and 7th Fighter Divisions, while the 4th and 5th Fighter Divisions were grouped together into the 2nd Fighter Corps as part of the 3rd Air Fleet (Sperrle). Thus the day and night fighters were incorporated into the defense organization of the Reich. This was to last almost to the end of the war. Since the night fighters came under my jurisdiction, I appointed inspectors of night fighters. Hermann was the first of these and later the successful night-fighter pilot Streib. Inspector of the day fighters in the east was Trautloft, and in the west and south, Lützow.

The foundation of the elaborate organization of Fighter Command suffered from the shortage of General Staff officers in the fighter force. The responsibility for this gap rested partly with me. I was, and still am, a supporter of specialization, from which alone I expected a thorough and extensive mastery of the subject of aerial warfare, which was becoming more and more complicated. Animosity against the General Staff was widespread in the Luftwaffe and was mutual. Energetic fighter officers had always tried to avoid being sent to the Academy of Aerial Warfare. They wanted to fly and to lead units. As a result of this attitude there was a majority of bomber pilots at the Academy. They were not very well disposed toward the fighter arm. Just when the leadership of the Reich's defense required so many Fighter General Staff personnel, they could not be found.

To fill the higher positions of command was also a problem. Göring did not believe that the reasons for the cumulative difficulties were often purely technical; he sought them in the person of the responsible command. He sometimes started from a preconceived and negative attitude originating from World War I or from the intermediate period. I regarded it my duty to stand up repeatedly for such personalities, but Göring did not like me any better for it.

Our opposed ideas on questions of personnel contrasted even more when he contended that to have command over a craft is only a burden. Experience had taught him that strong personalities without the ballast of expert knowledge were best suited for command. He acted according to this conviction. The changes of command became more frenzied. Things went so far that a newly appointed high commander, the moment he had managed to acquire the necessary theoretical knowledge for his new post, would be replaced.

These were by no means the only worries about personnel. The defense of the Reich against air raids caused such losses in personnel to the fighter arm that the shortage of flying officers, and thereby the shortage of suitable candidates for commanders, which already existed in 1941, took on disastrous dimensions by autumn, 1943. The Luftwaffe had about 70,000 officers and 400 generals. The number of officers who were leaders of units and instructors in the fighter arm never exceeded a total of 800 during the war.

There was never a shortage of boys in Germany who felt drawn toward the fighter arm. Propaganda in order to attract recruits, as is usual today in almost all countries with an air force, would have been unnecessary in Germany at the time. No obstacles should have been put in the way of those who were burning to become fighter pilots. As general of the Fighter Arm I received thousands of letters from lads who wanted to become fighter pilots but who never got into the air force in spite of an advanced glider training and their urgent requests.

The lack of recruits and the insufficiently trained young airmen became an increasingly urgent and ultimately a crucial problem. In the beginning training had suffered from the shortage of aircraft; later on there were no instructors and fuel became scarcer and scarcer, because the fighter arm was not strong enough to prevent Allied raids on our synthetic oil plants. It was a vicious circle from which the Luftwaffe could no longer escape.

What was achieved by the training establishments during the war in spite of overwhelming obstacles compares very favorably with the front-line achievements. I must also mention the immense casualties during training, which were only justifiable because of the extraordinary state of emergency.

In autumn, 1943, there remained no other way out but to shorten the training period once more. The urgent need for personnel created by losses, by newly formed units and increasing aircraft supply, had to be satisfied. The declining quality of the new pilots became all the more serious as the enemy forged ahead of us with regard to types of aircraft, quantity, and experience. Fledgling pilots could only be sent into action on the Eastern front, where they could gain experience step by step. In the Battle of Germany it was a question of being a veteran right from the start. A steadily increasing percentage of the young and inexperienced pilots were shot down before they reached their tenth operational flight—soon it was more than five per cent. The ratio of efficiency between the enemy and ourselves had shifted in our disfavor not only technically but also regarding personnel. We had long since lost the race of quantity.

The shortage of suitable and adequate replenishment of flying personnel points out fundamental weaknesses in the structure of the Luftwaffe. This basis for training was too narrow right from the start. An aggravation was the using up of the very substance of the Luftwaffe, as we did in the spring of 1942. Until the beginning of the war only two schools had grown from the Fighter Pilot School at Schleissheim, which I had attended during the "camouflage" period. At the end of 1944 only 15 of these schools existed and they could not satisfy the demand for the reasons I have mentioned above. The German fighter pilot was sent to the front after only 150 flying hours, the American with almost three times this figure. I must agree with General Koller, the last

Luftwaffe Chief of Staff, who states in a report that in the short building-up period of the Luftwaffe, the maximum of what was humanly possible had been achieved, but, like the army, it had no reserves of material or personnel. "Not counting 1940," Koller writes, "Hitler conducted every operation and almost every battle without reserves. One cannot improvise wars with only half-prepared forces, unless one risks everything, and this is actually what has been done."

In any case from the very beginning we did not have the strength to stand up to an extension of a war during which the Luftwaffe had to fight on fronts thousands of miles long and at the same time to defend the Reich against the attack of mighty air armadas. The strength of the Luftwaffe at the beginning of World War II was as follows:

30 squadrons of bombers (18 HE-111s, 11 DO-17s, 1 JU-86)
9 squadrons of Stukas (JU-87s)
1 squadron of battle fighters (HE-123s)
10 squadrons of destroyers (ME-109Ds)
13 squadrons of fighters (ME-109Es)
21 flights of long-distance reconnaissance planes (F) (19 DO-17Ps, 1 HE-111H, 1 DO-17F)
30 flights of local reconnaissance planes (H) (25 HE-126s, 5 HE-45-46s)

The British and American air forces were both weaker in number of units at the beginning of the war. But they were never so hopelessly overtaxed as ours were. When, at the opening of hostilities, the British and American air forces were faced with greater demands, they set aside a contingent of the potential manpower and of the war industry large enough to develop the air force on a sufficiently broad basis. Four years later they began the successful destruction of Germany with this arm.

Apart from some brief operations they always followed the principle of economy of forces, which despite losses and wear and tear, aimed at a steady increase of strength before anything else.

The inferiority of our fighters in number and performance was the theme of a discussion I had with Göring at Schloss Veltenstein in the autumn of 1943. As we talked Göring walked up and down the courtyard with me.

I was used to getting blamed by him for the failure of the fighter arm. I rarely accepted his reproaches lying down.

Whenever I thought them unjust I defended my fighter arm and its fighting spirit. I, for my part, pointed out to him shortcomings and neglects for which the fighters could not be held responsible. Thus I demanded better training and more and better aircraft. Göring was already very agitated by my contradictions. Now he broached a particularly delicate subject: the 5-cm. cannon which Hitler had ordered for the destroyers. The Führer developed the following theme: Naval battles had developed from boarding to broadsides, which today took place at distances in which the opponents never saw each other. At the beginning of the war our tanks could only open fire from a distance of 800 yards if they wanted to be sure of results, while our latest types were in a position to combat enemy tanks from a distance of 3000 yards. The Fighter Arm alone had not developed on these lines. They still had to close in to 400 yards before they could use their weapons effectively.

From this consideration arose the order for fighters and destroyers to use a large-caliber long-distance cannon against the American bomber formations. The result was as follows: an ME-410 destroyer, equipped with armored-car cannon KWK 5, weighing 2000 pounds (!), was reconstructed as an automatic weapon with a magazine holding about 15 shells, rate of fire about one shot per second. It was possible to fly with this monster sticking 3 yards out in front; firing was possible, too, although the cannon jammed hopelessly after about five shots. One could even hit something, not at 1000 or 3000 yards' distance, but at the most from 400 yards! Beyond that all chances of a hit were spoiled by having to fly the aircraft. Nothing was gained, therefore, and firing was reduced to single shots. We used to say ironically that we had only to shatter the morale of the bomber crew by a few artillery shots, then we could ram the Mustangs and Thunderbolts with our gun barrel.

Basically Hitler's idea was correct. What he had in mind was later realized by rocket salvoes but not by the 5-cm. cannon.

I explained to Göring once more the objections which had been made repeatedly by the troops, the engineering specialists, and me. But he was already too irritated to reason. He said I did not conform to his idea of a general. What he needed now was someone who could execute his orders with the troops by whatever means. He had not made me General of the Fighter Arm so that I should constantly protect the fighter arm and sabotage the orders he gave after deep and careful deliberation. Göring shouted so loud that I found it difficult to keep calm. I could not accept any more what he demanded of me. I thought it irresponsible to make such an obviously gross technical mistake at this decisive hour.

I therefore explained to Göring that I could not reconcile my conscience with the activities of a general such as he envisaged them. I asked him formally to relieve me from my command and to send me back to the front. Göring looked very surprised. After a long pause he said with accentuated curtness, "Granted!"

21

The Struggle with the Enemy—and Our Leaders

As I drove away from the castle on my way to the Nürn-
berg airfield through the little town of Veltenstein, the people
on the streets looked at me with a mixture of pity and curiosity.
They had heard the voice of the master of the castle. At the
field I received a telephone call from his chief aide-de-camp.
I was to remain in my post until further orders.

These indecisions about my further duties reflected the
atmosphere inside the German High Command, the strained
nerves and the tensions, which made the completion of any
plans and measures impossible. The High Command went
from improvisation to improvisation and often canceled what
had been decided and ordered only the day before.

A fortnight after the incident at Veltenstein I inquired
who was going to be my successor and when he would arrive
to take over. The reply was that there had been no order
yet, and I would be informed in due course.

Another fortnight passed. I was then told that the Reichsmarshal had decided that I was to stay at my post. Only
much later did Göring apologize for the incident. He asked
me to take his agitation into account.

This misfortune that had descended on Germany from the
air forced Göring once more to take a greater personal part
in the command of the defense of the Reich. Occasionally he
assumed the direct command of the fighter units during
enemy raids. However the enthusiasm of the group leaders
and at divisional headquarters was not so great when they
heard, "The Reichsmarshal is taking over." This was understandable since Göring had once sent all fighters chasing each
other as far as Pilsen. The operation went down in the
history of Germany's defense as the "Air Raid on Fort
Koepenick." An American force had attacked Düren in the
Rhineland from above a layer of clouds. The silver paper

foils dropped by the bombers had drifted with the wind to the east. While the bombs were already falling on Düren, radar sets picked up the metal slips right up to the Rhine, and OP's of the aircraft report service reported strong sounds of planes. The situation was clearly understood by the leading fighter divisions. But its voice carried no weight, because Göring was following the approach from Karin Hall and considered the situation in the air to be different. For a long time his distrust had spread to the command of the fighter divisions. He assumed that the bombers were flying on in an easterly direction toward Upper Franconia. It seemed to him that a raid on the ballbearing industry of Schweinfurt was imminent, so he ordered all fighter forces into this area. He thought that his fears were soon confirmed, because the aircraft report service was now reporting the sound of a large formation flying in the direction of Schweinfurt. Not a bomb fell there. They could not fall either, because for some time now the enemy bombers had been on their way home. Fighter Command knew this, but the Luftwaffe C.-in-C. believed he knew better than those "nincompoops." Actually what the aircraft report service had announced as enemy formations in the direction of Schweinfurt were nothing but our own fighters, flying high above the clouds, directed there by the Fat One in person. Naturally the fighter force could not locate Schweinfurt because of the clouds. They overshot it in search of the American bomber force. The aircraft report service now spoke of strong noises of planes east of Schweinfurt, on an easterly course. This made Göring expect a raid on Leuna. New orders to the fighter force: "All aircraft to proceed direction Leipzig." Here the same thing happened as at Schweinfurt. Fighter Command gave up trying to convince Göring of the real air situation as a bad job. Again our own fighter force flew over the Leipzig area, but no sign of any air raid.

"By whom, then?" we asked ourselves.

"What are the Americans up to?" Göring at Karin Hall asked himself.

A new idea: The Skoda works near Pilsen is probably the target. So the fighters were sent as far as Pilsen chasing themselves because of the sound of aircraft report service and because of Göring's judgment and evaluation of the air situation. It was a happy coincidence that the cloud cover slowly broke up and we could see the sky full of German fighter planes, but no sign of any enemy bombers. As the sun broke through over Pilsen, Göring suddenly realized that he had been backing the wrong horse. He took it with a sense of humor, knowing that he had made a fool of himself. He sent a telegram to all commanders and leaders of the units concerned in which he congratulated himself and all participants with engaging irony on the "successful defeat of the air raid on the Fortress of Koepenick."

The differentiation between friend and foe, the recognition, is one of the most difficult branches of radar technique. We never managed to solve this problem completely. It caused a lot of worries, troubles, and failures. But it is consoling that the English air defense also regarded the "identification of friend and foe" as a tricky affair.

New demands were constantly made on the radar industry, which had to struggle with great difficulties because of its late start and the heavy raids. The shortage of technical experts was increased by the fact that with each new set the factories delivered, special personnel had to be trained to operate it. Innovations did not replace the old stock, and mostly they were produced, fitted, and operated additionally. The gaps in personnel, caused by the demands of the army, could only be filled by the generous action of women. They were soon indispensable in hundreds of radar stations throughout the Reich and in the occupied territories. As a whole, German women worked and suffered unspeakably during the course of the war.

Later we managed to cope with the diverse and sometimes very cunning interferences by the enemy. The communication from the control centers and the Fighter Command stations to airborne units and single planes remained difficult. Especially at night the ether was full of silent and spoken direction beams, long, short, and ultrashort waves with their whistling or constantly sounding notes, atmospherics, commands, talks, music, and bells, creating for those who received them either in the air or on the ground the impression of a fair or an excited parliamentary debate. Nevertheless the enemy never succeeded in stopping all ways and means of communication at the same time.

The operation of the whole gamut of interference by the enemy made us realize the importance of listening posts and monitoring, which until then had not been fully utilized. The listening service tried to construct a picture of the situation on the other side by putting together, like a jigsaw puzzle, the countless radio messages of the enemy which were intercepted and decoded. The value of their reports was indisputable. The monitor system became only of practical importance with immediate effect when its observations were passed on directly to the leading centers of the Reich's defense for disposition and utilization for the operation in question. The inquiry into enemy preparations for a raid—the weather forecast for the approach route of the Allied formations and the target area; observation of assembling enemy forces; the enemy's radio navigation aids from transmitters in the air or on the ground; listening in to enemy radio as well as aircraft; radar sets—such information, if quickly evaluated and passed on, yielded a host of valuable data for Command. Important decisions were now often based on the reports of the monitor service alone.

In those days we found ourselves, in the realm of techniques and tactics, engaged in a constant race with the enemy in which, in spite of occasional successes, we were bound to be the loser because our potential was already overtaxed and on the wane. In their night raids the British presented us constantly with new methods in navigation and attack. By creating special pathfinder units the approach and the finding of the target were made easier for the following bombers and increased the efficiency of the raids. Course and turning points were marked by novel means of illumination. In each wave there were markers which staked out the respective targets with the famous "Christmas Trees." These were marker flares, checked in their descent, whose tinsel fire made them look like Christmas trees hanging upside down. The markers received their orders from the leader of the raid—whom we called the master of ceremonies—who directed the raid from a higher altitude and supervised its execution.

Our night fighters tried to adjust themselves to the new British methods, and profited by them to a certain extent, because the British markers showed the way not only to their bombers but also to our pursuing night fighters. In a certain way the disadvantages of the radio and radar interference were annulled by the effect of the markers. Another means of finding the bomber stream were the burning enemy bombers which had been shot down and which could be seen from a great distance. As a result, our night fighters found the whereabouts, course, and altitude of the bombers, which were visible in the glow of the fires that attracted our fighters from a distance of 60 miles as a candle attracts a moth. The British bombers were pursued until they were over the target and also on their return journey. The solid system of the *Himmelbett* and the limited defense areas were out of date. Now the fighters "traveled."

The radar eye in the aircraft became naturally of greater importance in this type of action. New types and developments were devised according to experience and front-line demands. It achieved its greatest success during a British large-scale raid on Nürnberg on the night of March 30-31, 1943. The coincidence of favorable factors, of which the most important was the rising of the moon during the raid, made it possible to shoot down 132 bombers (according to German reports).

The enemy did not remain inactive once the activities of our night fighters livened up again and caused them increasing losses. They sent out more long-distance night fighters against our night-fighter bases and against the assembly points. The nightly aerial warfare increased continuously in intensity, and its manifestations became more complicated and varied. The activity of interference extended further. The British had no end of ideas in this field. An entire formation, the 100th Bomber Squadron, specialized entirely in such activities as feints, diversions, radio blackouts, and interference. They provided many a surprise for us about which I shall still have something to say.

Following Hamburg the British night raids were mainly directed against targets in south Germany. Nürnberg was particularly heavily hit in several successive blows. Münich, Stuttgart, Frankfurt, Mannheim, and other towns in south Germany had their baptism of fire. In addition to these, Darmstadt, Kassel, Strassburg, Cologne, Aachen, Hagen, Münster, Hanover, and Bremen were repeatedly attacked and the towns on the Ruhr were raided until the end of 1943. A heavy raid was launched against Leipzig on December 3. On the night of November 18-19 the R.A.F. opened the Battle of Berlin, which lasted until March 24, 1944.

According to British statements, during the year 1943, 30 raids were made, each with a bomb load of 500-1000 tons, 25 raids with 1000-2000 tons, and 8 raids with more than 2000 tons. The R.A.F. dropped a total of 136,000 tons on Germany during 1943. The biggest bombs now used were incendiaries of about 2500 pounds and high-explosive bombs of about 10,000 pounds. The biggest bomb load during 1944 dropped on a single German city was 10,000 tons on Hamburg. Then followed Essen, Hanover, Cologne, each with 8000 tons; Mannheim and Ludwigshafen with 7000 tons each. All together in the period from March 1 until December 31, 1943, the R.A.F. made 96 large-scale raids on 29 different German cities. The effects and consequences of these raids were certainly overrated by the British. They calculated that because of the raids 2,400,000,000 working hours were lost, representing a 36 per cent reduction in the war industry. This was the reason—still according to English opinion—why the German fronts were weakened and why the Luftwaffe turned from the offensive to the defensive. This does not conform in the least to the facts. I have already tried to explain the main reasons for the regression of the Luftwaffe. Naturally the British raids also had their share in this, but this cannot be calculated and expressed in a percentage by either side. Reichsminister Speer expressed himself clearly in a postwar book on the damages sustained by the war industry. He wrote: "The consequences for the armament program from air raids were on the whole very small during the course of 1943."

Up to July, 1943 (Hamburg), the bag of the night fighters, directed from the ground, rose steeply. Then came a sudden drop. The Wild Boar tactics could bridge a gap and ease the situation, but it was no solution to the crisis. The enlargement of this force to three wings, ordered by Göring in September, remained an illusion as long as no pilots were available with the necessary standard of training for night fighting in single-engine planes. Moreover the required number of aircraft was not there. One of my worst ideas was the double use of the fighter aircraft for day and night operations. The moment greater demands arise the execution becomes unfeasible. Instead of "as-well-as" the result is usually "neither-nor."

The total number of twin-engined night fighters available in the entire Reich and its western forefront was never more than 350 aircraft during the year 1943. At best, an average of 50 per cent of these could be sent into action according to the tactical and the weather situation or because of insufficient technical preparations. If one considers further that only a smaller proportion of these made actual contact with the enemy, it is understandable that in the long run this was not the means of combating the large-scale night raids.

Faced with the steadily increasing devastation of the German cities, the High Command tried to compensate for the absence of the night fighters by forcing them into action, regardless of losses even in the worst weather conditions. Since early 1943 the R.A.F. had used the so-called "H2S" method (blind bombing technique), which made it possible to bomb area targets in large-scale raids without seeing the ground. Our night fighters, thanks to excellent instruments for blind flying and safety, were well able to meet weather difficulties, but with the enforced extension of the single-engine, night-fighter activities, the standard of the pilots sank so low that losses through bad weather were out of all proportion to the successes. The faith of these units was shattered because again and again they were sent into forced actions and chased hundreds of miles in all directions, zigzagging across Germany toward the raided objectives. A young arm, well proven, after its initial successes as an auxiliary to the night fighters directed from the ground, soon collapsed as a result of the mistakes of the High Command. Early in 1944 I received permission to capture the Wild Boar. The 30th Fighter Division was dissolved. From its units the 300th and 301st "Bad Weather" Fighter Wings were formed. The aircraft received additional special instruments. These all-weather fighters were used for day as well as night and bad-weather operations.

In the course of the year 1943 the accent of the Reich's defense shifted more and more toward actions against the daylight raiders. Even though numerically the British raids against Germany were still stronger than the American and were undoubtedly a great trial for the civilian population, the American precision raids were of greater consequence to the war industry. They received priority attention over the British raids on our towns.

Obviously, by raiding the German aircraft industry the Eighth AAF aimed at weakening the fighter defense, which had caused it a lot of trouble during the first unescorted heavy bomber raids deeper into Germany. During the summer of 1943 the Eighth AAF made 43 such raids on 14 different factories, dropping a total of 5092 tons of bombs. Although it would have been more important to bomb our motor industry, the consequences were nevertheless soon felt. The output program for ME-109s laid down by Milch, for example, fell from 725 aircraft in July to 536 in September, and to 357 in December. This again smashed all our hopes for an early recovery in strength of our fighter arm as part of the Reich's defense. The Americans were well aware of the result of their raids. They repeated their attack with a new series of raids at the end of February, 1944. This gave rise to a radical and major regrouping of the armament organization. The so-called "Fighter Staff" was created under Speer, the Minister of Armaments. He removed the production of fighter aircraft from the jurisdiction of the Air Ministry and provided additional personnel and a greater material capacity. He raised production to a height never dreamed of before.

But the effects were not noticeable before 1944. In the summer of 1943 there was no reason for such optimism. The raids on the aircraft factories were supplemented by attacks on the German ballbearing industry. The first air raid on Schweinfurt was a shock to the German High Command. If the German ballbearing industry, their Achilles heel, were to be destroyed or paralyzed, then the armament production of the whole Reich would suffer heavily. Speer, in the report I have already quoted, points out that with a continuation of the raids the German armament industry would be essentially weakened within two months and in four months it would come to a complete standstill. But luckily the first raid on Schweinfurt and Messerschmitt-Regensburg proved disastrous for the enemy: 315 reached the target area, 60 Flying Fortresses were shot down, and over 100 were damaged. For the first time the losses were 16 per cent of the airborne force and 19 per cent of the actual raiding force. So far the most important air battle of the war ended with a success for the German air defense. About 300 fighter aircraft took part. They assembled in the sector of Frankfurt, outside the range of the fighter escort, and were directed against the bulk of the bombers, in close formation. The success cost us 25 and not 228 fighters as the American communiqué claimed. The units which attacked Regensburg, according to plan, flew on in a southerly direction over the Alps, crossed Italy and the Mediterranean, and landed on the Algerian bases of the Ninth AAF. On August 24, this raiding force, which had started off with 147 Boeing bombers, returned to England with only 85. These first high losses shown by films, descriptions, and many reports, which were published later, caused deep depression among the American crews and a sort of crisis in the Command. Raids of this nature were not repeated before the fighter escort brought the solution.

Until September, 1943, the range of the American escort fighters covered only an area that ended roughly on the Reich's border between Emden and Cologne. The bulk of the escort fighters turned here and flew back to their bases, while a new wave of fighters met the bombers at this spot on their return.

It was our aim to break up the bomber formation and to destroy it. Thus we tried if possible to attack the same formation over and over again in order to weaken its defensive power, and also because high losses in one unit are felt more than if they are distributed over several or all the participating units.

As long as the Americans in the second half of the year of 1943 flew without or with insufficient fighter protection, and

179

usually on a course in a wide arc over the North Sea or the Baltic, both the fighters and the destroyers obtained good results. The 26th Destroyer Wing, which had so far two squadrons in Italy and one on the Eastern front, was now assembled in central Germany. Another wing was formed—the ZG 76, drawn from schools, night fighters, and reconnaissance planes and supplemented by the 1st Squadron of the ZG 1, which had been active from Brest to the Bay of Biscay. ZG 76 was sent first to south Germany and later to the Czechoslovakian sector.

The destroyer units were now fitted with ME-110s, 210s, and ME-410s. The ME-410 was 50 mph faster but did not bank so well and was susceptible to damage when attacked. When the craft caught fire, the crew had difficulties in bailing out. These two destroyer types were now mainly used outside the range of the enemy's fighter escorts, against the closed bomber formations. They had been fitted with larger and additional arms: 21-cm. rockets and 3-cm., 3.7-cm., and—unfortunately also—5-cm. cannons. With these weapons they were supposed to be in a position to break up the bomber formation, and the single bombers could then be attacked by 20-mm. weapons.

The last raid of the Eighth AAF of a deeper penetration into the Reich without fighter escort was again made on Schweinfurt. The target was of such importance to the Americans that they risked another raid in spite of the high losses of August 17. The 266 four-engined bombers which took part were only escorted by fighters as far as the Eiffel. But on this memorable day, October 14, 1943, we managed to send up almost all the fighters and destroyers which were available for the defense of the Reich, and in addition a part of the fighters of the 3rd Air Fleet, France. All together 300 day fighters, 40 destroyers, and some night fighters took part in this air battle which for us was the most successful one of the year 1943. We were able to break up several bomber formations and to destroy them almost completely. The approach and return routes were marked by the wreckage of shot-down aircraft. According to American reports only 25 aircraft of the entire force returned undamaged, 140 were damaged, and 61 were shot down. On the German side about 35 fighters and destroyers were lost.

The mortal danger which these precision daylight raids constituted for the ballbearing industry could now be regarded as averted for the time being. For the time being! Because now occurred what had been feared long ago and

180

what had been foretold and promised to the High Command for some time: the American P-47 Thunderbolt escort fighters increased their operational radius. From bases in south England they could now reach the line Hamburg-Hanover, Kassel-Frankfurt.

22

In Between Lay Germany

The aims and execution of the Allied bombing offensive were fixed after lengthy and in part very stormy discussions at the conference in Casablanca in January, 1943. The Allied Chiefs of Staff finally signed a document, stating the aim of the united Western air forces in the following words: "Progressive disruption and destruction of the military, industrial, and economic structure of Germany, and undermining the morale of the population to a point where the ability for armed resistance is decisively weakened."

For this purpose industrial objectives inside Germany were to be raided in the following order of priority:

1. Aircraft factories
2. The ballbearing industry
3. Synthetic fuel plants
4. Production of emery stones and other instruments for sharpening
5. Nonferrous industries
6. Buna works (synthetic rubber)
7. U-boat wharfs and accessory industries
8. Motor-car industry
9. Transport
10. Other war industries

The plan of the Combined Bombing Offensive passed by the Allied Supreme Command took on this aspect in May, 1943. It had been conceived by American and English experts of the military and political command, of the information service, and of private enterprise. It was often changed before it was put into action and during its execution. For example, U-boat construction and bases originally headed the list. During the first four months of 1943, 63 per cent of all American, and 30 per cent of all English bombs dropped on Europe were intended for the U-boats. Besides Emden, Wilhelmshaven,

Kiel, Hamburg, Flensburg, Lübeck, and Bremerhaven, the German U-boat bases on the Atlantic coast were repeatedly raided, in particular Brest, Lorient, Saint-Nazaire, La Palisse, and Bordeaux. Great destruction was caused in many of these places. Only the U-boat bases safe below thick concrete remained intact and in operation. In June, 1943, these raids were stopped because the results were unsatisfactory. U-boats could only be fought in open action. In this battle the English and American planes soon had great successes which were finally fatal for the German U-boat arm.

However the fight against the U-boat industry which, according to English wishes, had headed the list made at Casablanca soon descended to seventh place. First place was now given to the fight against the German aircraft industry, this time at the express wish of the Americans. From the fact that during the first 14 operations his bombers had sustained losses only from enemy fighters and none from flak, General Eaker, commanding the Eighth AAF, came to the conclusion that once he could wipe out the defense by the fighter air arm, it would be safe to penetrate into the heart of Germany. He knew quite well that the German fighter arm was going through a crisis during the winter of 1942-43. He was of the opinion that one ought to act quickly before the fighters had a chance to recuperate. In this way he managed to get priority for the fight against the German aircraft industry inside the Reich.

The American bombers made their first operational flights with an escort of Spitfires. As long as they did not have their own long-range fighters they reduced their unescorted raids on Germany to single daring operations, often at great loss, and in the meantime increased in quantity and quality the construction of their fighter-escort arm. An intermediate solution was the YB-40, a Flying Fortress that carried no bombs but whose sole task was to beat off the enemy fighters. A few were specially modified for this task. Each two or three bomb-carrying B-17s in the American formation were escorted by a YB-40. The successes were insignificant. We tried a parallel development in air defense. Four-engined HE-117s were fitted with cannons and rockets that fired vertically upward. We hoped that thus with these flying guns we could break up the bomber formations. These plans were also ruined by the American fighter escort.

As early as January, 1943, the first Thunderbolt escort fighter P-47 with the Eighth AAF arrived in England. By the beginning of April two squadrons were complete. A fortnight later the Thunderbolts made their first contact with the FW-

190, which was their superior in many aspects. But there was still a long way to go before it could be used in regular operations. Many improvements had still to be made. Its radius of action was not more than 150 miles to start with. Not un'il May was the Thunderbolt fitted with additional ejectable fuel tanks. It was autumn before the Thunderbolt escort came to its fullest effect with an increased active radius of over 300 miles.

Therefore the appearance of long-distance fighters over Germany should have been no surprise for us. But in desperation Göring not only refused to listen to reasonable predictions but also refused to accept undeniable facts of the Allied war in the air. Strength, altitude of approach, and extent of penetration of the enemy's fighter escort were simply denied or said to be exaggerated, all in the face of actual day-to-day experience. And when the American long-distance fighter in early autumn appeared in ever greater numbers over Germany and simply could not be explained away, Göring acted nevertheless as if they did not exist. His foremost demand continued to be the shooting down of bombers. The escorting fighters were to be ignored. Tactics of attack, equipment of aircraft, armament and training, all remained focused on the fight against the fighter escort in a limited area, in order to create better conditions for the following attack on the bombers. Finally I suggested sending all our fighters against the escorting fighters of one attacking force. Of course it would have been a very difficult decision in certain circumstances not to attack at all the carriers of the bomb loads, so disastrous for our cities. But to my mind it would have been a necessary attempt to stop the advance and the further extension of the fighter escort force. To fight the bombers before the escort fighters would mean in the long run to take the second step before the first.

But if instead of fighters, the bombers got the priority in combat, then the peripheral defense, which was still adhered to, was absolutely wrong. The continuous demand to attack the bombers as soon as possible could only be successfully fulfilled if the attacks were made in groups. This meant that each of our fighter groups, of about 20 aircraft in strength, would attack a greatly superior enemy force. In an action like this the results were naturally small, our own losses on the other hand considerable. Instead of attacking the bombers when they were as far as possible out of the range of their fighter escort, our fighters had to attack the enemy just when he was strongest.

When the time was up for our fighters they had to land on the nearest field, regardless of the unit they belonged to, reservice, and start on their second mission. Göring demanded categorically that at least two, if not three, flights be made in one action. This meant overtaxing the performance of crew, aircraft, and Command. Initially, however, good results were achieved. Many stragglers and damaged bombers could be caught on their return flight. Around autumn, 1943, the Americans tightened up their formation and flew with a stronger fighter escort. Our overtaxed fighter pilots then suffered great losses in their second and occasionally their third sortie.

And yet all their effort to protect the homeland effectively rarely brought satisfactory results. The bigger the American attacking forces grew, the more fatal became the operation on the periphery of the defense area by groups of our fighters, which were much too weak. The demand of the hour was quantity against quantity. The massing of our fighters was impossible at the periphery and could only be done in the center. That is why I proposed taking our fighter planes further back. It was only thanks to the fact that the German Command did not decide early enough to transfer the fighters from the outer areas back to the Reich that the occasional attempts of the Eighth AAF to break through into the inner Reich did not turn out to be more costly for them.

The Allied conduct of the war from the air went through a real and serious crisis. There was consternation about the fact that despite the raids on the aircraft industry the German fighters increased in numbers and in fighting strength. The British intelligence service, on which the USAF in England were dependent, had ascertained that from the summer of 1943 on, the number of German fighters in operation in the Reich and in the west had increased in spite of all their losses and the damage to production. How was this to be reconciled with the alleged results of the American raids on the German aircraft industry and the almost astronomical figure of enemy planes reported as shot down? Either one or other or even both were incorrect. The solution to this puzzle was found after the war. Today it is known in the United States that the figures of aircraft shot down were often exaggerated in those days. It is also known that the effect of the bombs was overrated and that the strength of resistance and the resiliency of the German war industry was underrated.

More important than the numerically insignificant increase of the German fighter arm was the considerable increase in fighting strength. We had found more effective ways of attack and had introduced new and more effective weapons. We were on the way to becoming master of the situation especially with the increase of fighter aircraft which was expected. Our group leaders were full of hope. They already predicted the breaking up and destruction of larger bomber formations. But once again things turned out differently.

In October General Spaatz was called to Washington in order to discuss the problems which the USAF had encountered in Europe. The result was a radical reorganization which was completed step by step during the next few months. The invasion of northwest Europe was planned for the following spring with a view to finishing the war. As a prerequisite for this huge operation the combined bombing offensive of the Allies against Germany had been planned and prepared in Casablanca early in 1943. This again assumed the achievement of air superiority over Germany. But this again was impossible without first defeating the German fighter arm. Aim and course were therefore clearly outlined. Decisive measures were needed in order to follow this course. Long-distance fighter escorts and bomber crews were recognized as obvious bottlenecks. Now every effort had to be concentrated on clearing these obstacles.

Simultaneously all the American air forces in the European theater of war were reorganized. At that time the Eighth AAF was stationed in England, the Twelfth AAF which had emerged from the Eighth, was in North Africa and the Ninth AAF was stationed in the Near East. Now the following new arrangements were made: The Ninth AAF passed on all their units to the Twelfth AAF. The skeleton of its command was transferred to England and when newly fitted out it became the Ninth (tactical) AAF. In spring, 1944, it was ready to assist the invasion. The Twelfth AAF in North Africa was also changed into a tactical air fleet in order to assist the operations on the Italian mainland. It had to transfer its long-distance bombers to the newly fitted out Fifteenth AAF, which with its base at Foggia (central Italy) was supposed to open the second air front against Germany. By raiding the aircraft industries in the southern German and Austrian regions it was to contribute to the primary goal, that of beating the German fighter arm defense. The necessary orders were signed by the Allied Joint Chiefs of Staff on October 22. The United States now had four air fleets in readiness in Europe, a strategical and a tactical, both in England and in the Mediterranean. With these they went into the final round early in 1944.

Undoubtedly the German High Command had not enough insight into the difficulties that the other side had been up against, and which are known today; in any case it was not recognized how critical the situation of the bombing offensive against the Reich had been. While the Americans reorganized themselves during the last months of 1943 and while they made their preparations for stepping up the raids for the winter, we were fully occupied with our own problems. There were plenty of them. One was the limited flying time of our fighter planes. It took about 50 minutes to assemble all available fighter aircraft and to lead them to one of the important battle areas which at that time were over Schleswig-Holstein, the Ruhr, and Frankfurt. After this the remaining time for combat was too short, although most of our fighters had been fitted with extra fuel tanks since April, 1943. Yet for the task demanded of them now they could have done with three hours' instead of the two hours' flying time possible with extra tanks.

Strangely enough the assembling of larger formations of fighters caused considerable difficulties. Since the Battle of Britain they had not flown in large formations. Wing formations only existed more or less on paper. Right up to the High Command the usual concept was in terms of squadrons. There were some wings whose squadrons were fighting in two if not three different theaters of war. The texture of squadrons that is so important for the combat in large formations had been destroyed.

But above all the withdrawal and concentration of the fighter units came too late. This took effect only when the Thunderbolt escort fighters were operating over Germany with increased range, and already there were signs of an even better American escort fighter coming into operation in the near future, the P-51 Mustang. At the start the American escort also made tactical mistakes. Instead of operating offensively against our fighter units, they limited themselves to a close direct escort. They tried to repulse our attacks in the close vicinity of the bombers. In doing this they went through the same negative experiences as we had done over England and Malta: the fighter pilot who is not at all times and at any place offensive loses the initiative of action. The American fighters learned and readjusted themselves. After January, 1944, they went over to aggressive free-for-all fights in the approach sector.

With the extension of the range of the American fighter planes the value of our destroyers, well established in the fight against unescorted bomber formations, decreased. They suffered heavy losses when they got into dogfights with enemy fighters, and from the end of 1943 this happened in nearly every raid. Lest we should lose them altogether for the defense of the Reich, they were transferred further back and received fighter escort.

At the end of 1943 the Americans had not only increased the range of their fighter escorts but had also considerably increased the operational strength of their bombers. After Operation Torch (North Africa) had absorbed most of the supply from the United States during the first months of 1943, the Eighth AAF now slowly reached its intended strength. In March it had not more than 100 bombers available for operations, in May it already had 12 squadrons with about 300 aircraft. To be able to send 300 bombers into action General Eaker demanded a strength at the bases of about twice that number. His request was fulfilled during the same year. In early November, 1943, he was able to raid Wilhelmshaven with 500 multiengined bombers. A month later, on December 13, 1943, he used 600 bombers in a raid on Kiel, dropping 1600 tons of bombs. Ludwigshafen was raided in the same strength at the end of December. These three raids by the Eighth AAF, outstanding amongst the events of the war 1943, were all flown with P-47 Thunderbolt escort. Rarer was the appearance of the P-38 Lightning, fitted with two additional tanks giving it an active radius of 500 km. At the end of 1943 the Eighth AAF had only two squadrons of these.

Naturally with the dispatch of stronger forces the losses rose proportionately. According to American data the losses of the American bomber force in Europe during the first ten months of 1943 were:

Jan.	18	*planes*	*lost*	*against*	46	*German*	*fighters*	*shot*	*down*
Feb.	20	"	"	"	73	"	"	"	"
Mar.	19	"	"	"	152	"	"	"	"
Apr.	28	"	"	"	146	"	"	"	"
May	72	"	"	"	357	"	"	"	"
June	82	"	"	"	271	"	"	"	"
July	108	"	"	"	558	"	"	"	"
Aug.	100	"	"	"	541	"	"	"	"
Sept.	99	"	"	"	312	"	"	"	"
Oct.	181	"	"	"	864	"	"	"	"

A total of 727 planes lost against 3320 German fighters shot down.

With regard to the number of fighters shot down, the Americans fared as our Luftwaffe High Command did during the Battle of Britain. Had the claims of planes shot down been only approximately correct the multiengined bomber should have met hardly any German fighters on their raids over the Reich. But in October, when the Americans claimed 864 kills, they suffered their most severe defeat since the war began at Schweinfurt. They did not hesitate, by the way, to admit their mistakes after the war, as is shown by an official report of the raid on Lille in October, 1942. Ostensibly 102 German fighters were shot down by the raiding Flying Fortresses. But the German archives, which became accessible after the war, showed that only two fighters were lost that day!

The relationship between our and enemy losses as shown by the Americans in the preceding table therefore gives a wrong picture of the situation. The American bomber losses had risen steeply in the autumn of 1943, while the losses of German fighter planes were still within bearable limits. The defense of the Reich had overcome the initial difficulties created by the Allied daylight bombing offensive and it was on the way to recovery. This development was interrupted not only by the increase in the enemy's fighting strength and range but also by another circumstance: in August, 1943, the Allies opened the second front in the air.

It started with the so-called "shuttle-bombing," with England and Africa being the two extreme ends. In between lay Germany, upon whom the bomb loads from both sides were released. A formation of 126 American bombers, which had attacked the Messerschmitt works at Regensburg on August 17, 1943, flew on in a southerly direction over the Alps and the Mediterranean and landed at an Algerian base. A week later this formation, by now reduced to 85 B-17s, returned to England, raiding the German U-boat bases at Bordeaux on their way. Already on August 1, B-24 Liberators from North Africa had raided the Romanian oil center of Ploesti in a low-level attack. The operation proved very costly to the attackers. Only 92 bombers returned to Benghazi, 19 landed on other Allied airfields, some of them heavily damaged, 7 sought shelter in neutral Turkey, 3 crashed into the sea, and 54 were shot down over land. In all, 532 airmen were lost. The success of the defense in this instance went mainly to the flak. The few fighters which were sent up gave chase to the returning bombers right out to sea. On August 13 the Ninth AAF stationed in North Africa sent its bomber force for the first time against Germany. Sixty-one Liberators raided the Messerschmitt works at Wiener-Neustadt. The Reich's defense had practically no fighters to encounter this raid. Hurriedly the conditions for organizing and commanding a fighter group in the southeast had to be created. The radar network, which was more or less intact in the west and the north showed considerable gaps in the south and the southeast. The Eastern Marches Group received two fighter and one destroyer squadron, which also had to be available against enemy aircraft approaching from the south. The raids of the Ninth AAF and later those of the newly assembled Fifteenth AAF, which started to operate in November, 1943, from Foggia in central Italy, added undoubtedly to the splitting of the Reich's defenses just as they were making a recovery. For the American Command they were of similar value to the extension of the range of their fighter escorts.

The weather has to be mentioned again as a last factor to our disadvantage that destroyed the balance between attacker and defender, which had somehow been re-established by a tremendous effort during the summer of 1943. While the attacking units flew in at an altitude of 21,000 to 24,000 feet, above the bad weather, in radiant sunshine, high above rain, snow, or the icing-up danger zone, completing their effective raids with excellent navigational aids and bombsights, and while they took off, assembled, and landed again in tolerable weather conditions in England or Italy, our defending units, by force of circumstances, often had to be sent up in the very worst of weather. Neither crews nor aircraft were prepared for such demands. The fighter aircraft had no instruments for blind flying, no de-icing of the cockpit, no safety arrangements for navigation or automatic pilots. Only a few pilots had sufficient training in blind flying. Most of them had no knowledge of instrument flying or bad-weather methods of landing. If, despite all the difficulties, they succeeded in breaking through the clouds, then the leader of the unit was faced with the insoluble task of assembling his unit above the clouds. Thus the planned operational strength never came into being. The result was that the attack had to be made by numerous small units. The defensive fire of the bombers and the escorting fighters took great toll of our force. Numerous German pilots were sitting in their completely iced-up cockpits, half blinded, to become an easy prey for the Thunderbolts. The appalling losses of this period were plainly due to the weather. The fact that, despite all objections, such forced actions of practically no value were demanded over and over again by the High Command shattered once more the confidence of the squadron in the leadership.

23

Chastisement

The winter of 1943-44 brought the heaviest burden of the
war so far for the Germans. The army was falling back on
all fronts. The Italian ally had seceded, the Axis was cracked.
No chance remained of winning the war against the manpower of the east and the material power of the west. Even
the hope for a just ending of the war no longer existed since
the formula of "unconditional surrender" had been decided
upon and announced at Casablanca. The "total war" had taken
on a form for which there were no parallels in modern history;
for each individual it was a fight for survival.

That this was the case was made quite clear by the Allied
air raids on the Reich's territory which increased that winter
to an extent that had never before been imagined. In 1942
during a secret session of the House of Commons, Churchill
had announced a bombing of Germany of unprecedented magnitude: "We must not allow false friends to deter us from these
difficult and terrible measures of war."

During the year of 1943 the R.A.F. had dropped a total of
136,000 tons of bombs on Germany, yet in the first two months
of 1944 it was already 36,000 tons. In March, 1944, 6000
British bombers raided Germany, dropping 20,000 tons of
bombs. Some German cities had reached such a degree of
destruction that further raids would have been uneconomical.
Only 20,000 of a population of 800,000 still remained in the
ruins of Cologne. Kassel, with five per cent, had the greatest
loss of civilians: 12,000 people lost their lives here during the
terrible raid in October. But the capital had to face the worst
during these months. In the night of November 18-19, 1943,
the R.A.F. opened its Battle of Berlin with a raid by 444
bombers. The number of bombers and the quantity and the
caliber of bombs dropped grew steadily. In January, 1944, six
heavy raids were made on Berlin during which a total of 9300
tons of bombs were released. In the night of February 15-16,
1000 aircraft dropped 2500 tons of high explosives and in-

cendiaries. On March 24, 1944, the R.A.F. reported that up to this date they had dropped 44,845 tons of bombs on Berlin. The Americans now took part in the extermination raids on Berlin. On March 3 American P-38 fighter aircraft made a reconnaissance flight over Berlin. The following day they sent over 30 Flying Fortresses with fighter escort. On March 6, 1944, Berlin had its first large-scale daylight raid by 672 Flying Fortresses with fighter escort. They dropped 1600 tons of bombs. The Reich's defenses could only muster about 200 fighters and destroyers against this force. Our losses were almost twice as high as those of the Americans.

In the previous months of January and February, 1944, the Eighth AAF in many large-scale raids had dropped 48,335 tons of bombs on German cities. This is a considerable increase in the monthly average compared with the approximate 150,000 tons of the year 1943. In the second half of 1944 nearly half a million tons of bombs were dropped by American heavy bombers on targets in Germany. The total at the end of the war was 2.7 million tons according to the American commission under General Anderson, studying the effects of the bombing war. In order to achieve this figure they flew 1,440,000 bomber missions and 2,680,000 fighter sorties. In a single year of the war (1944) the Americans spent billions of dollars on the air force. In the air battle of Germany they lost 18,000 aircraft and 79,265 flying airmen.

Discussing the British night raids and their terrible effects, Göring said to me, "The German people are bearing these raids like a chastisement by God." This was true. Yet it seemed as though the conflagrations in the cities had welded the people together, as though the misused phrase, "community spirit," had become reality for them in a common will to encounter the threatening extermination with all their strength. Only in this way can one explain the unbelievable achievements of this period regarding prevention of damage, reconstruction, and in the war industry, the year 1944 became the year with the highest output for aircraft production: 38,000 aircraft of all types were built, against 8295 in the first year of the war 1939!

The combined Anglo-American air offensive grew constantly in extent and intensity. Devastating nightly area bombing was complemented by daylight precision raids against our bottleneck industries.

The British and American governments were determined to see the plan through which they had devised together. They had prepared and started it with a terrific expenditure of energy and power. Now it was running. Not even the German retaliation raids could change this. During January and February not more than 275 tons of bombs could be dropped on London. The total for England in the same period was 1000 tons. That was exactly a twenty-seventh part of what the British bombers had dropped on Germany.

The only thing we could do to parry the destruction from the air was to concentrate all our strength on the defense of the Reich. Would what we had hoped for after the catastrophe of Hamburg at last materialize? Would Hitler and Göring be able to make up their minds at the very last moment to switch completely over to air defense? We hoped they would. Speer had passed on the charge of the Fighter Staff to Armament Supervisor Saur, and a new production program was designed. The accent was definitely on the construction of fighters. All other branches of the war industry had to stand aside in their favor. It was a realistic program which took the situation into account. Speer had clearly realized that the last moment had arrived for strengthening the air defense, and with it first and foremost the fighter arm, by centralizing and mobilizing all forces in order to create a prerequisite for the continued existence of the other branches of the war industry.

This emergency air force construction program was read to Göring in April, 1944, on the Obersalzberg. Bomber production had been curtailed, and the production of many other types was to be stopped. Night and day fighter aircraft were to be made as one unified type, which also had to meet the requirements of the other branches of the Luftwaffe. The quantities which were planned were absolutely adequate to the Anglo-American aircraft production. I was present at this memorable conference. I had the impression that Göring listened to Saur's disquisition with a premeditated attitude, on Hitler's orders. He did not seem to give it his full attention and replied immediately with many and definite objections. The radical curtailment of the bomber program, especially that of the HE-177 and the JU-88 and their further development, was regarded by him as impossible and he rejected it abruptly. On the contrary he demanded an increase and a guarantee of a minimum production of 400 HE-177 and 500 Junkers bombers per month. "The heavy bomber remains the kernel of the armament in the air," was his final shattering decision. This was, of course, possible only if the originally planned fighter production were heavily cut.

I spoke energetically against any watering down of the new fighter program. I was concerned not with higher or lower production figures but with the creating of strength in principle. I failed to understand what the High Command wanted if they were not prepared now to give highest priority to the fighter arm and to mobilize all lines of personnel and material. Speer's fighter program was changed according to Göring's directives and came into force eight days later in its diluted form. Even at this moment of the war in the air the German High Command regarded bombers as more important than fighters. The production of bombers went on at an increased rate. They could not prevent the raids on our synthetic petrol plants which started a little later, as a stronger fighter force could have done. In the end there was not enough petrol for the test flights of the bombers when they came from the assembly belt; they had to be wrecked on the benches where they had been built. The Anglo-American air force crossed the bomber off the German armament plan.

Speer cautioned me not to take the decisions as final, and promised to do everything in his power to increase the fighter production. I found him in complete agreement in his judgment of the situation. Moreover he had the courage to admit the consequences, even if those "on top" had refused to do so.

Now it was necessary to find a way to bridge the period until production got under way. An immediate strengthening of the Reich's defense was urgent. In December, 1943, the P-51 Mustang was introduced into the Eighth AAF, the technical details of which we had known already for some time. In the beginning of 1944 it was used more and more frequently and finally took over the task of escorting the American bomber units, while the P-47 Thunderbolt at first gave additional fighter protection and later operated mainly as a fighter-bomber.

The German destroyer, which so far had achieved good results in the fight against the multiengined bombers, now suffered unbearable losses because of the American fighter escort. The fighters that accompanied the destroyers were soon involved in dogfights with the numerically superior enemy, so that they were fully occupied themselves and the destroyers had to fend for themselves. In this way the ZG-76 lost a total of 26 out of 43 aircraft that took off on March 16, 1944, in the area of Augsburg. Another ten had to crash-land. Only seven managed to struggle home. The American fighter escort had attacked just at the moment when the destroyers were preparing to make their own attack. Only five bombers were shot down.

Even if this failure was exceptional, it was obvious that

such losses could not be sustained for any length of time. With the increasing strength of the Mustang fighter escort we also lost more of our fighters. Therefore we used the tactic of combat formations. The destroyers and heavily armed fighters assembled in the same area with numerous light groups of fighters. They attacked together.

A combat formation usually consisted of one attacking group and two escort groups. The former were to attack the enemy's bomber formation while the latter gave them fighter protection against the enemy fighters which were numerically many times stronger. These combat formations were an emergency measure forced on us by the enemy and it was anything but ideal. Anyhow they fulfilled the demand for concentration of forces up to the maximum which I always postulated. But other shortcomings soon appeared. The combat formations had become unwieldy forms, needing much more time for assembly and for climbing to the required altitude for the action than the single groups of fighters. But what was worse, the introduction of this tactic meant renouncing the fundamental principle of fighter action: at all times and in all places to be offensive. According to orders the combat formations were not to attack the American fighter escort, thus losing the initiative and making it easier for the enemy to take the decisive step from the defensive, which was their escorting duty, to the offensive. The results were devastating, because only the fighter that attacks has the advantage. Our losses rose irresistibly. Forced onto the defensive our units forgot how to conduct a dogfight. Now it had come to banking and diving away. Naturally any cohesion of the unit was lost, and singly our fighters were finished off by the enemy who outnumbered them greatly.

This development was undoubtedly catastrophic and it started with the order to attack the bombers only. This stage at which the German fighter arm had arrived represented only a link in a chain of disastrous mistakes. Only in this way can it be explained that the great struggle for air supremacy over Germany between the opposing fighters never took place.

In April, 1944, I said in one of my reports: "The ratio in which we fight today is about 1 to 7. The standard of the Americans is extraordinarily high. The day fighters have lost more than 1000 aircraft during the last four months, among them our best officers. These gaps cannot be filled. During each enemy raid we lose about 50 fighters. Things have gone so far that the danger of a collapse of our arm exists."

The destroyers could achieve satisfactory results only when they were lucky enough to find a heavy bomber formation whose fighter escort was momentarily busy elsewhere. On such an occasion the ZG 26 was able to shoot down 15 bombers of a formation raiding the synthetic petrol plants at Stettin, with a loss of only two of their own aircraft. During an attack on Budapest, 12 ME-140s of the 1st ZG 76 shot down eight American bombers without loss to themselves.

Single successes did not alter the fact that with the increase of American air superiority over the Reich, it finally became impossible to send destroyers into action. Therefore two remaining wings were rearmed with single-engine fighters during the summer of 1944. The destroyer aircraft with its great possibilities for putting into action new and stronger weapons had lost its operational possibility because of the American fighter escort.

The delicate situation of the defense of the Reich in the winter of 1943-44 gave birth to a new kind of fighter arm: The "storm" fighter. It was typical of the spirit of the German fighter pilots that they did not put up with the enemy's superiority, that they did not resign themselves, that they proposed to attack the death-dealing bombers to the point of self-sacrifice. In this way at the end of 1943, in addition to many other suggestions from the front, the following was brought to me: to ram the heavy bombers and in particular the leading aircraft. This idea was undoubtedly inspired by the example of the Japanese kamikaze pilots, who in order to destroy especially important targets dove their aircraft into them. Such self-sacrifice was rooted in the beliefs, the tradition, and the concept of heroism of the Japanese race. We Europeans could marvel at it, but it was foreign to our nature. Therefore I had to reject this idea of self-sacrifice on principle. On the other hand these ideas, whose keenest champion was Major von Kornatzki, gave rise to the formation of special elite units of fighters. Instead of ramming, they were to attack in tight formation as close as possible to the bombers. With more powerful armament they would have a better chance of a kill. Ramming was unnecessary. But it was imperative to wade right in and get as close as possible. The aim was to shoot the heavy bomber down at any price. If during such a storm attack their own aircraft was heavily hit, they could always ram and bail out.

After the initial successes of an experimental flight, a call for volunteers went out, which brought the expected strong response. The storm fighters were fitted with FW-190s armed with four 2-cm. cannons, later with two 2-cm. and two 3-cm. MK-108 cannons. The pilot was protected by additional armor. The first storm squadron was soon formed, the 4th (*Sturm*) JG 3 *Udet*. It proved first class. With entirely bearable losses they achieved high results. The foundations for further storm-fighter squadrons were laid down. It was my aim to add, up to September, 1944, one such squadron to each of the 9 wings which were defending the Reich. The execution of this plan was interrupted by the invasion.

The appalling seriousness of the situation in the air was brought home to me clearly when in spring, 1944, I took part in a fighter operation of the Reich's defense together with the Inspector of the Day Fighters, East, Oberst Trautloft. A Fat Dog, a large formation of enemy heavy bombers, was reported to be approaching the Dutch coast. We were following this, as we always did, from my little control room in Hottengrund. I ordered two Focke-Wulfs to be warmed up on the Staaken airfield and invited Trautloft to accompany me. He sprinted across the 50 yards to the plane that was waiting with the engine running. Ten minutes later we took off from Staaken. Course west; climb to 25,000 feet.

On the Reichs-fighter wave length we received details of location, course, altitude, and other important information concerning the major formation of about 800 B-17s and the other oddments which were flying in advance or safeguarding the flanks. We had just crossed the Elbe north of Magdeburg when we first caught sight of the enemy. We let the American formation pass at a respectful distance of from five to ten miles. Eight hundred bombers went by, 2000 tons of death, destruction, and fire inside their silver bodies, flying to their appointed targets in the heart of Germany. Something had to be done. Wave upon wave, endless formations of four-engined bombers! Right and left above them, with and without vapor trails, a vast pack of Mustang fighters. "The range of the enemy's fighter escort does not extend beyond the Elbe!" according to the General Staff. They had stopped talking about the Ruhr long ago, but they still refused to see what was written in realistic letters in the German sky.

Where were our combat formations? I switched over to the other Command wave length and found out that a part of our force after completing an attack were preparing to land and preparing for a second take-off to catch the enemy on their way back. The bomber formation did not look at all as if it had just been through a battle. No wonder, with such masses of bombers and their protective escort.

Further German combat formations were being assembled between Berlin and Magdeburg. I had to watch them in action. One of the last formations had just passed by. My fingers itched. Should I be passively watching this parade? I banked to left and closed in on the formation. Just then I saw a B-17 straggler trying to join another formation to the left. "Hannes," I called, "going in! We'll grab this one!"

There was nothing heroic in the decision. We should have headed right into a complete formation and shot down the leading aircraft. We should have been shot down for certain. Now with this straggler we had to act very quickly before he closed in on the other formation.

I was 100 yards on his tail. The B-17 fired, took desperate avoiding action. The only thing that existed in the whole world was this American bomber, fighting for its life, and me. My cannons blazed away. Pieces of metal flew off. Smoke poured from the engines. They jettisoned the entire bomb load. One tank in the wings had caught fire. The crew was bailing out. Trautloft's voice cried over the radio, *"Achtung, Adolf, Mustangs! I'm beating it—guns jammed!"*

And then—with the first bursts from four Mustangs—I sobered up. There was no mistake about the B-17; she was finished, but I was not. I simply fled. Diving with open throttle I tried to escape the pursuing Mustangs, which were firing wildly. Direction east, toward Berlin. The tracer bullets came closer and closer.

As my FW-190 threatened to disintegrate and as I had only a small choice of those possibilities which the rules of the game allow in such embarrassing situations, I did something which had already saved my life twice during the Battle of Britain: I fired everything I had simply into the blue in front of me. It had the desired effect on my pursuers. Suddenly they saw the smoke which the shells had left behind coming toward them. They probably thought they had met the first fighter to fire backward or that a second attacking German fighter arm was behind them. My trick succeeded; they did a right-hand climbing turn and disappeared.

24

The Beginning of the End

My operational flight confirmed that the decline of our fight-
ing strength was not merely a question of material but also
of personnel. The more the standard of the new pilots sank,
the more important it became for our units to be led by able
and experienced officers. But naturally there was a greater
shortage of these than ever. Good officers are the product of
careful selection and training. But the treasure of experience
can only be built up in operational combat, and this process
unfortunately causes a reduction of their numbers.

If we wanted to have well-commanded and larger operational forces, then the shortage of suitable commanders could
only be overcome by increasing the size of each unit. Therefore as early as 1943 I had suggested that the normal strength
of a flight should be increased from 12 to 16 aircraft and
pilots. This was started in autumn, 1943, with the 2nd and
26th Fighter Wings. Their strength was increased from 124
to 160 aircraft.

The next step I took was to weaken as far as possible the
forces at the front in favor of the Reich defense which was
nearly exhausted. The Southern front was already almost denud-
ed of fighter aircraft. Very much against the will of the Supreme
Command, the Luftwaffe Command had already extracted some
squadrons from the Eastern front, one by one. At last, by order
of the Führer, no more fighter units were to be removed any
more from the east. I found a simple way to by-pass this order
in favor of the Reich's defense. Because of Hitler's orders the
Eastern squadrons were taboo, therefore we had to be satisfied
with single flights, which in the end achieved the same effect.
Each fighter squadron on the Eastern and Norwegian fronts
now had to give up one flight for the defense of the Reich, with
orders to make up the missing flight immediately in action.
This was hardly noticed in the east, because the units were on
the average only 50 per cent of their nominal strength. At home

the extracted flights were immediately brought up to strength and were added as a fourth flight to the squadron stationed in the Reich. In this way we strengthened these squadrons from nine to twelve flights and from 124 to 160 pilots and aircraft. Incidentally, the pilots who had been transferred from the east to the west had a very difficult time owing to the completely different fighting conditions.

These efforts, however, showed results. They were continued tenaciously throughout the winter against all resistance. But it looked as though the results were to be annulled by the incredible intensification of the Allied air offensive. Against all attempts to increase our strength acted the continuous grinding of the Allied attacking mill, beneath which our defensive forces suffered heavily. When, by some rare chance, a unit had not been in action for a few days, its operational strength quickly reached 70 to 80 per cent of its potential once more. After the first action of course it sank again, and if there were two, three, or four further days with operational actions, it very often went down to 30 or 40 per cent, only to sink, if further action was demanded of it, to a tactical zero. But the Führer's order—and nothing could be done against it—stipulated that all available forces were to be sent up as soon as enemy forces were reported approaching the territory of the Reich. Another way out had to be found to prevent a numerical exhaustion of the units.

I suggested therefore to Göring that we should form a reserve, instead of pursuing the previous method of pumping personnel and material into the fighter force in order to maintain its action strength, or even to increase it. Experience soon showed that a third taken out of action collected not only the same but an even greater fighting strength than the two thirds of the units that remained in action. Göring agreed to my suggestion on condition that the effective strength of the units should suffer no weakening when in action. This condition could be fulfilled provided the aircraft of the recuperating pilots remained in action. Göring further demanded that by this means and with the reserve about to be formed, the strength of the fighters for the defense of the Reich had to be brought up to 2000. At last I had the right backing from above. The Air Fleet, Reich, the 1st Fighter Corps, all fighter divisions, the full training, and all complementary organizations at last worked with a common aim. Now we had some hope of achieving something decisive in the air defense in daylight. At that time a large reserve, if sent up in concentrated form to deliver a sudden blow, could substantially influence the situation of the war in the air. At the end of May, 1944, the reserve had already risen to 450 fighter pilots.

Then the invasion upset all our plans.

Naturally it did not come out of the blue. On the contrary, for a long time this threat had been hanging over the heads of the leaders and of all soldiers in the west, setting everyone's nerves on edge. Finally only the time and the place remained a surprise. Enough had been said and whispered about the invasion, the great event that would decide the war. In the beginning of 1944 the indications increased that actions would very soon follow words.

The task that faced the Allied air forces in connection with the preparatory phase of the invasion was clearly expressed in the New Year's Message of 1944 from the Supreme Commander of the USAF to Commanding Generals Doolittle and Twining (Eighth and Fifteenth AAF): "It is an undeniable fact that we cannot undertake an invasion before the German Luftwaffe has been put out of action. I therefore request you to destroy the enemy's air force wherever you encounter it, in the air, on the ground, or in the factories."

The necessity for this had been proved by the tenacious resistance, causing high losses, that the American and British bombers encountered during their day and night raids in the autumn of 1943. It appeared as though the Allied raids had mobilized rather than paralyzed the German war effort. Obviously the Allies had overrated the effects of the air raids to break the resistance of a nation in arms, just as we had done during the Battle of Britain. When we realized our error in 1940 we lacked the ability to intensify our raids. America and England, on the contrary, had not even reached the limits of their air potential in 1943. That year a new air offensive against the German aircraft industry was planned. Yet the weather conditions of the early winter made its execution impossible for the time being.

During November, 1943, there was not one day of good flying weather. Germany was nearly always covered by a thick blanket of cloud. For a long time there had been no protection against area bombing. On the contrary, the more the sky was covered and the darker the nights, the more certain one could be that the British bombers would be over. They were able to bomb their target areas with accuracy through thick clouds with the radar methods they had developed. The Americans on the other hand did not operate if cloud made the targets invisible during the daytime. They stuck to the principle of carpet bombing in well-aimed precision raids. Now they changed their tactics. So far apparently only expediency had made them refrain from area bombing. For their purpose the precision raids were more effective. But now, forced by the weather conditions, they went over to the technique that the English had used right from the start and always had championed.

A temporary change-over from the American to the British technique was therefore decided upon for the American daylight bombers. The H2S method had been extended and improved in the United States. We called it the H2X method. The American reports state that it was "no marvel of precision." On the screens of the sets in front of the bomb-aimer, water showed up dark and earth lighter. Towns could be seen as bright, gleaming spots. Individual targets, of course, could not be seen on this set.

The first raid of this kind was made on November 3, in very cloudy weather, by 539 B-17s on Wilhelmshaven with a strong fighter escort. Our fighters did not succeed in making a concentrated attack on the raiding force. The few of them that managed to get above the clouds found themselves hopelessly outnumbered by a host of American fighters. Only seven heavy bombers were shot down, the majority by flak. During November, 1943, there were nine such large-scale American raids. In December similar weather conditions prevailed. That month the Eighth AAF dropped the largest bomb load so far: 13,142 tons, for the first time exceeding the British monthly total.

With the radar method it was easiest to raid towns that lay either on the coast, at pronounced inlets, or on rivers. This is why Bremen, Kiel, and Wilhelmshaven were so often the targets during the first weeks of the American blind-bombing phase. They suffered heavily. Bremen had to withstand six large-scale raids during a period of five weeks. Although the Americans attached little importance to these raids, the effect on the fighting force and operational strength of the German fighter arm was serious. For the American crews it was a breathing space, a time for strengthening their morale. After the heavy losses they had sustained in autumn these raids were not much of a risk for them. An American combat report says, "This was my twenty-fifth mission. It seemed to be the least dangerous of all." But for our fighters these actions were heavy trials and caused crises. They were fought under the most difficult weather conditions, and high losses resulted. The fact that the Americans did not give us a rest during the winter months meant that we had to dip deeply into the barrel. This dashed our hopes of a forceful and successful riposte to the precision raids which were to be expected with the return of better weather. If we could not now succeed in our work of regenerating the defense of the Reich by the formation of reserves, there remained only one last salvation: the jet fighter and the V-weapons.

The Americans used the first fine day, January 11, 1944, to carry out a raid on the central German aircraft industry. How important they considered this target can be guessed from the fact that they decided on this raid although they had only one squadron of Mustang fighters to escort the raiding force right to the target. The 11 squadrons of Thunderbolts, two squadrons of Lightnings of the USAAF, and the six flights of R.A.F. Spitfires that made up the main escort had to let the bombers fly the last 60 to 100 miles alone. Only one of the three waves of bombers, composed of 663 B-17s and B-24s which passed over the Dutch coast, was protected right to the target by Mustangs.

That morning a thin layer of cloud at about 5000 feet lay over Holland and northwest Germany. East of the Weser there were gaps. There was good visibility over the target areas of Magdeburg-Halberstadt and Merseburg-Dessau. Further west, in the take-off area of our fighter units, a layer of clouds 12 to 1500 feet thick had to be pierced. Nevertheless nearly all the formations of the 1st, 2nd, and 3rd Fighter Divisions were able to approach the enemy in close formation. Of the 239 fighters which were sent up into action 207 made contact with the enemy. In the sectors of Rheine-Osnabrück, Hildesheim, and over the target areas there were heavy dogfights, in which we were very successful. On their way back the bombers were again attacked by our fighters on their second sortie. They attacked from south of Bremen up to the Dutch border, where the bombers met their fighter escort.

An American report said that the Luftwaffe had apparently lost more of its ability to make it a dangerous proposition to penetrate deeper into Germany without fighter escort. In certain respects the German tactics had improved since October (Schweinfurt). Never before had they remained in contact with the bomber formation for so long. They had skillfully chosen the moment when the fighter protection was at its weakest; they had first opened fire with rockets from outside the range of the enemy defensive weapons, before starting their mass attacks with the usual arms. Sixty bombers were destroyed. The war diary of the 1st German Fighter Corps calls this day an especially successful one. One can get some idea of the toughness of the fighting from our own losses, which were 39 fighter aircraft. The first reports of the action gave reason to believe that at least 105 bombers were shot down. Several kills had been counted double because usually several fighters took part in one kill.

This serious setback over Germany strengthened the decision of the Allied Command to put into action as soon as possible the planned large-scale operation against the German aircraft industry. According to U. S. Generals Spaatz and Anderson, the destruction of the German fighter production had become so urgent that they decided to go ahead with it, accepting the greatest risk and the very high losses. The operation bore the code name "Argument." It provided for precision raids coordinated between the American air fleets stationed in England and Italy, as well as for night raids by the R.A.F. against aircraft factories situated all over Germany and in particular against assembly plants of the fighter and destroyer production. The Fifteenth AAF operating from Foggia took little part, since they were urgently needed to support the Allied bridgehead.

On February 19 the weather cleared over Germany. The largest striking force ever was ready for action on their bases in the southeast of England: about 1000 heavy bombers and a fighter escort of 17 American squadrons and 16 English flights. During the night of February 19-20 the R.A.F. raided Leipzig following the Hamburg pattern in order to weaken the German defense in preparation for the following day's operation by the American units.

In the early hours of the morning of February 20 the air armada took off. The targets lay in the area of Braunschweig-Leipzig-Oschersleben and also further east up to Tutow and Poznań. Basing their calculations on the experience of January and October, the Americans counted on losing 200 bombers, but the German fighters could not repeat their earlier success. Twenty-one bombers lost was a low price to pay for what was accomplished. The following night 600 British bombers raided Stuttgart. On February 21 the American targets were aircraft factories in Brunswick and various airfields. The next day central Germany was raided again as well as Regensburg. A formation of the Fifteenth AAF took part in the action of February 23: they raided Steyr from Italy two days in succession. Simultaneously bombers of the Eighth AAF attacked Schweinfurt, Gotha, Tutow, Kreising, and Poznań. The "Big Week," as Allied propaganda called this operation, came to an end with a combined raid by the Eighth and Fifteenth AAF on Regensburg. The last day was another hard blow for the

Americans: they lost 64 heavy bombers. The main brunt of the German fighter attacks was borne in this action by those bombers that approached from the south. Their strength was 400, without fighter escort. Only 176 reached their target and of these 33 were shot down, i.e., 19 per cent. Such a percentage of loss was intolerable. Not even the Americans could afford to lose their crews and bombers after five or six missions.

Our new principle of "Mass against Mass," skillfully employed by Fighter Command, had brought us once more an impressive defense success. Allied propaganda on the other hand considerably exaggerated the effects of these raids. The Big Week was for several days the sensation in the Western press. The Allied Command also overrated the effect of the raids and underrated the resilience of German industry, as they admitted later. No repetition of raids on aircraft factories therefore occurred for the time being. Only months later did the enemy find out that our air armament was anything but finished. Despite the superficial damages we had sustained we hoped that the Allied planners would go on believing their errors and mistakes.

During the six days of the Big Week the Americans dropped 10,000 and the British 9198 tons of bombs on the German aircraft industry. For this the Americans made 3800 bomber flights, and the English 2351; and 3673 fighter aircraft made up the respective escorts. The Americans lost 226 bombers, 26 fighters, and in air crew 2600 men. The British losses were 157 bombers.

The comparison of American and English losses showed the remarkable fact that for the first time the percentage of losses of the English night operations was, with 6.6 per cent, higher than that of the American daylight operations which was only 6 per cent. Our night fighters had again reached a high degree of efficiency. They achieved their best result when the English raided Leipzig during the Big Week. They joined the bomber stream early in a battle that lasted several hours, and shot down 83 English heavy bombers. The R.A.F. suffered their greatest defeat at the hand of the German night fighters during the large-scale raid with 795 bombers on Nürnberg on the night of March 30-31, 1944. In favorable conditions Night-Fighter Command succeeded in directing concentrated formations into contact with the enemy. They decimated them during the approach, over the target, and on their way back. The result was 95 heavy bombers shot down.

In March the enemy day fighters were now allotted additional tasks. After the supposedly decisive blow against the

German aircraft industry, the American fighters received orders to abandon their defensive role, designed to protect the bomber formations over the territory of the Reich, and to go over to the offensive. General Kepner, in command of the fighter force of the Eighth AAF, was ordered by Spaatz to give battle to the enemy fighters wherever he could find them. Only now did the superiority of the American fighters come into its own. They were no longer glued to the slow-moving bomber formation, but took the law of action into their own hands. Wherever our fighters appeared, the Americans hurled themselves at them. They went over to low-level attacks on our airfields. Nowhere were we safe from them; we had to skulk on our own bases. During takeoff, assembling, climbing, approaching the bombers, once in contact with bombers, on our way back, during landing, and ever after that the American fighters attacked with an overwhelming superiority. Yet even this did not change our order: "Only the bombers are to be attacked"! The chain of mistakes with which the German fighter force was being dragged into the abyss had been enlarged by a few more links. The only hope that remained was the reserves that would increase the strength of the fighter defense to about 2000 aircraft.

The Big Week was the first of a series of carefully prepared air operations, all of which had the same aim: to make the European mainland ripe for an invasion. These operations extended over longer periods and sometimes overlapped in time and place. A precursor to each operation was a bitter internecine war for priority. This was waged by the leaders according to their different viewpoints and their different arms. Naturally the British Command thought that attacking the German flying-boat bases on the Channel coast was the most urgent task. Eisenhower championed a large-scale attack on transports and communications in France, to open the door to the mainland for his invasion troops. Spaatz for his part thought it vital to destroy the synthetic oil industry. Attacks against airfields and ground organization and against the Atlantic wall all found a place in the preparations for the invasion.

Eisenhower won the fight for priority. On March 25, 1944, he immediately ordered missions against the railway systems in the north of France and in Belgium. A plan, worked out by experts, provided for the paralyzing of the Western Europe transport network by raids on lines, bridges, stations, and junction boxes. A hundred railway junctions in France and 500 in Germany were earmarked for destruction. The plan had its disadvantages. The estimated casualty list of 150,000 French civilians was hardly likely to create a favorable mood in the country they intended to liberate. Only a fifth of the French railway traffic served German military purposes, and therefore great reserves could still be brought into action. The German skill in repairing damaged transport installations was not fully known but had to be assessed fairly high according to past experiences. Churchill therefore declared in a letter to Roosevelt in May, 1944, that he was not "convinced of the wisdom of this plan."

In March, 1944, the Ninth (tactical) AAF stationed in England began bombing French railway targets. At the end of April it had dropped 33,000 tons of bombs. The military results were unsatisfactory. In May the railway offensive reached its peak. Day and night, from England and Italy American and British light, medium, and heavy bombers attacked transport targets deep in Germany. During the first days of May hundreds of fighters and fighter-bombers were used in these operations. They chased moving trains: in France alone 475 locomotives were left standing on the lines, wrecked. Special Marauder commandos undertook the destruction of bridges. All together, up to the invasion, the combined strategical and tactical air fleets dropped the enormous total of 71,000 tons of bombs on transport targets in Western Europe. Nevertheless traffic was never brought to a standstill.

The attacks on our V-weapon bases were also a partial success. Since the beginning of 1942 the British secret service had received alarming information about German secret weapons which were being tested in Peenemünde. A year later, in May, 1943, the central office of photo air reconnaissance had in their possession aerial photos of the German experimental station for V-weapons. On these a tiny speck was recognized as the first V-I.

At the same time on the Channel coast opposite England extensive and secret building activities by the Germans had been observed. The British command was most concerned. The R.A.F. prepared for a large-scale operation. "Crossbow" was the code word for the battle against the V-weapons, either in the state of research, experiment, trial, production, on catapults, or even during their approach. On the night of August 17, 1943, 597 bombers of the R.A.F. raided Peenemünde. The damage and our losses were considerable. Among the 700 dead were irreplaceable scientists and experts.

Nevertheless developments and preparations for the V-weapon offensive continued. Eisenhower in a letter to General Arnold on January 23, 1944, pointed out that the Germans might conceivably finish their preparations before the invasion was ready and that they might possibly prevent it. Only the American precision method seemed suitable to cope with the steadily increasing numbers of firing platforms which appeared along the Channel coast. The English had discovered by now that with area bombing at night they could not achieve anything against these installations. On the experimental ground at Eglin Air Base in Florida replicas of the German V-weapon firing platforms were constructed as accurately as possible, at a considerable cost of material. On these the best and most successful methods of attack were tried out. Thunderbolts and fighter bombers in low-level attacks achieved the best results.

Up to the time of the invasion 36,000 tons of bombs were dropped on the V-weapon sites on the Channel coast. The losses caused by light flak were considerable, and the results doubtful. In any case it was presumed on the Allied side that thanks to the counteraction by the American and the British air forces the German V-weapon offensive had been delayed by at least three to four months. Only ten days after the start of the invasion the first flying bombs crossed the Channel. The last one was fired a few days before the capitulation. V-2 rockets were fired continuously after September 1.

The most successful operation of the entire Allied strategical air warfare was against the German fuel supply. This was actually the fatal blow for the Luftwaffe! Looking back, it is difficult to understand why the Allies started this undertaking so late, after they had suffered such heavy losses in other operations. Right from the start fuel had been the most awkward bottleneck for the German conduct of the war. Our total fuel consumption in 1938 had been about 7.5 million tons. Of this two thirds had to be imported. At the beginning of the war there were only reserves for six months. As the war drew out beyond all expectations, the synthetic petrol production was greatly increased. In 1943 the yearly production had already reached six million tons. Together with the yearly two million tons of crude oil from Romania and Hungary the demand was barely covered. In 1944 production rose steeply until the large-scale air raids which started in May.

Again the operation was based on a detailed plan worked out by specialists, and included about 80 different targets of the fuel industry concentrated in the Ruhr, in Silesia, and in the Ploesti area. Ninety per cent of the production came from 54 different works, 27 of which were of major importance.

The offensive opened in the second half of April, 1944, with raids by heavy American bombers from Italy on the installations at Ploesti. On May 12 the first daylight raid was launched on the German plants. During the morning 935 American bombers with escort of 1000 fighters crossed the Dutch-Belgian coast in the direction of Frankfort am Main, from where they turned toward the main German industrial area. About 150 bombers flew on eastward via Karlsbad into the area of Prague to raid the synthetic plant at Brüx.

The German air defense sent up more than 400 fighters, but only one unit managed to make contact with the enemy in close formation. Good results were attained in the Frankfort sector. The others were caught by the escorting enemy fighters while they were still assembling, and were soon involved in costly dogfights. Where we managed to break through the fighter escort or found an unaccompanied bomber formation, we were successful. A single wing of the Americans was attacked head on in a concentrated mass attack and broken up; within a few minutes it lost half its planes. It was only saved from total destruction because fighters from other groups came to their rescue. And again on the way back the bombers, which had released their bombs on Zwickau, Merseburg, Leuna, Brüx, Lützkendorf, and Böhlen, were attacked on a second sortie. This action was successful against stragglers and formations which were not covered at the time by escort fighters. The Americans reported the loss of 46 bombers. The German record shows a definite bag of 72 bombers against a loss of 65 of our own aircraft.

We had gathered all our strength but we knew that we had neither succeeded in preventing a raid on one of our most vital war industries, nor inflicted such losses on the enemy as to deter them from a repetition of such attacks. The raided works were heavily damaged. The Americans insist that in this raid on the Leuna works a building was destroyed in which experiments with heavy water for the splitting of the atom were being made.

While the raids of the Fifteenth AAF continued on Ploesti and on the oil centers of Austria, Hungary, and Yugoslavia, the R.A.F. dropped mines nightly in the Danube to stop all transports to the Reich (the river had become more and more important through lack of railway tankers). On May 28 and 29 the Americans made further raids with slightly smaller forces on our synthetic plants at Ruhland, Magdeburg,

Zeitz, Luena, Lützkendorf, and Pölitz. The R.A.F. also added targets of our petrol industry to their nightly program.

As early as June, 1944, the month the invasion started, we felt very badly the effects of the consolidated offensive. Fuel production suddenly sank so low that it could no longer satisfy the urgent demands. Speer, when interrogated by the Allies, stated that from June on, it had been impossible to get enough aviation fuel. While it was possible with the greatest effort to keep up at least a minimum production of motor and diesel fuel, the repair work on the plants where normal fuel was converted to octane constituted difficulties which were impossible to overcome. The enemy soon found out how much time we needed for reconstruction and for resuming production. Shortly before this date was reached under tremendous strain came the next devastating raid.

By applying the strictest economy measures and by using the reserves of the OKW (Western High Command), it was possible to continue the fuel supply to the army during the summer months of 1944. Yet from September on, the shortage of petrol was unbearable. The Luftwaffe was the first to be hit by this shortage. Instead of the minimum of 160,000 tons monthly, only 30,000 tons of octane could be allotted. Air force operations were thereby made virtually impossible! For the army similarly disastrous conditions did not arise before the winter.

The raids of the Allied air fleets on the German petrol supply installations was the most important of the combined factors which brought about the collapse of Germany. The enemy was surprised at the results. With only 5166 tons of bombs they had scored a bull's-eye against Germany's material strength of resistance. Seven times this weight had been dropped on V-weapon firing platforms and 14 times that weight on railway installations. Only after the start of the invasion did the Allies realize the true strategical importance of the German synthetic oil plants. They were now given top priority on the list of targets.

The direct preparations for the invasion started on May 11 with concentrated American and English air raids on airfields and ground installations for the Luftwaffe in Western Europe. The targets chosen were about 100 airfields within a radius of about 300 miles in Normandy, the intended point of landing. Most of these airfields were not in use. They were so repeatedly and thoroughly destroyed that when our fighters wanted to use them after the invasion had started they found only chaos.

The fortifications of the Atlantic wall were simultaneously attacked. For security reasons these attacks could not be concentrated on the invasion area alone. For each target in this sector two outside the area had to be raided. The expenditure was colossal, the results debatable. Up to the date of the landing, 23,094 tons of bombs were dropped on the concrete blocks along the Channel and the Atlantic coast. The bombing reached its peak 20 minutes before the landing started.

The Luftwaffe was not in a position to interfere with all these operations. The Allies had 12,837 aircraft available for the invasion, the German fighter aircraft of the 3rd Air Fleet confronting them had between 80 to 100 planes! The total amount of aircraft in the whole Luftwaffe on all fronts was 3222 (of which only about 40 per cent were serviceable), composed of 1195 fighters, 434 night fighters, and 153 destroyers. In France we still had only two fighter wings, which were sent up day after day against the overwhelming enemy. The majority of fighters were used for the defense of the Reich. Contrary to the surmise of the German Command that, during the days just prior to the invasion, the entire enemy air force would be concentrated on this sector of operations, the Americans and the British continued their strategic bombing offensive against the Reich almost without interruption. One of their aims was to tie down and to weaken the German fighter defense.

On the cue words, "Threatening Danger West," all units operating in the defense of the Reich, with the exception of two wings of bad-weather fighters and the destroyers, were to be thrown into the invasion sector—a total of about 600 aircraft. The High Command gave orders that for this purpose 50 per cent of all units were to be kept in readiness to support the army as fighter-bombers in low-level attacks. In case of emergency the fighters were to assist 100 per cent in the land fighting.

The High Command started from the correct assumption; that the invasion had to be repulsed immediately or at least within ten days. If this were not possible the invasion had to be regarded as a *fait accompli*. The immediate urgency was to get the forces in time to their action stations. However this demanded a knowledge of the time and place of the landing. During the last weeks and months the forces in the west were often alerted in vain. From the point of view of weather and tide conditions the probable date for the landing was the end of May. The OKW suspected that the landing would be staged between Dieppe and Dunkirk, or possibly at the Seine Estuary. The Allied disguise of their real intentions by sending out special reports did not remain without effect. Sufficient and effective air reconnaissance over the Channel and the embarkation ports was impossible because of the air superiority of the enemy. The German Command actually groped in the dark until the moment of the landing and even for some time after.

During the evening hours of June 5 preparations for attack by the Allied air fleets were noticeable. The British radio gave sabotage instructions to the French Resistance fighters and just before midnight even announced the imminent start of the invasion. A few minutes later the first paratroop landings started between the Seine and the Orne. The gigantic mechanism of the invasion by Allied air, sea, and land forces was in action.

According to the evaluation of the situation by the C.-in-C., West, the main landing was still to be expected at a different spot, and the first operation was regarded as a feint or a side show. In this way a lot of time was wasted and the issue of the cue word was delayed. Finally the Luftwaffe acted on its own initiative and started regrouping its forces. This was the delayed opening move to the bitterest fighting phase in its history.

25

"Where Is the Luftwaffe?"

When the first news of the strong Anglo-American landings was confirmed and it was quite clear that the invasion which was to decide the fate of Germany had started, the first reaction was one of relief. The threat that had been considered in all its possible aspects and discussed until everyone was sick of it had at last became reality. The uncertainty that had paralyzed all military planning and preparation was over. Nobody underrated the difficulties that lay before us, and yet we had almost hoped for this day. Now it had arrived and we knew where we stood.

During the night, while two British and two American paratroop divisions landed in Normandy, the invasion fleet drew near under an umbrella of American and British fighters, to force the main landing. The Allied air forces available for the assistance of the landing operation consisted of the Bomber, Fighter, and Coastal Commands, as well as the Second (tactical) Air Force of the R.A.F. and the Eighth and Ninth (tactical) AAF, a total of 6000 to 7000 aircraft. On the other hand the German 3rd Air Fleet with 9th, 10th, and 2nd Flying Corps, the 2nd Air Division, the 2nd Fighter Corps, and the reconnaissance group 122, reported on June 5 a fighting strength of 481 aircraft, 64 of them reconnaissance and 100 of them fighter aircraft. On the day the invasion started not more than 319 aircraft could meet the enemy. This represents a ratio of forces of about 1 to 20.

During the night it had still been possible to attack a convoy approaching the coast, with a force of bombers, with insignificant results. In the daytime the Allied fighters formed a solid air umbrella over the landing sector, and they sent up fighter forces outside the invasion area which closed off the whole zone. Only in two instances, on the first day of the landing, did German fighter-bombers penetrate the defensive frame and the air umbrella and drop their bombs on the bridgehead. From the very first moment of the invasion the Allies had absolute air supremacy.

Therefore the enemy, our own troops, and the population asked the obvious question, "Where is the Luftwaffe?" The American and the English crews who had flown over Germany knew that the German fighter arm, although weakened, was still in existence and was still an opponent to be taken seriously. But where was the Luftwaffe now? The enemy asked this question in a tone of relief, but the German soldiers, on whose shoulders alone rested the whole burden of the invasion front, asked it with daily increasing bitterness.

They could not guess that through the delay in giving the cue words our preparatory measures could not start early enough. They did not know that orders for the transfer of almost all the fighter forces of the Reich's defense into France, to support the army—a move which had been planned long before down to the smallest detail—was given by the OKL (High Command Air) only on the second day of the invasion. Up to June 8, therefore, the 3rd Air Fleet in France relied solely on the 80 serviceable fighters of the 2nd and 26th Fighter Wings. According to statements by its commanding general, the 2nd Flying Corps at Compiègne learned of the start of the invasion only on June 6 at about 8 o'clock in the morning. Communications had been greatly disrupted and disorganized by the preceding air raids.

The transfer of the air force units defending the Reich, and the reserves, which, as far as I remember, consisted of about 600 aircraft, started on June 7 and 8. The circumstances in which this transfer was executed were highly unusual. It began under a baleful star. Weeks before, a special transfer staff had been appointed to make all necessary preparations. A destination airfield, prepared and provisioned, was chosen for each unit. Yet the continuous raids against the ground organizations in France made redispositions necessary at the last moment and forced a complete abandonment of the original bases in favor of quickly improvised front-line airfields. But for the most part our pilots were used to the well-equipped and smoothly functioning fighter bases of the Reich's defense, and they could not adjust themselves quickly enough to the primitive front-line conditions in France. Also in the choice of location and in the layout of these emergency airfields, not enough regard had been paid to efficient camouflage, which our air inferiority demanded. As a result our bases were constantly shadowed and threatened by Allied fighters and fighter-bombers.

The transfer itself brought us unusually high losses. It all happened in a great rush and under a nervous strain that can easily be understood in the circumstances. The intermediate touch-down airfields were overcrowded. The destination of the units often had to be changed in flight because the intended landing field had been put out of action at the last moment by an enemy attack. The advance commandos very seldom met with the main force of their unit. In any case large parts of each unit had remained in Germany including many unserviceable aircraft. Thus each unit was already partially disintegrated. The fighter corps lost its bearings because of the bad communications. The Command did not know the units' strength or immediate needs, where they were or if they had arrived at their destinations. Almost half the units got involved in dogfights on the way to their action stations. They suffered losses, were dispersed, and without a leader often did not find their new bases. Their cross-country training had been insufficient because they had been sent up too soon on defensive operations by the defense centers. There were an incredible amount of crashes. The repair squads were so overtaxed that they were unable to get a sufficient amount of aircraft back into service or to salvage the crashed planes. Soon everything was in a hopeless chaos.

A major operational disadvantage was the fact that the bulk of our fighter forces had to be based north or northwest of Paris. The ground organization there was more compact and less damaged. Although from here the beachhead was within the range of our fighters, we could only approach it from the flank. This made it easier for the Allies to patrol the area and to intercept the German fighters during the approach. Thus most of the dogfights took place far away from the invasion area, not because our fighters preferred it this way, but because the superior Allied forces dictated it so. Whenever we managed to penetrate the area over the beachhead, it was only to the east, while the western section, that of the Americans, was nearly free from German planes. Cherbourg was completely out of range. The ideal position for drawing up our fighter forces, south of the invasion coast, was impossible because of terrain difficulties and the complete destruction of the few existing airfields.

The chaos caused by the transfer gradually cleared up. New combat units were formed in the operational area. During this arrangement hardly any of the wings got their own squadrons: some of them got three strange ones. This resulted in disadvantages for united action that have been greatly underrated. The wings which now only had fighter-bombers and bombers, representing about a third of the total

215

force, came under the command of the 2nd Flying Corps (close combat corps). The remaining fighter units came under the command of the 2nd Fighter Corps (air defense corps). The two corps had to work in close cooperation.

Obviously from the very start the German High Command lacked a sober judgment of the situation and a clear concept of how the few German fighters should be employed in the fight against the invasion, so that they should have some chance of success against a 20-to-1 superiority of the Allies. Faced with so many tasks, there was again the temptation to split up the weak forces and to fritter them away. Principles of fighting, which had been successful in the east and in 1940 in the west, were retained although conditions were entirely different. Experiments were tried, but they all led back to the old realization, seemingly almost banal now, that nothing could be done either in the air or on land without air superiority.

The program of the High Command originally envisaged bombing attacks in daylight with fighter escort against the invasion forces. Luckily the Luftwaffe Command in the west succeeded in having this suicidal idea canceled. Instead of this the fighters and fighter-bombers were to attack continuously the bridgehead from the first day of the invasion onward. This action broke down against the wall of enemy fighters which bolted up the area, as I have already mentioned. Now the protection for the fighter-bombers was increased and the approach was tried from a very high altitude. But we hardly ever managed to assemble for such an attack because of the constant watch kept on our stations. The fighter-bombers therefore changed back to fighters and in the future were employed in their natural function. They had been considerably decimated without having been able to ease the situation in the least. At the end of June the 2nd Flying Corps was dissolved and its units incorporated in the 2nd Fighter Corps. Under its command were also the 4th and 5th Fighter Divisions. Up to this time 1000 aircraft had been lost on the invasion front, including those lost during the transfer. Up to July 7 a reserve of 998 fighters had been brought up. Therefore the numbers of aircraft in action were approximately maintained in spite of the enormous losses.

In the meantime the strength of the Allied fighters had considerably increased because they could now operate from the French mainland. In bitter fighting and under the protection of a screen from the Allied ships' artillery the small bridgeheads had extended into a continuous strip of land

216

several miles deep. Sapper units had been among the first to land and they completed the first emergency landing strips on the first day of the operation. Two days later the first front-line airfield could be taken over and from June 19 all American fighter-bombers operated from airfields in Normandy. Two artificial harbors and a pipeline that had been laid across the Channel allowed the landing of heavy material and the continuous supply of fuel. Up to June 24 we observed 23 Allied airfields, most of them in the English sector.

Under the protection of the consolidated Allied air forces, 25 landing divisions were built up by June 15: 427,000 men, 62,238 vehicles, and 105,175 tons of material were already on the mainland. The German counterattacks, particularly fierce around Caen, collapsed under the hail of bombs from the Allies; British bombers appeared again, for the first time in daylight. On June 18 the enemy managed to break through to the west coast of the Cotentin peninsula, thus cutting off Cherbourg. This fortress fell on June 29. One of the first important operational goals of the Allied invasion plan had been reached and a deep sea harbor was in their hands.

They had reckoned with a German strength of 25 to 30 divisions. They met not even half this number. And yet considerably stronger forces were available. Hitler decided too late to throw them into the battle, because long after June 6 he still expected further Allied landings at other places. The bringing up of the army reserves was therefore much too late. Because of the enemy's air supremacy the army got into similar difficulties during its move, as did the Luftwaffe. It took a whole week to transfer a combat unit of the 265th Infantry Division from Quimper in Brittany to the front in Normandy. The 2nd SS Armored Division left its station at Limoges on June 11 with marching orders for the front. It reached the Loire between June 14 and 16. Only parts of it reached Le Mans with great difficulties because of destroyed railway bridges. From here progress was only possible on foot. Its first units only went into action at the end of the month, much weakened by low-level attacks and partisan actions. The 9th and 10th Armored Divisions received their marching orders to the west on the day the invasion started. After a few days they arrived in Metz. Because of the hopeless transport conditions only the armored units were transported to Paris for the time being. The last 200 miles from there to the front was almost impossible by rail—the only way of transporting heavy armor. In moves up and down the country, lasting for weeks, 1400 miles instead of 300 were

217

covered. These urgently needed armored units were only able to go into action at the end of July.

The English and American tactical air forces successfully extended their attempts to interrupt the bringing up of German reserves deep into France. They had made any move by daylight almost impossible. In June alone they destroyed 551 locomotives. A report by the commander of the 2nd Panzer Divisions says: "The Allies have total air supremacy. They bomb and shoot at anything that moves, even single vehicles and persons. Our territory is under constant observation. . . . The feeling of being powerless against the enemy's aircraft . . . has a paralyzing effect . . ."

The German fighter arm, despite its tremendous effort, was unable to bring about any change in this desperate situation. We sustained unusually high losses in hopeless attempts to defend ourselves against superior enemy forces. The total strength we were able to send up daily was never more than 250 fighters. The squadrons, which only a few weeks before had been replenished with new pilots and new planes, melted away in the kiln of the invasion. Besides our losses in the air we were almost reduced to immobility by continuous raids on our airfields, by the interruption of the flow of reserves, by the overstraining of the supply and repair service, and by the entire complicated apparatus needed by technically highly developed, and therefore highly vulnerable troops.

I had sent Fighter Inspector Trautloft with a communications staff to the 2nd Fighter Corps, to keep in constant touch. He was in close personal contact with the squadrons in action and was able to give the corps valuable information, inspiration, and suggestions. Until the fall of Paris I spent several days with the units in the west. My impressions were shattering. In addition to the appalling conditions there was a far-reaching spiritual decline. This feeling of irrevocable inferiority, the heavy losses, the hoplessness of the fighting, which had never before been so clearly demonstrated to us, the reproaches from above, the disrepute into which the Luftwaffe had fallen among the other arms of the forces from no fault of the individual, together with the other burdens the war at this stage had brought to every German, gave the greatest sense of solidarity ever experienced by the Luftwaffe.

Our pilots in the west were waging a real jungle warfare. Wherever a fighter plane rolled out of its camouflaged lair, an enemy immediately pounced on it. The danger of being detected and destroyed by the enemy was ever present. At last we retired into the forests. Before and after each sortie the planes were rolled in and out of their leafy protection with great difficulties and much damage. Soon the Allies applied carpet bombing to those parts of the forests suspected of hiding German fighter planes. Those squadrons which did not perform masterpieces of camouflage and improvisation, and have a good run of luck in the bargain were beaten up in no time.

Fourteen days after the invasion the units had sunk so low in their fighting strength that neither by driving the personnel nor by material replacements could they be put on their legs again. I therefore made a second attempt to form reserves. Receiving permission to do so from the Supreme Command was to me a proof that my conviction was right: it would have made sense from the start not to throw all our forces into the invasion front but to keep at least two squadrons as operational or exchange reserves back in the Reich. This suggestion had been rejected at the time.

Now nothing else could be done except to withdraw one squadron after the other and to send it home. The remaining aircraft and some of the pilots were passed on to the squadrons remaining in action to fill them up. The regroupment went at a satisfactory speed. The production of fighter planes was fortunately high. The training of new airmen and the courses for converting already experienced pilots into fighter pilots proceeded at high speed despite the great petrol worries. In August 1000 fighter pilots left the schools. Their standard was by no means satisfactory and their training needed an additional 15 flying hours either with the newly formed squadrons or with units standing by for action.

At the start the refreshed squadrons were sent straight to the invasion front, but the situation in the Reich had become so acute that the building up of new reserves had to be pursued with all pressure and with all available means. A lessening of the strategic bombing offensive against the Reich only occurred during the first days of the invasion. We had assumed that the enemy would concentrate the full strength of his air force, including the strategical force, on the extended invasion front. The British military leaders were of the same opinion. They had demanded from the Allied High Command that the heavy bombers should desist from their usual strategical tasks during the fighting at the bridgehead, and stand by in case any critical developments arose. Spaatz however asked that the bombing of Germany should continue to be a priority. Eisenhower decided in favor of the latter idea. The Allied strategical air forces received orders to continue their bombing offensive against the Reich provided the front did not need their assistance by a deterioration of the situation. For the bombing of the Reich there was available at the time:

2100 heavy bombers of the Eighth AAF in England
1200 " " " " Fifteenth AAF in Italy
1100 " " " " Bomber Command of the
R.A.F. in England

Works and installations of the fuel industry now became the primary targets in the Reich. The plan provided the following allocation of tasks: The Fifteenth AAF from the south should raid the refineries, the depots, and other installations at Ploesti, Vienna, Blechhammer, and Oderthal (Upper Silesia). The 205th R.A.F. Bomber Squadron stationed in Italy was to continue dropping mines in the Danube. The Eighth AAF from England was to raid works and installations at Pölitz, Zeitz, Magdeburg, Leuna, and Ruhland in Lower Silesia as well as refineries at Hamburg, Harburg, Bremen, and Hanover. Ten targets on the Ruhr were allotted to R.A.F. Bomber Command.

Against such a concentrated large-scale raid, as was made ten days after the start of the invasion, the remnants of the German fighter defense were powerless. On orders of the OKL only the 300th and 301st Bad Weather Fighter Wings had stayed behind in Germany. Finally the storm-fighter squadron, which had done so well in the defense of the Reich, in the second week of the invasion could be transferred back to the Reich.

When the new large-scale offensive against the petrol industry started from Italy on June 16 with a raid on Vienna, and the Eighth AAF raided Hamburg and central Germany with more than 1000 multiengined bombers and an escort of 700 to 800 fighters, we only could meet them with grotesquely inferior numbers but effectively enough to inflict considerable losses. On June 20, out of 1361 bombers 48 were shot down and 468 damaged. The American report that gives these figures even speaks of a temporary loss of air superiority. Twenty-eight German fighter planes were lost in this action.

On the following day Berlin had a 2000-ton raid which had caused a lively argument on the side of the Allies. A few days before, the attack on London by V-weapons had started. As a retaliation the British suggested bombing the German capital with a ferocity never before employed. Harris was even prepared to send his night bombers over Germany by day; and 3000 British and American bombers were to have turned Berlin into a heap of rubble. Spaatz energetically opposed this plan, which he called pure terrorism. Eisenhower and the High Command of the AAF in Washington were of the opinion that in such a large-scale raid only military viewpoints should be considered. The British proposal did not materialize because Harris withdrew his offer when he thought that with the fighting heavy in Normandy perhaps he might not be able to find sufficient fighter escort for the bombers. Now the Americans flew alone and bombed aircraft factories, railway installations, and government buildings. They lost 44 heavy bombers.

Part of the raiding forces, consisting of 114 Flying Fortresses and 70 Mustangs, turned off just before the main target and set a course for Ruhland in Lower Silesia, raided the local synthetic petrol plant there, and continued their flight in an easterly direction: destination, Soviet Union. This event caused a considerable stir in the German High Command. Did this mean the opening of a third air front? Had we now to expect three-cornered raids instead of shuttle raids? Had we to fear strategical bombing from the east? Would all our troubles of removing the essential industries to the east be in vain? After the west and the south, should we be forced to form an eastern defense of the Reich?

The fears were not unfounded. Allied strategy was moving in this direction. The idea of shuttle bombing had long been favored and the Americans supported the idea enthusiastically, although the first practical example on August 17, 1943, when American bombers stationed in England, after a raid on Regensburg, flew on to North Africa and returned via Bordeaux to England, had a sobering effect. Neverthless the Soviet government was approached soon afterward with a request for some bases near the front to be made available. The wish to prove to the Soviets a willingness to cooperate more closely and to give direct military assistance also played a great part in this approach. Yet the Kremlin did not seem very keen. Nor were the more conservative British air strategists. However in November, 1943, USAF Generals Deane and Vandenberg went to Moscow for discussions. The Soviets were very cagey, but Molotov finally agreed "in principle."

Roosevelt took the opportunity at the Teheran meeting to discuss the matter personally with Stalin. The President's son Elliot became an enthusiastic advocate of the idea. Finally, after many objections Stalin appeared to be in agreement, but months passed without anything happening. In February, 1944, Harriman, after a long conversation, succeeded in convincing Stalin. The dictator of the Kremlin declared his willingness to

221

equip six airfields capable of receiving 200 American bombers and their fighter escort, but for the time being he rejected a similar arrangement in Siberia for strategic raids on the Japanese.

After this go-ahead signal General Spaatz immediately dispatched a military mission to Russia. The originally promised six bases had shrunk to three, and these were in a pitiable condition: Poltava, Mirgorod, and Piryatin. Moreover they lay much too far east for the liking of the Americans. During the months of April and May the repair and extension work started while American convoys were on the way across the Arctic Sea and through the Persian Gulf to bring up the necessary material, equipment, fuel, and anything else the bombers needed. The manpower was provided by the Russians, in short measure and not as skilled as the Americans required. In the meantime the date of the invasion drew near and a special shock effect was expected from the coordinated American air raids on Germany from west and east.

At the end of May, after the lengthy and tedious formalities required for the entry of the 1200 American ground crews, the three Soviet airfields were ready to receive the first U. S. bombers. Operation Frantic Joe could start. Since the Eighth AAF was fully employed on preparations for the invasion, the Fifteenth AAF was ordered to make the first flight. General Eaker, Commander of the USAF in the Mediterranean, flew himself in the van of 130 Flying Fortresses that took off on June 2, protected by 70 Mustangs. The target was Debrecen in Hungary. Originally it was intended to raid aircraft factories in Riga and Mielec in Poland. More or less as a polite gesture Spaatz had asked the Russians if they agreed to these targets. Moscow was very much against them. There was a long diplomatic palaver, but the Soviets stuck to their guns. They suggested that targets in Hungary and Romania should be attacked, and thought that for the targets proposed there had been no need for a landing in Russia. Greatly annoyed, the Americans started the operation. The crews had been issued strict orders how to behave when mixing with their Red brothers-in-arms. No fraternization! Faultless behavior! No political discussions under any circumstances!

The units landed in paradelike fashion. The flight went off without incident. One aircraft exploded in mid-air for reasons unexplained. In Poltava the Soviet dignitaries were standing by for the reception. It was drizzling slightly as everyone shook hands with measured politeness. Moscow could announce the successful execution of the first shuttle raid between Italy and

222

the Soviet Union. On June 11 the unit returned to Italy. In Germany the news of the event was drowned in the whirl of the invasion. The expected shock effect had not come off. Only when the Americans repeated the operation on June 21, this time with a unit which branched off from the large-scale raid on Berlin by the Eighth AAF, did we sit up and take notice.

Apparently a German HE-177 brought the first news of this event. It hung onto the American formation and kept in touch with it. The German Command acted with lightning speed. Two hundred bombers of the 4th (strategic) Flying Corps took off in the early evening of June 22, 1944, from their bases in East Poland to attack this worthwhile target 600 miles away. Our units had adopted the technique of the night raids, with bomber stream, pathfinders, and flares, which the English had brought to perfection. The weather was favorable, the defense minimal. Without losses to themselves the German bombers dropped their load on the aircraft parked with peacetime carelessness on the airfield of Poltava. Forty-three Flying Fortresses, 15 Mustangs, and several Soviet aircraft were destroyed and 26 damaged, and 300,000 gallons of fuel, which had been brought half around the world with so much trouble, went up in flames. One American and 25 Russians lost their lives. The following day Mirgorod and Piryatin were raided. Although the Americans had brought their planes into safety this time, the bomb and fuel dumps were destroyed. The German Luftwaffe had proved that it was still able to wage offensive air warfare.

Naturally this was the last successful operation of this sort. On June 23 the Soviet started its large-scale offensive which could never be halted. All forces of the Luftwaffe on the eastern front were called to the aid of the army.

The raids on Germany remained fatal even without the use of the Russian bases. Hardly a day and rarely a night passed without heavy raids, mostly by more than 1000 four-engined bombers. One German town after another sank into ruins. In his memoirs "Bomber" Harris says: "It must be expressively mentioned, that, except for Essen, we never chose any particular factory as a target. The destruction of industrial plants was always regarded as a special task. Our aim was always the center of the town." Thus in most of the German towns it was always the center with its culture, hundreds or even thousands of years old, that was destroyed, and the modern industrial districts, which resemble each other all over the world, although they received some damage, remained more or less intact.

The summer months with good weather and good ground visibility offered the best possibilities for precision raids. On our synthetic petrol plants alone 20,000 tons of bombs were dropped from the beginning of the invasion until the end of June. In this month the reduction in petrol production was already felt as an obstacle to the conduct of operations. The fuel production sank from 927,000 tons in March, 1944, to 715,000 tons in May, 1944, and down to 472,000 tons in June, 1944.

The American fighters over Germany, assisting the bomber offensive, went over to a free chase against our fuel supply by single attacks on petrol transports and stores. In London a mixed commission had been created in the fight against the German fuel supply, to coordinate the individual operations of the Allies. In order to encounter the continuous and heavy devastations, Speer created the Geilenberg Special Staff, which, with an army of 350,000 laborers, mostly foreigners, kept up the reconstruction and decentralization of synthetic petrol plants by erecting new buildings widely dispersed and well camouflaged. After the war an American expert could only say: "The English and ourselves could do nothing else but marvel at the speed and the thoroughness with which this work proceeded." Naturally this army contained agents of the enemy's secret service, numbering more than the strength of a regiment.

In the meantime on the invasion front the Allied strategic bombers were only sent into action at particularly important points. Thus on July 18, 1600 heavy and 350 medium English and American bombers intervened in the particular bitter fighting at Saint-Lô. Within a few minutes 7700 tons of bombs came down on the battlefield. So far this was the heaviest bombing of the war of this type. A few days later von Kluge reported to Hitler the result of a conference of commanders. In face of such complete air supremacy nothing else could be done except to give up territory. The report ended with the words: "The psychological effect on the fighting troops, especially on the infantry, caused by the cascades of the falling bombs, of the elements, is a factor which gives cause for serious consideration.'

A week later, on July 25, the attack was repeated on the same target area, but in much greater strength: 1,507 heavy, 380 medium, and 559 fighter-bombers attacked the position. According to a statement from the commander of the Panzer Training Division, 70 per cent of his troops were either "dead, wounded, or had a nervous breakdown," and von Rundstedt called the bombing "the most effective and most impressive use of the air force I ever witnessed." In fact the psychological effect seemed to be the most important effect of such mass bombing of battlefields. The material effect was not rated so high, especially by the American armies. A territory pockmarked with craters hindered the advance and offered good defensive opportunities to the opponent. Furthermore, during such a mass release of bombs some always fell short and caused losses amongst one's own troops. Nevertheless the Allied pilots solved their task of "throwing bombs at the feet of the invading army" so well that Eisenhower could state with truth in his book, *Crusade in Europe,* that without the air force taking part the invasion would have turned into the greatest disaster in the history of the war.

Therefore it may not be incorrect to state that the mass bombing on July 25 was the overture to the collapse of the German defense and to the breakthrough of the Allied invasion army into the unprotected hinterland. On July 26 and 27 fighting at Saint-Lô was still swaying backward and forward. On the evening of that day the German resistance broke down at different places, and the enemy achieved deep penetrations. On July 31 they reached Avranches, and the next day the breakthrough was a fact. Through the bottleneck which was still narrow at the start, the Allied army of millions streamed to the south and the southwest without encountering any resistance of note.

The battle of Normandy had been decided; the invasion was a success.

The hope of the German Command to close the gap again was not fulfilled. The desperate counterattacks at Falaise did not penetrate. The war diary of the Seventh Army reports: "The attack failed because of unusually lively activities on the part of enemy fighter-bombers." The Luftwaffe, or rather what was left of it in the west, took part in this desperate attempt to stem the enemy with all available aircraft. When the weather permitted and when the constant observation of our take-off points and the battle area eased a little, our fighters even had successes. On August 2, the Americans noticed for the first time effective daylight attacks by German fighters on their armored and motorized columns. Our daily active strength had increased to about 400 fighter planes. Up to now we had been imprisoned in our forest hide-outs, but now heavy dogfights occurred all the time. We had to pay with great losses because of the unequal odds. The American observation that our pilots showed "more fighting spirit than ability" was sad but true.

The fighter activities in the defense of the Reich stiffened once more. The Fifteenth AAF operating from Italy sustained heavy losses in their raids on Ploesti and the Vienna area. In July, 1944, they reached the record figure of 318 bombers. In August their losses of flying personnel were even higher than those of both the American armies fighting in Italy. Harris made a similar observation during a discussion with Allied air force chiefs: During the few weeks after D Day the losses of Bomber Command were greater than those of the Second British Army on the invasion front.

During this summer the Luftwaffe lost an average of 300 aircraft per week. The German figures are shattering: from June, 1941, until June, 1944, there were 31,000 flying personnel. In the following five months, June till October, this figure rose by 13,000 to a total of 44,000 airmen!

Spaatz informed the American headquarters at the end of July that the German Luftwaffe was by no means dead, and that all signs pointed to a revival of the German fighter strength. The fact that our efforts to build up new fighter reserves created concern among the Allies gave us reason for new hope. Numerous new units were being formed and trained for action in daily maneuvers. By the beginning of August this second reserve had reached a strength of 700 pilots and aircraft.

What could we not have done a year before with such a force! But now? Was it right to throw everything into the great conflagration in the west? Or was it a crime? On my second journey of inspection to the invasion front I tried to find an answer to these weighty questions. Out of the breakthrough at Avranches arose the threat to Paris. Everywhere there were signs of the beginning dissolution. The remains of the fighter units, except for the Northern forces, had to be taken back into the area east of Paris. Neither airfields nor supply nor communications had been prepared in the hurry of the retreat. The Command was completely at sea as to where, when, and how the Allied offensive could be stopped, even if only temporarily.

Fantastic to think that the 3rd Air Fleet was able in those conditions to send up in one day 250 fighters and 180 fighter-bombers; the facts do not emerge from the very detailed and factually indisputable battle reports. At headquarters they only saw in the reports from the West: 430 fighter and fighter-bomber actions—57 lost—not even 15 per cent! Where was the Luftwaffe? In one day 430 sorties by fighters and fighter-bombers! And the report was passed on higher up. But it did not say in

226

these reports that on the same day 27 aircraft were burned out on airfield X; that on the landing strip Y in the park of a castle, a squadron was annihilated by enemy fighter-bombers while taking off; that Z squadron lost 50 per cent of its strength while transferring from one base to another. Who was interested in the daily loss of material and men? Where was the Luftwaffe? Who cared that the daily sorties of 430 aircraft had no other operative effect than for the fighter-bombers and fighters to be routed by the enemy?

In the west I had seen for myself what value could be attached to the actions under the given conditions. This insight could not be achieved by discussions of the situation with the leading corps, the air fleet, or even with the High Commands. On the contrary, the further one is removed from the battle the more it is necessary that prestige and Command routine replace the realities of the battle. During my visit to the different units at the front I realized the disproportion between the effort and the result of our actions. I knew that never before did we have to fight under such desperate conditions. And the orders were to continue the fight with increased vigor. When he heard that German reserves had arrived, Montgomery said cynically that they would increase the German defeat. What could we do? Should we continue to fly this expensive demonstration that was of no practical value except to burn to death in it, to die in it? I came to the conclusion that there was nothing else to do but to inform the leaders of the real situation, if any could spare the time to listen to me.

On my arrival in Berlin I asked for the latest figures of the fighter reserve. They had increased to nearly 800. But with this good news I received orders from OKL to send immediately the total fighter reserve into the defense battle in the west. That was absolutely irresponsible! They were bound to get into the stream of the retreat and be overrun. They could do nothing any more to change the critical situation of the army, even had there been a ground organization to receive them. One cannot throw fighter wings into gaps like infantry regiments! These squadrons, which consisted of 80 per cent unexperienced pilots, could have found their feet with tolerable losses in the defense of the Reich. The order to protect the German war industry from total destruction would have justified their action in the defense of the Reich and would have made it worthwhile! But in the west they were doomed to be destroyed in the air or on the ground without achieving any operational effect.

My objection, which I raised with the Luftwaffe staff, only

227

received the answer, "The Führer's orders!" I could not speak to Göring. He had retired because he was "not well." The real reason was probably his collapse under the continuous reproaches which were leveled against him and the Luftwaffe. Until the last moment he had tried to keep the real situation hidden from those above. Now there was no longer anything to hide or to falsify. The naked facts of the war in the air spoke realistically and inexorably.

Since I could not count any more on Göring I turned to the Minister for Armaments, Speer. Even in this desperate situation he remained sober and strictly realistic as ever. He asked for information as to what the fighter arm could undertake against the strategic day bombing. The key industries and transport had been hit so severely that things could not go on like this for more than a week. I reported to him that the Führer had irrevocably ordered the last fighter reserves to be transferred to the beginning retreat in the west.

Speer said, "If the Reichsmarshal does not act then it is my duty to act. Please come with me immediately to the Ministry. We will fly and see the Führer at the Wolf's Redoubt. This order must be canceled." Four hours later we landed at Rastenberg. Soon afterward we were standing in the Führer's bunker. Hitler gave me the impression of being very irritable, overworked, and physically and mentally overwrought. Speer explained briefly and precisely the situation of transport and the armament industry which had become more acute through the increase of the American mass attacks. As usual he accompanied his exposé with actual figures. Hitler listened with increasing irritation. When Speer requested a strengthening of the fighter forces in the Reich even if necessary at the expense of the situation on the Western front, and that the fighters which had just been ordered to France should be used for the defense of the Reich, he could not complete his sentence. He had just started, "Galland has just arrived from the west, and can give you, my Führer . . ."

Hitler interrupted him like a maniac. Speer was given a berating that was particularly embarrassing because it was quite unjustified. The Führer forbade any interference with his operational measures. "Please look after the war industry!" And as an aside to me, "See that my orders are immediately executed!" And to both of us, "I have no time for you any more!"

We were thrown out.

26

The "Great Blow"

After this abrupt ending to our fruitless discussion Speer and
I wanted to fly back to Berlin the same night, but we were
told that the Führer wanted to see us again the next day.
This hardly boded anything good. In order to be well prepared I asked for the details of actions at the front and from
the home defense by telephone. Soon afterward I learned that
Saur had produced a document. Neither the person who con-
cocted it nor the sender nor the person who presented it could
have had an inkling of how Hitler would react to it. The
sender, a representative of an aircraft factory in Paris, had
conferred with one of our commanders, who had probably
unburdened his heavy heart during the conversation. The outcome was a "Factual report by an unprejudiced outsider on
the real conditions of the aerial warfare at the invasion front."
This report got into the hands of the higher officials much
more quickly than usual, and of all people it came into the
hands of Saur. He believed that he could now prove that the
fatal paralysis of the Luftwaffe could not be blamed on his
section of the war industry. This letter strengthened the
thesis that the fighter arm had become a Danaïd vessel, into
which the gigantic production figures were poured in vain.
Hitler in his turn drew the most amazing conclusions from
this letter. He said to us the next day, after an icy reception,
that he had received news that the German fighter pilots in
the west, because their aircraft were inferior in performance,
no longer sought out the enemy but bailed out before it came
to a dogfight. I wanted to reply that this could only apply to
isolated instances. I wanted to prove to him with figures that
the will to action and the fighting spirit of the German pilots
had not been impaired in spite of incredible strain and losses.
I felt an urge to point out the reasons for the momentary
unbearable situation, but Hitler would not let me speak.

He worked himself up into a screaming rage: "I will dissolve the fighter arm. Apart from a few fighter squadrons

229

equipped with modern aircraft, I will continue the air defense with flak batteries. Speer, I order you to furnish me immediately with a new program. Production has to be switched over from fighter planes to antiaircraft guns and must be increased considerably."

Speer too was not given a chance to reply. He was given ten days to produce the new program. Then Hitler closed the short and completely one-sided discussion. As we stood outside the building in which one of the most monstrous orders of the war had just been given, doubts assailed me. I wondered if logic had gone by the board. I probably seemed very distraught, because Speer told me that I should not let my mind dwell any longer on this order. Things were not as bad as they looked.

"During the next days," he said, "I will prove, that a changeover from light metal armament to the production of guns is nonsense."

If the Führer wanted, he could increase the flak output by switching over to it the capacity of the locomotive-building program. The limit for the AA gun program did not lie in guns, manpower, or output, but in explosives. There was already a shortage of ammunition. If the fighters were no longer in the position to protect the explosive and fuel industries, then in a very short time all the war industries would come to a standstill.

These sober and lucid words were convincing. Speer had been right. There was no more talk about dissolving the Luftwaffe. It is difficult to explain how the order from the Führer ever came about. It is only fair to put on record that Hitler knew perfectly well how important his air arm was at the time. Among the secret documents at the Führer's headquarters a shorthand note was found of the "discussion of the Führer with Generaloberst Jodl on July 31, 1944, at the Wolf's Redoubt, starting at 23:53 hours." In this document, marked "Top Secret," Hitler's opinions on the cause of the German collapse in the west are given as follows: "One must realize that in France a turn of the tide can only come about, if we manage to re-establish air superiority even if only for a certain period. I am therefore of the opinion that we ought to do everything possible—however hard it may be at the moment—to hold the air force units now being formed in the Reich, in readiness as a last reserve for an extreme emergency, so that they may be ordered to a spot where it might be possible to bring about a change of events. Today I cannot say where the last dice may be cast." This was recorded a few days after the abortive assassination attempt on July 20 and a few days before Speer's and my visit to his headquarters.

In the meantime the transfer of the fighter reserves conflicted with the retreating stream of the western armies. A large proportion of these fighters, about 800 planes in all, never got into action. Many had to be scuttled because they had been directed to fields which had been already evacuated. Others fell into the hands of the enemy as they had orders to land on airfields which in the meantime had been occupied by the enemy. More than 200 fighters had no other choice than to land in the open country, where because of the ignorance of the situation they were soon steam-rollered by the enemy. The number of aircraft shot down during the transfer has never been established. One thing is certain: this considerable force, which was sent to the west, did not shoot down more than 25 enemy planes, while about 400 fighter planes with a large proportion of their pilots were sacrificed to no purpose. They were shot down, fell into enemy hands, were scuttled, destroyed, or went up in flames.

The retreat of the Luftwaffe from France may have been no better but certainly not worse than that of other branches of the forces, which were forced to a headlong retreat and evacuation after the Allied breakthrough at Avranches. Any front-line troops in these conditions will present a picture of disorganization and of demoralization. It must not be forgotten that the ground and supply organizations, the aircraft industry, and especially air intelligence and communication services were largely employing emergency personnel civilians and female assistants. This did nothing to improve the military picture of these turbulent events. If one further considers that the preparations for a retreat according to plan were not only forbidden but regarded as defeatism, then it is a marvel that a general panic was avoided.

It is characteristic of an air force that a relatively small group at the front has a huge machinery at the rear. It is difficult enough to maintain aggressive strength when advancing, but in a retreat the weight and bulk of these supporting services have a proportionately negative effect the quicker and more disorganized the retreat becomes. This was incidentally the reason for the speedy collapse of the French air force in 1940. Many of its members showed skill and courage as pilots with the voluntary formations of the R.A.F. after the collapse of France. The *Armeé de l'Air* was not so much beaten in the air as destroyed on the ground; drawn into the eddies of the French retreat it was drowned.

231

Something similar seemed to have started with the Luftwaffe during the evacuation of France. In any case the enemy considered us as already finished. From American documents the fact emerges that the Allied Command never expected the Luftwaffe to rise again. Actually the Allied air fleets met not only with stronger AA fire in the summer of 1944 when raiding the German towns but with the resistance of the German fighter force. Yet most of the reports of the American and British units on the Western front closed with the words: "No enemy resistance." During this summer another 18,000 tons of bombs were dropped on the German aircraft factories. On August 27, 1944, the R.A.F. night bombers made their first raid in daylight on a German town in the west.

As I have mentioned, our fighter units arrived at the Rhine in a chaotic condition. The wings, squadrons, and even the flights had got into a complete mix-up, and except for a few had shrunk to a fifth of their normal strength. It took a long time for the decimated ground crews to find their units. They had sustained great material losses. The *Todt Organisation* did well in salvaging aircraft that had been shot down, damaged, or grounded, as well as spare parts, vehicles, and equipment. It was also invaluable in preparing airstrips on the Rhine front. The existing ground organizations on both sides of the Rhine were in no position to cope with all these new units. Each aircraft Command now had additional airstrips under their care. Careful camouflage and dispersal was of greatest importance because of the constant danger from the air.

For the sake of re-establishing order within the fighter arm we introduced a complete regrouping. The 3rd Air Fleet was changed by Göring into the Air Force Command, West. It now comprised the replenished 2nd, 26th, 27th, and 53rd Fighter Wings. The 5th, 54th, 51st, and 52nd Fighter Wings were fighting at the Eastern front. The 3rd Wing was added to the 300th and 301st Wings for the defense of the Reich. My main desire was to create a new reserve. For this purpose I brought the 1st, 16th, 11th, and 17th Fighter Wings up to strength and reformed the 4th, 76th, and 7th Fighter Wings. The reconstruction made good progress. Oddly enough my proposal to give priority to the replenishing and the formation of reserves instead of sending forces to the front was accepted without demur by the Supreme Command. As in my two previous attempts in this direction, I maintained that this was the only possible way to deliver the necessary great blow in the defense of the Reich. This phrase was taken up in the highest quarters. The Great Blow became the slogan. It seemed that wings had been given to all who worked for the reconstruction of the fighter arm in the hope of meeting the enemy once more with some decisive chance of success. It should have been possible to reverse things in the air at home with about 2000 to 3000 fighter planes. This was now our aim for the next month.

At about this time, the middle of September, 1944, the Allied advance came to a standstill at the approaches to the West Wall. Only at one spot, at Aachen, did the enemy cross the border of the Reich. The West Wall, which had been hurriedly and scantily manned for defensive action, was not the reason for the unexpected halt to the Allied offensive. The enemy thought it necessary to reorganize and to improve his supply lines after his several-hundred-mile advance. Perhaps he believed he could force our unconditional surrender by merely increasing the air offensive against the Reich's territory, with no further casualties to the army. After the collapse of the front in France a belief that the war would soon be over at least before the end of 1944 was prevalent in the western camp. Paris fell on August 25. Three Allied army groups crossed France by forced marches: the 21st Army Group under Montgomery in the north, the 12th under Bradley, and the 6th under Devers, which had landed in the south of France on August 15.

Rome had already been occupied by the Allies on June 4, the first Axis capital to fall. Once the resistance at Monte Cassino ceased on May 21, the enemy was able to unite his forces advancing from the south with those which had landed at Anzio-Nettuno on May 25. At the time Churchill pleaded insistently that the Allied superiority in Italy should be used for a quick advance toward the Po River in order to start operations in a northeasterly direction and, assisted by landings at Trieste and Fiume, to advance to Laibach and gain a foothold on the Danube, thus taking the initiative in southeastern Europe. This plan was dropped only after Roosevelt exerted pressure and requested that troops from Italy should be made available for the landing in the south of France. Thus Kesselring succeeded in falling back in good order onto the so-called Gothic line in the Appenines, and along the Arno River. Here he held out almost without any support right to the end of the war.

When the Red army in August-September, 1944, with its advance on the Balkans, came into the operational range of the western air forces stationed in Italy, the American bombers received orders to assist the Russians by suitable raids. Ignoring the agreement of Teheran, the Soviets did not open their counteroffensive against the European Fortress simultaneously with the landing of the British and American armies in France but waited until June 22, when the invasion could be regarded as definitely successful and any chance of a setback had clearly been eliminated. The German front in the east had been so weakened by the crisis in the west that the Russians won quick and easy successes. On August 23, Romania broke its pact with Germany and on September 5 Bulgaria canceled her obligations. Von Weichs' army group, on its retreat from Greece, Albania, and Yugoslavia, tried desperately to make contact with the main German front which had retreated back to Hungary. To prevent this was the main aim of the American raids to assist the Red army. For better coordination General Eaker sent a liaison staff to Tolbuchin's army group H.Q. Moscow disliked this independent contact, but tolerated it until one day American fighter-bombers by mistake attacked a Soviet column at Nis, destroying 20 vehicles and killing one general, two officers, and three men. The Soviets then energetically forbade any further aid by the Americans and also any flying over the operational area of the Red army.

Almost simultaneously the last act of the west-east air cooperation in strategic bombing was played. After the successful raid by German bombers on Poltava only small units, mainly fighter-bombers, used the air bases which the Russians had lent them. When the Red army approached Warsaw in August and a national rising started in the Polish capital under General Bor-Komorowski, the British and the Americans thought it was time for a new large-scale operation. The anglophile rebels should be assisted and supplied by a mass operation of Allied heavy bombers. The only way of achieving this successfully was by intermediate landings. Stalin, whose troops had stopped at the gates of Warsaw, refused to give his sanction. Churchill and Roosevelt intervened personally, but in vain. Only when the rising forces were nearly exhausted did the Soviet permission come through. On September 18, 107 Flying Fortresses dropped 1284 containers with food and arms. Nine tenths of these fell into German hands. Soon afterward Stalin canceled his permission, and British bombers flew a last demonstration nonstop flight to Warsaw. They dropped a laurel wreath on the scene of the tragedy. A few days after the Polish rising had collapsed, the Red army entered the suburb of Praga, east of the Weichsel.

234

In the west Eisenhower decided to concentrate his forces on the left flank. The advance of Montgomery's army group received absolute priority. On September 4 he took Antwerp, a useful port for supplies. A breakthrough into the north German lowlands and an encirclement of the Ruhr seemed possible from the north. The British war leaders especially welcomed Montgomery's advance because it would liquidate the "rocket coast," as the Allies called the firing bases of the German V-weapons.

Eight days after the start of the invasion the first four V-1s had exploded in the British capital. The Allied bomber offensive could not prevent this. The landing had forced us to action even before preparations were finally completed. After a pause of three days the landing started on a large scale: 300 flying bombs were fired in the course of 24 hours. The surprise, especially at this critical moment of the invasion, had a great effect. On June 16 Churchill called his war cabinet for a very grave session. It came to the decision not to break off the battle of Normandy. London had to "take it," although no effort would be spared to master this latest danger.

The V-1 was a jet-propelled, gyropiloted, horizontal flying bomb with a high explosive load of 2000 pounds, an average speed of 400 mph. It was therefore relatively easy to bring down. The British air defense states that it destroyed 46 per cent before they reached their target, 5 per cent by the balloon barrage, 17 per cent by AA fire, and 24 per cent by fighter planes. Finally 2800 AA guns, 2000 barrage balloons, and all available fighter aircraft were mobilized against the "doodle bugs." Further, the bombing of the launching platforms was continued, although the results so far had to be regarded as unsatisfactory. In June the R.A.F. dropped 28 per cent of its total bomb load on German V-weapon bases. In July it rose to 42 per cent. All together during June, July, and August, English and American planes dropped more than 100,000 bombs on this new offensive weapon. Thus they absorbed about a quarter of the total amount of bombs dropped by the Allies.

Nevertheless the V-bomb attack continued. It must have been a discouraging discovery for the Allies that their great effort had no other result than to reduce the monthly total of the V-bombs sent over from 3000 to 2667. The R.A.F. had tried their new Tallboy bomb, weighing 10 tons. The Americans directed their radio-controlled B-17 filled with 20 tons of explosives against the firing ramps. All kinds of retaliation had been considered, including the use of poison gas, although this was once more discarded. A section of the war cabinet had to meet daily with Churchill presiding. Even during the Blitz and the Battle of the Atlantic such measures had never been taken.

Anderson finally suggested attacking the production and fuel sources for V-weapons "instead of continuously attacking nothing but the firing ranges in a blind rage." Spaatz, too, as opposed to Tedder, was of the far saner opinion that the best way to fight the German V-weapon offensive would be to paralyze the German war industry.

The Allied advance brought the discussion and the worries to a temporary end. On September 1 the last V-1 was fired from a mainland base at London. Eight days later the British Minister of Defense announced the "end of the battle against the flying bomb." The following day a London suburb was shaken by a heavy explosion. The first V-2 rocket had exploded on English soil, carrying a ton of explosives and traveling five times as fast as sound through the stratosphere. Against it there was practically no means of defense. The V-1 attack was also resumed launched from aircraft—only a speedy end of the war could save England from this new danger.

Between September 11 and 15 preparatory discussions were held for Montgomery's advance over the Maas, Waal, and Lek into the north of Holland and northern Germany. The greatest air landing operation of the war was to secure the Allied bridgeheads on the other side of the rivers. Two American, one British paratroop division, one Polish brigade, and smaller units were mobilized in England for this operation. Simultaneously on land Montgomery was to break through the German lines and make contact with the paratroops. The entire Allied air force was to assist this operation. This amounted at the time to 12,182 planes, 4294 of which were fighter aircraft. The Luftwaffe Command had 431 fighters available, at least on paper. The Allies therefore expected the greatest resistance from flak and decided to make the operation in daytime.

At night on September 16 and 17 bombers of the R.A.F. made a heavy attack on the dangerous flak positions and the airfields in the operational area. In the early hours of the morning these were followed by 852 American four-engined bombers, with fighter escort directed against the same targets. Finally more than 2000 transport aircraft and gliders landed 34,876 soldiers, 1927 vehicles, 568 guns, and 5227 tons of material. The landing and the consequent supply flights were all heavily protected by fighters. Over the landing area itself the Allies placed a strong continuous air umbrella.

To strengthen the German fighters in the west three wings of the reserve, which were just forming, were called upon and sent into this defensive battle. Naturally they could neither prevent this landing nor essentially influence it. Nevertheless in this action the Allies according to their own statement lost 240 aircraft and 139 gliders, most of them shot down by flak.

The British had the misfortune to land in the middle of the 9th and 10th S.S. Panzer Divisions which were on the march. The enemy had not noticed this movement. Also Montgomery's advance did not progress as planned. Already on September 21 the operation had to be regarded as a failure. The general gave as a reason for his failure insufficient air support by the Americans. But an American inquiry commission sent out by General Arnold found these facts: Too great an optimism regarding an early collapse of Germany, insufficient British land forces, and faulty timing. In any case a conclusive American report states: "The combined air and land operation, on which the Allies had based their greatest hopes, ended in failure."

Arnheim killed the hopes of an early end of the war. The expectation that Germany would now surrender unconditionally came to nothing. After the high spirits aroused by the quick advance there was a bad hang-over in the Allied camp. This feeling was increased when the enemy's reconnaissance found an unexpected rise in the numbers of the German fighters. At the front not much attention was paid to this, although the strongest German fighter resistance since the war was evident during the air operation in Holland and during the ensuing supply airlift. In the course of this month, September, the German fighter arm received 3013 single-engine fighter aircraft, newly built or repaired. The German aircraft production with a total of 4103 aircraft of all types per month reached the absolute peak of the war.

And this after a year of systematic raids! In the summer of 1944 alone the Allies dropped 18,500 tons of bombs on the German aircraft industry. After the Big Week, which was supposed to be the death blow to our armament, Speer had contrived the reconstruction and the dispersal of the industry. So far it had been concentrated in 27 larger works arranged on production, technical, and economical lines. Now it was spread over 729 medium and very small plants. Some were situated in tunnels, caves, or disused mines, some were hidden in forests, ravines, and villages. They were admirably

237

camouflaged and not only made air observation difficult for the Allies but also their spying and sabotage. The unbelievable difficulties of bringing air armament to such heights by "home industries" are impossible to describe.

From the end of September on, forces from the new reserves, could occasionally be sent out against American daylight raiders. On September 27 and 28, 64 four-engined bombers were shot down by fighters and by flak. On October 6 an American bomber force with fighter escort raided Berlin. We did not succeed in penetrating the fighter protection, but a single fighter squadron managed to outclimb the last bomber wing, dove on it, and, before the escort fighters got to the spot, destroyed the flight down to the last bomber. On the next day, October 7, 41 bombers were shot down. In those days the reports of the missions created great anxiety at Allied headquarters. Doolittle complained to Spaatz about insufficient fighter protection. The ratio of 2 to 1 between bombers and fighters was no longer adequate. It should be raised to 1 to 1, or better still two fighters to each bomber. A few days later at a conference of the General Staff he even demanded that strategic targets in Germany should temporarily be given precedence, in the shape of another Big Week against aircraft production.

In Washington these developments were considered gravely. A larger allocation of fighters was impossible. Production, and the dispatch of personnel and material had already been slowed up in expectation of the approaching end of the war. There was talk of reducing the number of bombers sent into action if they could not be protected, a consideration to which attacker and defender would certainly have reacted quite differently. Anyhow the large four-engined bomber formations were now divided into smaller groups of 20 to 25 aircraft. Greater alertness, greater discipline in formation flying, and the maximum effort by the accompanying fighters were ordered.

The German fuel supply was still top target for the new offensive. Up till the end of September, of 91 plants producing petrol only three were undamaged, and 24 only partly so. The fighter defense and the flak concentrations, which the enemy feared so much, had been unable to prevent this. In order to render the revival of the petrol industry impossible, the Allies renewed their precision raids as far as the autumn weather at the end of September permitted. During October about 13,000 tons of bombs were dropped on these targets, and during November 37,000 tons, increasing the total of bombs dropped so far on the German petrol industry to 100,000 tons. The fact that production did not sink any further, but increased from 23 per cent to 31 per cent of capacity, was due only to an almost unimaginable effort. Nevertheless the petrol supply became so short that at the start of the Ardennes offensive the stocks available to the German High Command were only big enough to last for five days.

During the resumption of the Allied petrol offensive the British night bombers were sometimes more successful than the American daylight raiders. The R.A.F. managed to paralyze completely the synthetic petrol plants of the Ruhr at Nordstern, Scholven, Wesseling, Homburg, Wanne-Eickel, Sterkrade, Castrop-Rauxel, Kamen, Bottrop, and Duisburg. They had obstinately improved their tactics and instruments. Our night fighters were blinded again in May and June by new methods of interference, and during the raids on Kiel and Stuttgart they were unable to shoot down a single British plane. Moreover there was certainly no lack of ingenuity in the use of new methods on the German side.

There was no shortage of night-fighter aircraft. From the middle of 1944 on we could even speak of a surplus. The decrease of the German night-fighter successes in this period was mainly due to interference, shortage of fuel, and the activities of the 100th Bomber Squadron. The task of this special unit was to mislead our fighters and to befog our conception of the air situation by clever deceptive maneuvers. This specialist unit finally performed its task so well that it was hardly ever absent from any of the British night operations. The 100th Bomber Squadron can claim to have set really difficult problems to the German Night Fighter Command. The British increased their raids at the end of 1944 from month to month, with decreasing losses.

At the end of October, Tedder advocated a plan which was to bring about the collapse of Germany within a few weeks by a concentration of all Allied air forces on the destruction of the German traffic network. A conference of international traffic experts and Allied information officers was called. They worked out a plan dividing Germany into nine zones, in which all traffic was to be laid waste. During the first weeks of November the plan was put into action. The German war industry was in great difficulties caused by the paralysis of transport, and it led to the fatal crisis.

The civilians had to suffer heavily once more during this last winter of the war. Not only did the British continue

239

their terror raids in addition to their attacks on military targets, but the Americans started blind bombing as the bad weather began. In the last four months of 1944, according to American statements, 80,000 people were killed and 130,000 houses destroyed during the blind saturation raids on German towns. But neither panic nor disorganization occurred to the degree "Bomber" Harris and others had forecast.

The offensive against German petrol supply, on the other hand, was bound to lead to the suffocation of the war production. Speer understood the inevitability of this development only too well. The Saar and Upper Silesia of course were still in German hands. In spite of the nearness to the front, the German mines were still working at full speed. But already the situation that arose a few months later could be foreseen; the time had come when it would be impossible to transport the coal produced, either by rail or by waterway. If it were impossible to stop the destruction from the air, then productively, technically, and also militarily, it would be impossible to continue with the conduct of the war. For the time being production was still running and in some branches had only just reached its highest output. During the year 1944, 40,593 aircraft of all types were produced and in no other year of the war had such a figure been reached.

The Great Blow had been carefully planned and worked out in all details. All commodores and commanders were called together for a rehearsal at the 1st Fighter Corps in Treuenbrietzen, during which four or five different action and approach flights were practiced with all variations. It was wholly agreed that in the frame of the planned action the following points had to be achieved:

1. In the first action at least 2000 fighters in 11 combat formations of the 1st Fighter Corps were to be brought into contact with the approaching bomber formation.

2. During the fly-in and the return of the enemy about another 150 fighters of the Luftwaffe Command, West, were to be sent up.

3. In the second action another 500 fighters were to be brought into contact with the enemy.

4. About 100 night fighters were to screen the borders toward Sweden and Switzerland to catch damaged or straggling single bombers.

5. To shoot down an approximate total of 400-500 four-engined bombers against a loss of about 400 aircraft and about 100-150 pilots.

This was going to be the largest and most decisive air battle of the war. On November 12, 1944, the entire fighter arm was ready for action: 18 fighter wings with 3700 aircraft and pilots. A fighting force such as the Luftwaffe had never possessed before. More than 3000 of these were expecting the Great Blow.

Now it was a question of awaiting favorable weather. Good weather was one of the essentials for this mass action. It was a difficult decision to hold back the defensive fighters, which were standing by in face of the air armadas dropping gigantic bomb loads daily. But contrary to my previous experience the leaders kept calm and did not insist on vain and costly forced action.

The enemy began to sense the strong German fighter potential in those days, but the main object of these combats was to train those units intended for the Great Blow.

In the middle of November I received an alarming order, the whole impact of which I could not foresee. The fighter reserves were to be prepared for action on the front where a great land battle was expected in the west. This was incredible! The whole training had been aimed at action in the defense of the Reich. All new pilots should have had some training in the totally different conditions at the front, but petrol shortage forbade this. With regard to the supply situation it would have been irresponsible to use the stores accumulated for the Great Blow for training purposes. Moreover the internal organization of the units, the tactics, the armament, the equipment, were only suited for the special task of the defense of the Reich. A readjustment within a fortnight, as had been ordered, could not be undertaken. The experience and standard of the unit leaders and pilots could be regarded as just passable for the defense of the Reich, but for action at the front they were absolutely out of the question. Besides the squadrons had now without exception a strength of 70 aircraft and were therefore much too large for the airfields at the front.

On November 20 the transfer to the West was ordered regardless of my scruples and objections. Only the 300th and the 301st Fighter Wings would remain in the Reich. I must admit that even now, as I took part in the discussions for the mobilization of the fighters in the west, it had not occurred to me that all these preparations were for our own counteroffensive. Until the very last I was kept in the dark, and only a few days before the start of the offensive in the Ardennes was I informed of the plan. Only then did I realize that the

High Command from the beginning had understood something quite different by the Great Blow, and that the intention to go over to the offensive in the west already existed at the end of July.

On October 11, Hitler was presented with the operational plan that had been worked out by the General Staff; and for the most part he sanctioned it. Right from the outset he had guaranteed a strong fighter support for the army under suppositions that, of course, did not exist.

By this time the preparations were much too advanced to make any serious attempt at changes. Also my influence with the High Command had sunk so low that any such attempt would have been hopeless. At the time I was merely tolerated, because no one knew who was to be my successor. The third and last formation of a reserve was to be the last major task as General of the Fighter Arm. The reserve was there; then it was taken away from me.

For me any sense in continuing the struggle collapsed at this moment.

Now that the Red army was prepared to push open the door to the west, the German leaders should have had no other aim than to throw all their forces against this enemy. If the German divisions were sent against the east instead of to the Ardennes, then it would still have been possible to stem the Red flood. If our fighters, about 4000 strong, were not to be used for their intended task of regaining air superiority over the Reich, then they might as well be used to assist the army in the last great battle of the war. They could have achieved quite different results against the enemy in the east than against the one in the west. Today it is an established fact that the German offensive in the west strengthened the position of the Kremlin against the Western Allies in the fateful decisions taken at the Yalta Conference.

At the end of January the Allies had won back heavily all the territory they had lost during our offensive in the Ardennes. In February the second German advance north and south of Strasburg was also repulsed. But in the east the storm broke on January 12; five Soviet army groups steam-rollered the German lines.

The Luftwaffe received its death blow at the Ardennes offensive. In unfamiliar conditions and with insufficient training and combat experience, our numerical strength had no effect. It was decimated while in transfer, on the ground, in large air battles, especially during Christmas, and was finally destroyed. Operation Ground Slab was the conclusion of this tragic chapter. In the early morning of January 1, 1945, every aircraft took off: some fighter units flying night fighters or bombers. They went into a large-scale well-prepared, low-level attack on Allied airfields in the north of France, Belgium, and Holland. With this action the enemy's air force was to be paralyzed in one stroke. In good weather this large-scale action should have been made correspondingly earlier. The briefing order demanded the very greatest effort from all units. According to records about 400 Allied planes were destroyed, but the enemy was able to replace material losses quickly. In this forced action we sacrificed our last substance. Because of terrific defensive AA fire from the attacked airfields, from flying through barrages intended against V-1 bombs, and from enemy fighters, and because of fuel shortage we had a total loss of nearly 300 fighter pilots, including 59 leaders.

Only by radically dissolving some units was it possible to retain the remainder. But this task fell to my successor.

27

What Possibilities Did We Have?

It was a bitter moment for me when in January, 1945, I was relieved from my post as General of the Fighter Arm. Yet today when time, experience, and insight into past events have shown the divergence of the concepts by which the war was waged so opposed to mine, I am glad I was able once more to join the ranks of the army of millions of German soldiers who even during this hopeless state of the war still did their duty and did not stop for military and political considerations. As soon as I was back at the front in action, no matter how hopeless, this thought was a great relief to me.

The material and personal disputes have also lost the bitterness I felt about them at the time. I only propose to relate those details necessary to an understanding of the crisis in the Luftwaffe Command that broke out openly near the end of 1944 and the beginning of 1945.

Göring's prestige and influence had suffered continuously since the Battle of Britain and had weakened so greatly after the catastrophe of Hamburg that it was doubtful if he could ever have recovered them again. The man who had been chosen to be Hitler's successor, "The Führer's most faithful paladin," as he called himself with pride, the creator of the Luftwaffe, perhaps the only one of the National-Socialist leaders who had ever enjoyed real popularity with the mass of the German people, now retired from leadership and public life. At the end of 1944 Göring made his last strenuous attempt to regain the confidence of the Führer, the Luftwaffe, and of the people. It was too late. Mistakes and omissions had started a chain reaction which could never be halted.

As the central force that the Reichsmarshal had represented for the Luftwaffe since its birth weakened, other forces surged into the lead of the air force. Certain circles formed that fought for influence and position. Decisions were not made on a realistic plane but as a result of the tough struggle which had started between the overlapping circles. This grew more bitter from day to day.

Following the special heavy raids on our fuel production before and during the Anglo-American invasion, the petrol shortage made it necessary to dissolve a whole series of flying units whose further existence could no longer be justified. Besides bomber, reconnaissance, and transport units, all units of the 9th Flying Corps and the corps itself were axed. Originally it had been formed out of the "Assault leaders against England," to counter "terror by terror."

The wings of the 9th Flying Corps were transferred to the Prague area and retrained for fighter planes; this demanded fighter instructors and trainers, and blocked our reserve squadron and our leader pilot training courses. It was now called KG (J) (J = fighter).

From now on Bomber Command gained more and more influence in the fighter arm. As a result of this development the last act of the jet-fighter tragedy, of which I shall speak in the next chapter, took on a specially dramatic character. Comparable with the cogwheels of a gearbox the circles of different interests in the Luftwaffe no longer interlocked properly.

It could not remain hidden from Göring that a first-rate crisis, concerning trust and leadership, was brewing in the fighter arm, from the leader right down to the last man. How far he had estranged himself from the fighter arm, and how little he still knew of its spirit and its heavy struggle, could be seen from the way he tried to alleviate the precarious situation. He called together the leaders of all day- and night-fighter units, as far as they could be reached, to a meeting at the headquarters of the Air Fleet, Reich, near Wannsee. It was supposed to be the last beating of the drums before the Great Blow. It turned out a fiasco. Göring lost his control and raved. His insulting aggressiveness achieved not the inspiring effect he intended but only bitterness and revolt. One can only speak like that to a group if one still has their trust and respect. The units at the front openly made sharp and derogatory remarks about the Reichsmarshal. We fighter pilots were indeed prepared to fight and to die, as we had proved often enough, but we were not prepared to let ourselves be insulted or blamed for the disastrous situation in the air over the Reich. Most unnecessarily Göring ordered on top of all this that his impossible speech should be recorded. The record was to be played at intervals to the pilots at action stations. I cannot vouch for the execution of any other order given to the fighter arm less than this one.

The mistrust of the leaders was not restricted to the fighter

245

arm. By forming various fanatical rival groups the officer corps of the Luftwaffe had lost the homogeneity on which depends the fighting strength and the value of any unit. Up to January, 1945, my position remained unchanged. But when I was sent on leave without a successor being appointed, the news created some unrest among the fighter arm. This was the last of a series of reasons why several wing commanders, some of whom had simultaneously been relieved of their posts, approached Lützow and Trautloft and after serious consultation arrived at the conclusion, "It cannot go on like this any more." A delegation was to try and get an audience with Hitler to make a direct report and to press for a radical change. But this never came about. The upright and courageous Oberst Lützow was then chosen as speaker for the fighter arm. At the instigation of Chief of General Staff Koller and the senior pilot of World War I, the Commander of the 4th Air Fleet, Ritter von Greim, a delegation headed by Lützow was received by Göring. After he had been told the seriousness of the situation in the fighter arm with great frankness, he called all commodores of fighter wings that could be contacted for a meeting.

The meeting was held in Berlin in the *Haus der Flieger* and it took a very dramatic turn. Lützow had drawn up the suggestions and demands of the fighter arm in the form of a memorandum. This referred essentially to the following points: Overwhelming influence of Bomber Command in the fighter force; equipment of bomber instead of fighter squadrons with the ME-262; impossible demands for bad-weather operations; insults to the fighter arm and doubts about its fighting spirit expressed by the Commander-in-Chief; distrust of the Reichsmarshal's influential advisers; and the dismissal of the General of the Fighter Arm.

Lützow's suggestions and criticisms exploded like a bomb. As the demands presented in the name of the fighter arm coincided with those I had always brought up, Göring saw me as the instigator—the ex-general of the fighters who could not take part any more in the conferences. Göring in a fury closed the meeting, called the action of the fighter pilots mutiny, and left the room addressing Lützow: "I'll have you court-martialed." And 48 hours later Lützow was exiled from Germany. The ban included the ruling that he was not allowed to communicate either with me or any other fighter pilots except on matters directly concerning the service. He became a squadron commander in Italy.

Next morning I was called to see the Chief of the Person-

246

nel Department, who informed me of Göring's indignation and his suspicion that I was the driving force behind the "mutiny" of the fighter pilots. I was ordered to leave Berlin within 12 hours, I was to keep myself in readiness for being called up and to report my whereabouts. Simultaneously all fighter units were informed by teleprinter.

I knew what it was all about, but I had not expected the measures taken against me. I was about to be drawn into the whirlpool that the sinking of the Reichsmarshal's ship, already drifting on stormy waves, keel uppermost, would cause when it was sinking. Naturally I had committed many mistakes, although they were different from the ones of which I was now accused. The intention to use me publicly as a scapegoat is understandable when one realizes the desperate situation in which the Luftwaffe and especially Göring found themselves.

During the chaos that prevailed I had returned to Berlin without permission. I came to the conclusion that the choice of possibilities remaining open to me was not large. But things turned out quite differently. I was unexpectedly ordered to report at the Reichskanzlei. Here one of Hitler's air force adjutants declared to me that the Führer had known nothing of the measures taken against me, that he had now seen through the game and had given an order to "stop this nonsense at once."

The Galland Affair was closed herewith. The last little mistake on the part of the government could do nothing more than amuse. Göring called me to Karin Hall, not knowing that I was already informed about Hitler's decision. I was no longer impressed when the stern judge finally declared that he had decided to take no further action against me in recognition of past services to the fighter arm.

In conclusion, Göring told me that Hitler had granted my petition, had revoked the grounding order against me, and had ordered that I should be given the opportunity to prove personally my constantly repeated statement about the fighting value of the jet fighter. I was to form a unit with ME-262s. I could choose my own pilots. He recommended to me the obstinate and recalcitrant commanders and commodores whom he had recalled, headed by the "leader of the mutiny," Lützow. The new General of the Fighter Arm was to have no jurisdiction over my new unit. On the other hand it was to be in a sort of quarantine and to have no connection with any of the other units. This had the advantage that as far as operations were concerned I was completely independent and under no jurisdiction of division, corps, or fleet.

The ring was closing. As lieutenant and flight captain I went into the war; I should end it as lieutenant general and flight captain. That was a task for me. A fighter section which as far as jurisdiction went was so to speak airborne. A few selected German elite fighter pilots! Jet fighters in what we thought to be the best planes in the world! And I was the fortunate man who was allowed to form and lead this strongest flight of fighters in the history of the war.

Since the end of World War I, scientists, designers, and daring spirits had devoted their genius to the development of rocket and jet propulsion, and they tried now to utilize this principle, which had already been used for missiles, for the propulsion of aircraft. Suddenly, when they succeeded in directing the released energies of rockets, burning fluid fuel, and later as the turbojet blower was developed, jet propulsion for aircraft became the focal point of interest. Both methods made it possible to develop energies, allowing speeds up to the sound barrier, which so far had been regarded as impossible. Even supersonic speeds came theoretically within the reach of the practical. This announced a complete revolution of aviation.

Since the years 1937-38 intensive experiments were made in Germany with the aim of exploring the new means of propulsion for military aviation. The principle of using the reaction effect of very rapidly escaping exhaust gas as a thrusting force for aircraft propulsion appeared in three main forces:

Rocket propulsion uses fluid fuel oil that is continuously burned, and the necessary oxygen for the combustion is contained in one of the fuels carried. Theoretically such an engine can work under the water as well as in the stratosphere. For aircraft propulsion it is independent of altitude.

The *turbojet engine* works on the same fundamental principle but the oxygen is taken from the surrounding air and is conducted into the engine via a many-chambered turbine. Its aviation ceiling is determined by the oxygen content of the atmosphere it passes through. Rocket propulsion uses about 17 times as much fuel as the turbojet engine.

Jet propulsion differs from the turbojet principle only in that it receives the oxygen by the natural pressure of air created when flying, instead of by a turbine. Therefore it is dependent not only on altitude but also on the speed achieved.

The first fighter plane of the world to exceed the speed of 600 mph had rocket propulsion. It was built by Messerschmitt

248

in Augsburg before the outbreak of World War II, in April, 1939. Its designer, Dr. Alexander Lippisch, developed it from a tailless glider, which was flown by the unforgettable Günther Grönhoff until his fatal crash in 1932. The other forerunners from the tailless propeller planes to the final rocket aircraft were tested by Dittmar, until he had a bad accident. Rudolf Opitz continued his work. Other representatives of the German glider-pilot elite like Hanna Reitsch and Wolfgang Spate sponsored and flew the plane. Several prototypes had been already built by the beginning of the war and bore the mark ME-163.

Professor Walter in Kiel developed the rocket-propulsion engine. The same designer also introduced revolutionary innovations in the field of U-boat construction and the propulsion of torpedoes as well as power units for different rocket projectiles and other flying missiles, which were later employed as V-weapons. His rocket engine HWK 509, which was used in the ME-163, ran on so-called T- and C-fuel in a mixture of 3 to 1. The problem of finding a workable solution for bringing fuel consumption and the necessary degree of safety during operation into a suitable relationship with the required performance of the aircraft gave the development experts the greatest difficulties.

In the autumn of 1940, when the Battle of Britain was already dying down, I had an opportunity to acquaint myself more thoroughly with Dr. Lippisch's planes. Generalluftzeugmeister Udet introduced them to me at Luftwaffe High Command H.Q. and discussed them with me in detail. He thought this first rocket-fighter plane in the world was of very great importance for a possible air defense of the Reich. To speak of such a possibility was at the time still regarded as defeatism by the Luftwaffe Command. In his opinion experiments, development, and designs in the realm of revolutionary, novel ideas, and together with these the entire development of aviation, were decisively retarded by the order from the Führer which had just been issued demanding that all technical experiments and development jobs not likely to be ready for utilization within 18 months be postponed indefinitely. The order was based on the expectation of a speedy termination of the war. The entire capacity was therefore to be concentrated on this aim. It is a proof of the high standard of German science and technique that they were able nevertheless to achieve such a great step ahead of other countries in the field of V-weapons and jet planes. Udet undoubtedly deserves the credit for the fact that the work in the planning departments and the designing offices of the aircraft and motor works continued despite the Führer's orders, because with the authority of his position he gave full backing to the firms concerned. Naturally in these conditions he could not give matters the priority and assistance they deserved, but he saw to it that the work was continued at least to a modest extent. Only because of this had we something to build on when in the face of defeat the cry for special weapons was raised. That Germany had V-weapons during the last phase of the war, even at a moment when the conditions for their effective use had vanished, justice demands that credit be given to those men who continued their developments against the will and the express orders of Hitler.

Until the engine was completed, the ME-163 was tested as a glider by Dittmar in an almost vertical dive at a speed in the region of 550 mph. This speed had not yet been reached in horizontal flight by the so-called cold rocket engine. But the performances achieved were absolutely extraordinary right from the start. Particularly remarkable was the high rate of climb, which later for the mass-produced plane was about 300 to 360 feet per second, so that the normal altitude of approach of the American bomber formations could be reached in three to four minutes including the take-off.

The world speed record at the time of 475 mph was already exceeded during the fourth test flight at Peenemünde. And at last the day came! Heini Dittmar described his attack on the speed of 600 mph, which had been regarded as impossible, as follows:

"The tension grew daily as the speed increased from one flight to the next. From now on a measuring basis was established for each take-off, so that in each case the exact flying speed could also be registered from the ground by the three kinotheodolites. The next flight was registered with 550 mph and the following one with 570 mph. Because the rudder started to flutter at this speed I once lost the whole rudder-control connection. Nevertheless the landing went off well.

"Now things got serious. Another three or four flights were necessary in order to reach our goal, because the engine always stopped when I got near the 565-mph mark. The next time in order to save fuel, I let myself be towed by an ME-210 up to 300 feet, then I cast off and climbed on my own power to 12,000 feet and flew with full throttle over the accurately measured course. The airspeed indicator already showed 565 mph and rose steadily, 580, 585, 590 were reached. The engine did not fail me this time. When I looked again at the instruments the speed was surely over 600. The needle of the airspeed indicator was jumping. The left elevator started to vibrate, at the same moment the nose dipped, the plane dived out of control with the usual increase in speed. I cut the engine and regained control immediately, although during those few seconds I thought that the end had come. An exact evaluation of the taken measurings resulted in a speed of 601 mph. This was on May 10, 1941!"

More than three years passed before Wolfgang Spate could form the first ME-163 test group in Brandis near Leipzig. Its aim was to provide additional protection for the Leuna synthetic petrol works which were raided particularly heavily and frequently at the end of 1944. A further group was stationed at Stargard near Stettin to protect the large synthetic plant at Pölitz. Further defensive barriers of rocket-fighter formations were planned for Berlin, the Ruhr, and the German Bight.

This type of air defense of a single object suited the characteristics of the ME-163. The "power-egg," as this aircraft was called because of its squat build and its incredible ability to develop power, could, with its five tons of fuel, only fly for a few minutes under power between take-off and landing. At an operational height of 30,000 feet, its tactical operational range was about 50 miles. It was directly guided by a ground directing post, attached to the group and equipped with one or two radar sets. If an enemy formation or a single aircraft approached the 50-mile radius the rocket planes of the group took off singly, calculated to the second, one after the other in quick succession. They climbed in loose formation on a course given to them by the directing post. On sighting the enemy formation they climbed another 3000 feet above it. From this position they made one or two attacks and then glided or dove back without power to their base. Following the enemy was out of the question. For the landing operation a few seconds' fuel reserve was saved. They landed on a skid. The undercarriage was dropped immediately after the take-off. Take-off and landing were the weakest points of the ME-163. Experiments with catapulting or take-off ramps as well as towing by aircraft were under way. The operational safety of the engine still created trouble. The armament also had to be considerably improved. After long delays it went into action during the second half of 1944, too-hastily under the pressure of the situation. Much valuable time was lost, but finally the Allied offensive also paralyzed the production of the ME-163, of which 100 aircraft per month were being

251

turned out. The fact that it had the same fuel basis as the V-2 and other novel rocket weapons which were in preparation during the last phase of the war, had not been considered early enough.

Thus one of the epoch-making, revolutionary technical developments of Germany during the last war passed without having any practical effect. It would have been ideal to prove the correctness of my contention that superior technical achievements—used correctly both strategically and tactically —can beat any quantity numerically many times stronger yet technically inferior.

Most of the ME-163s fell into the hands of the Soviets during the collapse. Also the development of the ME-163, the JU-263B went the shortest way from Dessau to Moscow. Dr. Lippisch, the designer of the ME-163, has been working since 1945 for the Northrop works in the United States; and fundamental principles of his construction ideas can be seen in many of the fastest supersonic trial planes of the USAF. It is an undeniable fact that the Russians too have benefited greatly from the pioneer work of German scientists and designers of jet-propulsion engines and aircraft construction.

Four days before the declaration of World War II, on August 27, 1939, the test pilot van Chaim flew the first jet aircraft in the world, the Heinkel 178. Only a small circle of people directly concerned knew of this event, which for that time was of great importance. Exactly a year later, on August 27, 1940, the first Italian jet plane, the Caproni-Campini made its first flight. It reached 300 mph, and the event received great propaganda. The British followed with their Gloster-Whittle E. 28/39 on May 15, 1941. But of this we learned as little at the time as we did of the fact that chief pilot Robert M. Stanley in the United States flew the Bell Airacomet on October 1, 1941. Thus jet aviation was not, like all significant inventions, including radar, invented in one country alone, but matured simultaneously in different countries with high scientific development. At the beginning of this development Germany was indeed clearly ahead of the Western Allies by 18 months, but no strategical benefit matured from it. The following pages will give an insight into the tragic chain of circumstances that were the cause of this.

With us the development of the first jet fighter, prototypes progressed under such secrecy that even I, as General of the Fighter Arm, learned about it relatively late. This secrecy, which in technical matters was not always so complete in Germany, can be explained by the fact that the necessary work had to be done against the order of the Führer. Only in the beginning of 1942 did I attend a conference held by Generalluftzeugmeister Milch with the chief test pilot and the designers Messerschmitt and Heinkel.

Already in the earliest stages of the development of jet planes the question arose: bomber or fighter? At the first conference in which I took part I stated my point of view clearly:

"I must put on record that it is fundamentally wrong to plan our development one-sidedly, to specify a superfast bomber without considering simultaneously that the same aircraft, or perhaps a similar one, may be needed most urgently as a superfast fighter even before the fast bomber."

As the question "bomber or fighter?" later assumed a tragic importance for the development of the ME-262, I think it only right to say here that Professor Messerschmitt, according to the minutes of the meeting, replied to my remarks with the words, "I am of the same opinion." He asked to be allowed to produce at the same time "at least a few hundred fighters with jet propulsion."

A year later, in May, 1943, Messerschmitt informed me that the test flights of his ME-262 prototypes had now progressed so far that he begged me to fly one and judge for myself. He was convinced of the future of the developed type. If my judgment was favorable, we would try with a demonstration to win the Supreme Command over to the mass production of the jet fighter. Feldmarshal Milch declared himself agreeable to our plan. With the ME-262 we had a hope of being able to give the fighter arm a superior aircraft at the very moment when Allied air superiority was opening up catastrophic prospects for Germany in the war in the air because of the increased range and overwhelming number of the American fighter escort.

I shall never forget May 22, 1943, the day I flew a jet aircraft for the first time in my life. In the early morning I met Messerschmitt on his testing airfield, Lechfeld, near the main works at Augsburg. Besides his designers and technicians and the jet-engine experts from Junkers there were the Commander of the Luftwaffe Testing Station, Rechlin, and his chief fighter test pilot, Behrens, who later crashed fatally in Argentina while testing the jet fighter, Pulqui II. After the introductory speeches by the specialists who had taken part in the construction, there was a tension full of expectation.

We drove out to the runway. There stood the two jet fighter ME-262's, the reason for our meeting and all our great hopes.

An unusual sight, these planes without propellers. Covered by a streamlined cowling, two nacelles under the wings housed the jet engines. None of the engineers could tell us how much horsepower they developed. In answer to our questions they feverishly worked their slide rules and only determined x-kilogram thrust at y speed at x altitude which, with the flying weight in question, would correspond to a developed force of H.P. propeller propulsion. This caused distrust among us pilots, who were not yet accustomed to the properties of this hitherto-unknown force of thrust. But the engineers were right in their strange calculations. Comparisons with the propulsive properties of propellers were indeed unsuitable. If the characteristics of performance, which the firms had calculated and partially flown, were only approximately correct, then undreamed-of possibilities lay ahead. And this was all that counted!

The flying speed of 520 mph in horizontal flight, which was fantastic at that time, meant an advance of at least 120 mph over the fastest propeller-driven aircraft. Inferior diesel-like oil could be used as fuel instead of octane, which was more and more difficult to get.

The chief pilot of the works made a trial demonstration with one of the "birds." After it was refueled I climbed in. With many manipulations the mechanics started the turbines. I followed their actions with the greatest of interest. The first one started quite easily. The second caught fire. In no time the whole engine was on fire. Luckily as a fighter pilot I was used to getting quickly in and out of a cockpit. The fire was quickly put out. The second plane caused no trouble. I took off along a runway, which was 50 yards wide, at a steadily increasing speed but without being able to see ahead. This was on account of the conventional tail wheel with which these first planes were still fitted instead of the front wheel of the mass-produced ME-262. Also I could not use the rudder for keeping my direction: that had to be done for the time being with the brakes. The runway is never long enough! I was doing 80 mph. At last the tail rose. I could see. The feeling of running my head against a wall in the dark was over. Now, with reduced air resistance, the speed increased quickly. The 120-mph mark was passed. Long before reaching the end of the runway the plane rose gently off the ground.

For the first time I was flying by jet propulsion! No engine vibrations. No torque and no lashing sound of the propeller. Accompanied by a whistling sound, my jet shot through the air. Later when asked what it felt like, I said, "It was as though angels were pushing."

Yet the sober reality, conditioned by the war, did not allow me any time to enjoy fully this new feeling of being pushed while flying. Flying characteristics—maneuverability, top speed, rate of climb—during that few minutes' flight I had to formulate my judgment of this new aircraft.

Just then the four-engined Messerschmitt flew over Lech-feld. It became the object of my first exercise in jet-fighter attack. I know that from below they were watching me with more technical than tactical eyes and that my maneuvers would worry them. These first products of a highly developed technique could be handled more carelessly than raw eggs, but what could be achieved with them exceeded all conceptions and ideas so far; therefore safety factors were of no possible interest for the moment.

On landing I was more impressed and enthusiastic than I had ever been before. But feelings and impressions were no criterion, but the performance and characteristics were ascertained. This was not a step forward; this was a leap!

We drove back to the factory for the final discussion. In the distance on the runway stood the two ME-262s. They appeared to me like "silver streaks on the horizon." Today I still believe that it was not exaggerated optimism to expect from a mass action of ME-262 fighters a fundamental change in the German air defense even at that late hour. I was only afraid that the enemy might catch up to us in the development—or even surpass us. This worry remained one of the few that was unfounded. But large-scale operations by ME-262s never matured for quite different reasons. I could not guess these reasons when I sent the following telegram to Feld-marshal Milch following my first test flight:

"The aircraft 262 is a very great hit. It will guarantee us an unbelievable advantage in ops., while the enemy adheres to the piston engine. For air-worthiness it makes the best impression. The engines are absolutely convincing, except during take-off and landing. This aircraft opens up completely new tactical possibilities."

28

The Jet-fighter Tragedy

Any soldier knows that during a war it is not always the pon-
derables that count, but that a great deal depends on luck.
After this flight I believed that I was in luck. This was no
dream or fantasy, no daring project that would become reality
in some distant future. The jet fighter ME-262, the fastest
fighter aircraft on earth, was a fact. I had flown it. And I knew
that with it we could beat any other fighter plane. Of course
it still had to be nursed through its infancy. But all of us, who
sat down for a round-table conference were convinced that
everything had to be done to make use of this unique opportunity. Risks had to be taken and unusual means had to be
found. Thus a joint suggestion was worked out proposing an
immediate start on the construction of a first series of 100
aircraft to serve simultaneously first technical and tactical
tests. Such a procedure was contrary to the usual care applied
in German aircraft construction. We wanted to prepare immediately for the final mass production, and we thought of
using the time it would take until production really started
to gather the necessary experiences with these first 100 aircraft.
The changes we found necessary could then be applied to the
first production series.

This suggestion, together with the report of the flight, was
worked out then and there and signed. A duplicate was sent
to Milch, and I traveled on the same day with the original to
Göring in Burg Veltenstein. Göring shared our enthusiasm.
He would not have been a fighter pilot had he not shown full
understanding for the train of thought resulting from my first
trial flight with the ME-262. In my presence Göring telephoned
to Milch, who also had the report and the suggestions in hand.
He too was in complete agreement. All suggestions were accepted with amazing speed and enthusiastic resolutions. I
thought that I had already won all along the line. The Reichsmarshal first had to get Hitler's sanction, which was necessary

256

for such an important decision; but this would undoubtedly be granted, since we had such determined support from the experts. First thing next morning Göring wanted to see the Führer and inform him personally of all the details. In the meantime I was to hold myself in readiness to tell him my impressions and judgments if necessary.

The next days passed without any news or orders from above. I was very eager to win Hitler over to our plan. As days passed I had an idea that our hopes for a quick development of the German jet fighter would not be realized. Hitler had refused to give his sanction. He had already conceived a great distrust of Göring and the Luftwaffe, and wanted to convince himself personally about the soundness of our suggestion. He told Göring—and not without justification—that the Luftwaffe had disappointed him too often in the past with promises and announcements of technical innovations and improvements. The heavy bomber, the HE-177, had been promised him not later than 1941, and even today no one could foresee when this aircraft would go into action. The ME-262 should not be rushed. Nothing was going to be done about it until he had decided.

The fact that he did not call any member of the Luftwaffe to the conference of experts that he held showed how great Hitler's distrust really was. He even forbade their participation. The Reichsmarshal took this obvious affront quite passively.

The Führer demanded from the assembled engineers, constructors, and specialists binding promises and guarantees, which they were unable to give. With these securities our plans would have implied no risks. But we had started from the premise that the great possibilities in view would justify the acceptance of certain risks. Hitler himself in most of his plans had accepted much greater factors of uncertainty! He overrode even Messerschmitt and the other responsible men who a few days before had worked out with me the plan under discussion. He hardly let them speak, and ordered that the technical tests of the ME-262 should be continued with a few prototypes, expressly forbidding any kind of preparation for mass production. This far-reaching decision was taken without the agreement of the Supreme Commander of the Luftwaffe.

Thereby the production of the ME-262 received a further delay of six months after it had already suffered a delay of about two years, due to the previous order given in autumn, 1940, to postpone all research developments. I believe that in this way about 18 months were lost in the development of the ME-262. We fighter pilots knew what such a length of time meant in the technical advance of aerial warfare. At the fronts and over the Reich we experienced daily the growing supe riority of the enemy not only in quantity but also in quality.

At the end of 1943, under conditions that were much more unfavorable than those a year and a half before, the High Command became interested once more in the ME-262. Suddenly they wanted its full mass production. It received a very high priority in the armament program. On November 2, 1943, Göring visited the Messerschmitt works to learn how the work was progressing. In a conversation with Willy Messerschmitt on this occasion they discussed a subject which was to be of decisive importance to the growing tragedy of the German jet fighter. Göring asked Messerschmitt how far the ME-262 would be able to carry one or two bombs, to act as a surprise fighter-bomber, and he continued, "I want to tell you the trend of the Führer's thought. He discussed this matter with me a few days ago and he is deeply concerned with the solution of this problem . . ."

Perhaps Hitler was already worried about the imminent Anglo-American invasion. As a defense against this he must have had hopes for the jet fighter in addition to the V-weapon project. That was the reason why the jet fighter was now demanded and advanced from higher offices. But instead of using it to take away from the Allies, step by step, their air superiority, without which the invasion, according to Eisenhower, would have been the greatest disaster in the history of the war, the jet fighter was now to become a fighter-bomber as a supplementary weapon for the army.

Messerschmitt answered Göring evasively. Naturally it was possible to fit the ME-262 with fixtures to carry light bombs, like any other fighter, if the known loss of performance were accepted. During the Battle of Britain the question, "fighter or fighter-bomber?" had been decided once and for all: The fighter can only be used as a bomb carrier with lasting effect when sufficient air superiority has been won. Already over England this first condition did not apply on our side, but now it could not even be mentioned.

When I was present at a demonstration of the latest Luftwaffe technical developments in December, 1943, at the aviation center at Insterburg in East Prussia, I did not know anything about the possible considerations not to use the ME-262 as a fighter. Hitler had come over from his nearby headquarters. The jet fighter ME-262 caused a special sensation. I was standing right beside him when he suddenly asked Göring, "Can this aircraft carry bombs?"

Göring had already discussed the question with Messerschmitt, and replied, "Yes my Führer, theoretically yes. There is enough power to spare to carry 1000 pounds, perhaps even 2000 pounds."

This was a carefully formulated answer which objectively could not be disputed. Among aviators this reply would have created no disturbance. Because any expert knew it was purely hypothetical. The ME-262 possessed no fixtures for releasing bombs and no bombsights. According to its flying properties and its safety conditions it was highly unsuited for an aimed-bomb release; diving or gliding were out of the question because of the unavoidable excess of the permissible top speed. At speeds of over 600 mph the aircraft became uncontrollable. At low altitudes the fuel consumption was so high that the operative range became unprofitably small; therefore low-level attacks, too, were out of the question. There remained high-altitude bombing, yet here the given target had to be at least the size of a large town to be hit with certainty under the given conditions.

But who could explain all this to Hitler at the moment? In any case, who would have had a chance of his argument being understood, to say nothing of being accepted? Of course it was the duty of the Reichsmarshal, with whom Hitler had spoken on these questions, to point all this out to him. I did not know if he had done so. Anyhow the Führer gave neither Messerschmitt nor ourselves an opportunity to explain.

He said, "For years I have demanded from the Luftwaffe a 'speed bomber,' which can reach its target in spite of enemy fighter defense. In the aircraft you present to me as a fighter plane I see the 'Blitz bomber,' with which I will repel the invasion in its first and weakest phase. Regardless of the enemy's air umbrella it will strike the recently landed mass of material and troops creating panic, death, and destruction. *At last this is the Blitz bomber!*—Of course none of you thought of that!"

Hitler was right. Indeed no one had thought of that! And we were still not thinking of it. The existing program for production and tests for the ME-262 continued unchanged. In collaboration with the Luftwaffe research unit and the Messerschmitt works, I formed a commando of experienced fighter pilots, who started with tests in real action against English Mosquito daylight reconnaissance planes. At last we had a fighter which was superior to the fastest Allied aircraft. Soon the first kills were achieved.

The tactical and technical trials went hand in hand as we

had planned from the start. One detachment of the commando was stationed at the Messerschmitt aircraft factory at Augsburg, a second at the Luftwaffe research station at Rechlin, north of Berlin. The collaboration between all military and industrial departments developed extremely well and quickly. Everybody knew that we were concerned here with a really decisive and important weapon at a more than critical point of the war.

But the Allies also knew what it was all about. The first single encounters with the new German rocket fighter ME-163 had already alarmed the enemy. The Americans had not yet made the acquaintance of the ME-262. But information from the Allied intelligence service and the observation reports by the British Mosquito pilots made General Doolittle arrive at the conclusion that if the German jet fighters appeared in sufficient numbers they would make daylight raids impossible.

The concentrated raids by the entire Allied air fleet in February, 1944, under the code name Big Week directed against the German aircraft industry also caused heavy damage to the production of the ME-262. Because of the damage to the factories at Augsburg and Regensburg the tardily ordered series of 100 planes could not be delivered. Increased difficulties in personnel and material retarded the final course of production further until the end of March, 1944. When four weeks later the first batch was ready to leave the assembly works at Leipheim, they were hit by a heavy American daylight raid on April 24. Because of Hitler's interference we were not much further advanced than a year before, when, directly following my first test flight, we wanted to start mass production. At that time we would have had less difficulties to overcome.

About that time, April, 1944, at an armament conference, I gave a résumé of the situation in the air as I saw it:

"The problem of fighter aviation—I am only pointing out here the problem of the fighters—which the Americans have created is simply that of air superiority. The development as it is proceeding now already borders on air supremacy. The ratio of numbers which we fight in daytime lies approximately between 1-to-6 and 1-to-8. The standard of the enemy is extraordinarily high. The technical performance of their planes is so considerable that one must say: Something has to be done about it! Daylight fighting in the last four months has caused a loss of more than 1000 men of the flying personnel. Among these of course were many of the best flight

260

captains, squadron leaders, and wing commanders. We have trouble in closing these gaps, not with numbers, but with experienced pilots.

"Which path must we follow to lead us out of this situation?

"First, the ratio of numbers must be changed; this means that the aircraft industry must guarantee the delivery of enough aircraft to allow us to build up the fighter arm. Second, the technical performance must be higher, especially as we have less planes and always will have. Of this we are fully aware. . . . I am of the opinion that already with a small number of technically superior planes, such as the ME-262 or the ME-163, we could achieve a great deal, since the conflict between the fighters—which is a prerequisite if we want to shoot down any bombers in daytime at all—is for the most part a question of morale. The enemy's morale has to be broken. With the aid of these two components, number and performance, the fighting value of our units will rise, and also the standard of training. I do not expect that we shall ever achieve an equal footing, but I think that we shall achieve a reasonable ratio.

"During the last ten attacks we have lost, on the average, over 50 aircraft and about 40 pilots. That means 500 planes and 400 pilots in ten raids. At this rate we cannot replace them in the existing training conditions.

"We need quality of performance, if only to restore in our own force the sense of superiority, even if our numbers are smaller.

"For example to give some idea of values: *At the moment I would rather have one ME-262 than five ME-109's."*

The armament department accepted my point of view. The part which the ME-262 played in this planning became more important from month to month. Three months after the beginning of this program its production figure was to exceed 1000 aircraft monthly. But Hitler rejected this plan. He still refused to think in terms of air defense.

This was shattering enough, but the tragic climax of the history of the jet fighter was reached when the Führer, at a discussion on the emergency program, came to talk about the ME-262. After the situation of tests and construction had been debated, he asked suddenly how many of the finished aircraft were able to carry bombs. Milch, who because of a quarrel with Göring had not been present when Hitler had expounded his ideas on the Blitz bomber at Insterburg, answered true to the facts, "None, my Führer; the ME-262 is being built exclusively as a fighter aircraft."

Hitler foamed with rage. Officers who were close to him told me later that they had rarely witnessed such a fit of temper. He raged against Milch, Göring, and the Luftwaffe at large, accusing them of unreliability, disobedience, and unfaithfulness. Soon afterward Milch was dismissed from his post.

Hitler's reaction was all the more surprising because no one present at Insterburg had taken the idea of the Blitz bomber for more than the idea of a layman, a strange, transitory idea. Nobody had taken it seriously, quite obviously not even Göring or Milch, who must at least have heard about it. All that had been undertaken was a provision for a bomb as an alternative to the auxiliary tank under the fuselage. One hundred and twenty aircraft had so far left the factory. A considerable percentage of these had been already destroyed, either on the ground during raids or by accidents. Not a single one of them had been fitted out in such a way that it could perform Blitz bombing.

We felt the effect of the Führer's outburst when a few hours later Milch, Bodenschatz, Messerschmitt, the commander of the testing stations, and I were called to the Reichsmarshal. He communicated to us the Führer's orders regarding the readjustment and rearming of the whole series of ME-262 as bombers. To avoid all misunderstandings no one in the future was allowed to refer to the ME-262 as a fighter or even as a fighter-bomber, but only as the "Blitz bomber." One might as well have given orders to call a horse a cow!

As he had already stressed at Insterburg, Hitler wanted to beat off the invasion with this Blitz bomber. According to the minutes Göring had said, "This action can be performed at once over the English coast by raiding the embarkation points and especially on the beaches, then during the landing by dropping bombs among the landing crafts and the landed tanks, etc. I visualize the operation in this way: The aircraft flies along the beach and blasts the hordes, which at the beginning will be uncoordinated. This is how the Führer sees the action and it is to be prepared in this manner."

Messerschmitt and I tried desperately to storm against this faulty decision. The German fighter pilots had a right to demand this superior fighter aircraft for themselves. Perhaps more than sober military consideration it was the knowledge that we must claim this right which gave us the strength to leave nothing undone to change Göring's mind. I had the impression that at the bottom of his heart he was himself convinced of the correctness of our argument. But to the world he had made Hitler's decision his own. He concluded, "So that we may understand each other clearly, I must repeat that a debate or a discussion of the fundamental question cannot be thought of any more."

The fighter arm and the defense of the Reich, which had seen in the jet fighter the savior from an untenable situation, now had to bury all hopes. The whole testing, training of personnel, and preparations for action were taken away from the General of the Fighter Arm and given to the General of the Combat Fighters (bombers).

During the few weeks until the opening of the invasion while town after town, armament factories, transport installations, and synthetic petrol plants were destroyed in the unprotected homeland, the General of the Combat Fighters tried to make a bomber out of the ME-262. Pilots had to be trained; bombing had to be practiced; tactical methods had to be found; and numerous changes had to be made on the aircraft. When the invasion finally started on June 6, not one of the Blitz bombers, which were supposed to have repelled the invasion, was ready for operation. Even in the following weeks, as long as the front still contained a bridgehead, no Blitz bomber went into action.

At last, in August, 1944, the first Blitz bombers went into action against the Allied invasion army, but the chances of a success had now become very meager because of the Allied advance. During these actions a few bombs were dropped daily somewhere on enemy territory. Very rarely was one able to say what, if anything, they had hit, or with what result. How different was the picture Göring had painted to us of "how the Führer sees the action!"

It must be pointed out here that the Bomber Command and its units never demanded the ME-262 for themselves. It was passed on to them with the order, "The command of the Führer has to be obeyed."

Thus the jet fighter had been declared to be a Blitz bomber. Now the bomber units that were to fly this plane were bastardized, because they were also to fly the Blitz bomber as a fighter. There was method in this madness. The fighter arm, which had so to speak lived on the hope of superiority of the ME-262, felt this decision not only as a blow against common sense but also against themselves. I tried to fight this decision with all the means and arguments that seemed to me irrefutable. I explained my conviction to Göring that now, in the

263

increasingly difficult conditions of the war in the air, it was impossible to transform a fighter into a bomber just like that; that only the most experienced and first-class pilots would be in the position to achieve results with the ME-262, and not re-educated bomber pilots. Further I argued that the bomber pilots in their new training could not change immediately to the jet fighter without training first on ordinary fighters; that they could not see enough in the air; that they could not aim because of the great speed of approach, even if they were at all able to distinguish between friend and foe. But everything was in vain. I got the reply that the bomber pilots were used to flying with two engines; that in contrast to the fighter pilots they were able to fly blind; and that they could see better anyhow if only from a pure sense of self-preservation; and that they would quickly learn a bit of shooting.

Then I tried to suggest a compromise: We should equip at least equal numbers of the ME-262 as bombers and as fighters. Action would show then which of the two was able to achieve the greater results. But this too was rejected. Then I made a final suggestion which, as desperate and as daring as it was, would have been much better for the Luftwaffe. I foretold that the operational results of the combat fighter squadrons would be nil; they would only block aircraft and fuel supply as well as our training capacity. It would be the best thing to send the entire 9th Flying Corps on leave into the Bavarian mountains until the end of the war.

These words were insulting. I knew that. But I had no gift for diplomacy and hiding my true opinion. I was never forgiven for my malicious prediction, especially since it unfortunately came true. The KG 51 was already in action with Blitz bombers. Now the refitting of the KG(J) 54, 27, and 6 began. It took weeks before it really started. Their pilots overflooded our replenishing troops and the unit leader training course. For the training of a pilot for the 4th Flying Corps (fighter), 65 tons of fuel were needed, while at the same time for the training of an ordinary fighter pilot only 25 tons were allocated, and this only in theory. Until the end of the war practically no KG(J) got successfully into action either as a Blitz bomber or as a fighter.

For the moment I could get only a small fighter test commando with a few ME-262s. According to the opinion of the leaders the plans for the Blitz bomber could not be crossed with these. They left it to me as a sort of hobby. It certainly would have died a natural death had Speer not supported me. It was through him that now and then one or two ME-262s found their way to us. It was not always easy, because Hitler, after the big row had taken the control of the turbojet production into his own hands. Each week the production figures had to be brought to him. He checked them carefully and with distrust and made the allocations personally. Thus at this period of the war the Supreme Commander of All Forces disposed not only of infantry battalions and flak batteries but also of individual aircraft!

In the meantime I tried to influence all competent leaders of the Luftwaffe and of the armament departments—as far as I had access to them—and also men of the government and leaders of the party to share and to second my point of view: A change in the disastrous situation in the air could only be achieved by a clear stressing of air defense and by sending into the defense of the Reich all the ME-262s that emerged from the now-accelerated production line, and by using them as fighters. I cannot judge in detail how far I succeeded in this.

Perhaps the steady flow of attempts may have finally broken down the existing lack of comprehension. The developments confirmed my argument so emphatically that it could no longer be overlooked. The V-weapon offensive came to a standstill because the bases were lost. The planned and ordered complementary bombing offensive did not even reach the gate. Fuel shortage paralyzed everything. The bomber fleets that in record numbers rolled out of the factories into the works yards remained there and had only salvage value. On his own initiative Speer ordered the stoppage of bomber production. What could have gone on in the hearts and minds of those exhausted workers, technicians, and engineers who had to see that the product of their devoted labor was now good for nothing else except to be wrecked on the spot?

Also the provisory solution of fitting out the bomber units with ME-262s had come to nothing and they had received no aircraft replacements and were now without planes. The craziness of the situation could not have been demonstrated more clearly than by an American daylight raid on the Messerschmitt works at Augsburg and the neighboring airfield of Lechfeld. Here were stationed the KG(J) 51, being refitted with ME-262s, and our test commandos. Six jet fighters were all that we could send up to meet the attackers. They were unable to prevent the 60 ME-262s, which were to be used as Blitz bombers, from being destroyed on the ground.

At last, in October, 1944, I received orders from Göring to form a jet-fighter unit of the two test commandos in Lechfeld, which were to be sent to the west. Their successes were to convince Hitler that the ME-262 was a really excellent fighter plane. It was revealing that this suggestion came from Himmler and that in order to put into action such a modest decision, which concerned only the Luftwaffe, Göring needed the backing of the man in a strong position! Welcome as it was that Himmler took the initiative in this way, it also had the disadvantage that from now on the S.S. meddled not only in questions of V-weapons and production of jet planes but also in purely operational questions.

The allocation of ME-262 for fighter service was more ample now. In the meantime the first planes of the Arado jet bomber had been produced. The AR-234B was fitted with two Junkers jet units; it had a top speed of 425 mph at an altitude of 18,000 feet, and could carry a maximum bomb load of two tons together with about 800 gallons of fuel. This interesting aircraft did some very valuable service until the end of the war, especially as a reconnaissance plane. For each AR-234 that went to bomber and reconnaissance units Hitler permitted one ME-262 to go to the fighter arm.

He entrusted the formation of the first ME-262 fighter unit —the permission for this had at last been granted—to Nowotny who, with a bag of 250 enemy aircraft, was then one of Germany's most successful fighter pilots.* The unit was formed at Achmer near Osnabrück. Nowotny took up his job with great enthusiasm and energy.

The unit made rapid progress, although it had to cope with many difficulties. The losses from faults in servicing and through technical hitches were greater in the beginning than those from enemy action. Yet the numbers of enemy aircraft shot down by ME-262 in a few weeks rose to 50.

On October 8, 1944, I visited the first jet-fighter squadron at Achmer. On this occasion I had invited Generaloberst Keller, the leader of the NSFK (National-Socialistic Flying Corps), who had been chosen for a very important post in the defense of the Reich. I wanted to give him some idea what could be demanded from a jet fighter.

The next morning: Alarm! Action stations! Strong American heavy bomber units approaching. The squadron made ready. Already the vanguard of the raiding force were over the airfield. We feared for every ME-262 taxied out for the take-off. A flight of piston-engined fighter planes that had the

* The Luftwaffe employed a more liberal system of certifying "kills." Both the USAAF and the R.A.F. required witness of: (1) the crash of enemy aircraft or (2) the bailing out of pilot and/or crew. Thus many kills registered by enemy German pilots would be listed as "probables" by the Allies

266

job of covering the take-off and the landing of the ME-262s was already involved in heavy dogfights. A large number of light flak guns posted all around the field were barking away furiously. Mustangs and Thunderbolts did not manage to prevent the take-off of the jet fighters, but it was critical and exciting. Nowotny took off too. Over the wireless we heard his commands for the attack. Then he reported his first kill. But one of his engines dropped out. He would try to get home. He could not be far off. We stepped out into the open. Visibility was not good; six tenths clouds. Soon we heard the whistle of an ME-262. That must be Nowotny. We clearly heard the report of the quick-firing cannon and the machine guns. Dogfight! Seconds later an ME-262 appeared out of the cloud and dove vertically to the ground. A black cloud and an explosion—it was the last fight of the first commander of a jet-fighter unit. This action and its success had a great bearing on Hitler's decision in November, 1944, to permit the formation of the first jet-fighter wing.

After what had happened nobody could have had any illusion about the possibility of putting into effect the following plan: The Flying HJ (Hitler Youth), boys of 16, 17, and 18 years of age, were supposed to pilot the new Volksfighter, a single-engine jet-fighter. Without training in power flying or any fighter-pilot schooling they were to make the last attempt to defend the Reich.

Thank goodness this "civil defense of the air" never came into being.

29

The Last

Toward the end of 1944 it seemed as though the ME-262 fighter would at last go into action in the defense of the Reich after a delay of years. Nowotny's squadron became the base of the first jet-fighter wing, which Steinhoff formed as the JG 7. Yet, in the meantime, the necessity to undertake something decisive against the Allied war from the air gave rise in the armament ministry to the politically inspired idea of mass-producing the jet Volksfighter and using as little material as possible and the lowest possible man-hours.

Almost all construction groups of the better-known aircraft firms tendered their design for this aircraft. Messershmitt and Tank agreed with me that the specifications and conditions were bound to lead to an aircraft that, in its technical and tactical performance, could only be uninteresting and possibly a total failure. The results of the calculations already showed a minimum in every respect.

Because the bombers were struck from the program, the aircraft industry was not working to capacity and had room for more work. This applied especially to the Heinkel aircraft factories. The Ministry of Armament and the Technical Department for Air Armament had already decided upon Heinkel's design, which was known as the HE-162. From the beginning I had strongly opposed the Volksfighter project. In contrast to the creators of this idea, my objections were based on factual reasons such as insufficient performance, range, armament, bad conditions of sight, and dubious airworthiness. Furthermore I was convinced that this aircraft could not be brought into worthwhile operation before the end of the war. The terrific expenditure of labor and material was bound to be at the expense of the ME-262. To my mind all forces ought to be concentrated on this well-tested jet fighter in order to make the best of the possibilities remaining to us. If we scattered our strength once more in this last phase of the war, then all efforts would be in vain.

On September 23, 1944, at the headquarters near Rastenburg the decisive discussion on the Volksfighter was held. From previous discussions I had hoped that the majority of the participants would support me in my rejection. But in my demand to supplant the HE-162 with the ME-262 I remained alone except for the Chief of the General Staff. My suggestion was to increase mass production of the ME-262 by having it built under license by all aircraft factories that were not working to capacity, and further to use all these planes only for the air defense of the Reich. This earned me a sharp rebuke from Göring which ran something like this: "This is unheard of! Now the General of the Fighter Arm refuses a jet-fighter plane which the armament production is offering him by the thousands within a few months!" Hitler, who had obviously detailed someone to report to him, was fully informed about the course of the discussions with the Reichsmarshal, and within an hour he demanded from me a written statement of the motives for my rejection of the Volksfighter. This was an additional reason for my being replaced as General of the Fighter Arm.

But the plan was put through and preparations were made for mass production. It was planned to use boy pilots after a hurried training on gliders, while production and service were to be assisted and controlled by the Gauleiters. The Volksfighter was to represent a sort of *levée en masse* in the air. Incredibly schedules were fixed, astronomical production figures were planned. Göring himself became a victim of the national frenzy with which the planning of the Volksfighter had infested almost everyone connected with air defense. "Hundreds! Thousands! Umpteen thousands!" he cried. "Until the enemy has been chased back beyond the borders of Germany!"

This project had one advantage: It was technically quite impossible to hang a bomb under the tiny aircraft and to declare it a Blitz bomber. Compared with the ME-262, the HE-162 meant a considerable step *back*ward in every way.

The construction was completed in two and a half months, mass production was ready to start on a grand scale as the prototypes were ready. In the history of aircraft design and construction this must have been a singular feat. On December 6, 1944, the HE-162 flew for the first time. A few days later—far too soon—it was displayed to a large circle of interested experts at Vienna-Schwechat. Before the eyes of the spectators the test pilot Peter yanKed the insufficiently tested plane too strongly in an attempt to loop. The aircraft started to disintegrate in the air, beginning with the right wing. Peter was killed.

In March, 1945, the planes of the first series were ready. Until the end of the war about 200 were produced. The question whether the Volksfighter could still have played a successful part in air defense was left in abeyance. The details of construction and a considerable number of half-finished planes fell into the hands of the Russians, and a few finished aircraft were seized by the Western Allies.

During the first days of 1945 the leaders of the Allied air forces apparently had no clear idea of how far Germany had collapsed. Under the impact of their own difficulties created by the offensive in the Ardennes, they obviously overrated her ability to continue the war. There is no shortage of Allied documents dating from this period that reveal an outspoken depression. The offensive in the Ardennes had been repelled. For a whole month the strategic air forces of the Allies had to be used extensively in tactical operations, supporting the English and American armies and thus diverted from their original task of raiding Germany. On January 8, 1945, Arnold declared, "Either we have been too optimistic in our conception of the possibilities of raids, or we have made a fatal error in calculating the effect which the destruction would have on the German war machine."

On January 11, the chiefs of the Allied air fleets met for a conference at Versailles. They considered a complete readjustment of their air strategy, taking it that the war would still last for a long time. General Anderson in particular pointed out the fact that the German aircraft production had recuperated during the lull in the offensive. Doolittle agreed with him, and Spaatz stressed the danger of the German jet fighter. It was calculated that to date already 700 ME-262s had been built. That was approximately correct. Up to the end of 1944 the industry had reported the completion of 564 planes.

A letter which the Commander of the American air forces wrote to Spaatz on January 14, 1945, clearly reveals two points:

1. That the command of the Allied air forces was nervous and uncertain.

2. The possibilities which would have resulted from a decisive and resolute action from the German side.

In the letter it says: "At the moment we have a superiority over Germany of at least 5 to 1, and yet, undoubtedly against our hopes, calculations, wishes, and plans, we have not been able to act on such a scale as we would have liked. Air raids perhaps will not force Germany to capitulate. But on the other hand it seems to me that with this enormous attacking force we should be able to achieve much better and more decisive results than we have actually done so far. I am not criticizing because frankly I cannot see any solution myself. What I am doing now is only to give my thoughts free rein in the hope that in this way I may ignite some spark, some light or idea or something, which may help us to bring this war to a quick end."

The Allies never found this new idea, but the fight against the German jet-fighter production and its mobilization was given priority, with immediate effect. Furthermore, all efforts were continued to paralyze the German war potential by raids on fuel supply and on the transport network, to break the morale of the people by a tremendous stepping up of the terror raids. But all this was merely a continuation of the previous methods at an increased tempo. The light of which Arnold spoke and for which he hoped never dawned.

The conference of the Allied Chiefs of General Staff held in the presence of Churchill and Roosevelt on January 30, 1945, in Malta, shortly before the Yalta Conference, was under the sign of the unhappy situation which had arisen at the beginning of 1945 between the Western Powers and their Russian ally. On January 13, the last large-scale offensive of the east had started with terrific masses of Soviet tanks and infantry breaking out of the bridgehead at Baranow. Equally strong advances occurred at the northern and central sectors of the Eastern front. A fortnight after the start of the Russian offensive, Upper Silesia and four fifths of East Prussia were lost. Königsberg and Breslau had become frontline towns. The capital of the Reich was seriously threatened by Soviet armored columns which had advanced to the Oder-Warthe line. In Moscow hardly a day passed without salvoes in honor of a new victory.

In contrast to these Russian successes in the communal struggle against Germany, the Western Powers for the moment could only point to their air supremacy. In order to play this up and to prove the good will for a collaboration with the Soviet, the Allied bombing plan was revised as a result of the conference of the General Staff at Malta. Top priority were now "Berlin, Leipzig, Dresden, and other German cities where heavy raids caused great chaos among the civilian population which had been swelled by the refugees from eastern Germany."

271

Four days later, on February 3, 1945, the capital of the Reich was raided by 1000 multiengined bombers. According to American statements, 25,000 Berliners died in this raid.

The result was reported to Churchill and Roosevelt at Yalta. The conference started the following day. Its known results still dominate world politics. The words of Stalin, which were quoted at the time by the English press, give proof of the arrogance with which the Russian dictator confronted his Allies. Referring to the separate meeting of Churchill and Roosevelt, Stalin is supposed to have greeted his partners with the ironical words, "I said Yalta—not Malta!"

This conference closed on February 11. On the evening of February 13 about a thousand British four-engined planes started to bomb Dresden from 22:09 until 22:35, followed by raids the next two days by American units. Although much has already been written about this sinister chapter of the war, its files are not yet closed. No one has yet been able to establish the exact number of victims of this most devastating area bombing raid of the entire war.

A week after Dresden, Operation Clarion began. The Allies had already planned it in the autumn of 1944 after their advance to the western border of Germany and after their unlucky operation at Arnheim, in order to bring the war to a quick end. All serviceable aircraft of the four air fleets stationed in England, a total of 9000 bombers, fighter-bombers, and fighters, made a unique demonstration raid which spread over nearly the whole of Germany. Essentially it was directed against transport targets, but it was also intended to illustrate to the German people that in practically no corner of the Reich were they safe from the Allied bombers. Therefore preference was given to smaller cities and little towns that had not yet been raided; villages and even single farms were attacked. The same operation was repeated the next day on the same scale. During this action, bombs were dropped by mistake on the Swiss principality of Schaffhausen. The intended target for this "precision raid" was Freiburg in Breisgau.

On February 26, 1945, Berlin experienced its fortieth large-scale raid; actually the four hundredth raid, this sorely tried city had suffered. From above the clouds, 1112 American bombers dropped 2879 tons of bombs. During March the American and English raids increased, delivering an almost continuous shower of bombs. Night after night, day after day, death and destruction descended upon the ever-diminishing area of the Reich. Hardly a town remained untouched. On March 12 the largest amount of bombs ever dropped during a night raid on a German town was registered as 4899 tons on Dortmund. The last week in March is entered as a record in the statistics of the R.A.F. with a total weight of bombs dropped of 67,365 tons. On April 6, Harris stated that there were no worthwhile targets for his strategic bomber fleet in Germany. A day later the large-scale R.A.F. air raids stopped. The bombing commission that functioned in London under the code name "Jockey" telegraphed to the Allied headquarters: "Jockey has unsaddled." Three days later, on April 10, American four-engined bombers raided Berlin for the last time. A fortnight later the Eighth AAF was transferred to Okinawa in order to bomb Japan in conjunction with the Twentieth AAF, already stationed in the Far East, until she was ripe for capitulation.

The last air battle of this war over Germany in which the Americans suffered impressive losses was delivered by the German fighter arm on March 18, 1945, over Berlin. The capital of the Reich was attacked by 1200 bombers that had an escort of 14 fighter squadrons of P-51s. Although many flak batteries had already been removed to the nearby eastern front, 16 bombers were so heavily hit that they had to make emergency landings behind the Soviet front line. The enemy suffered much greater losses at the hands of the jet fighters of the JG 7. From American flight reports one can see that the ME-262 broke again and again with ease through the American fighter screen and shot down one bomber after the other from the tightly closed formations despite an inferiority of 100 to 1. Besides those shot down by flak, the Americans had to report a loss of 25 bombers and 5 fighter planes. The next day the Americans again suffered losses from German jet fighters, while our piston-engined fighters could achieve nothing against the mass of the Allied fighter escort. Doolittle and Tedder now demanded decisive measures to prevent the operation of German jet fighters, without stating what these measures should be.

In January, 1945, we started on the formation of my unit that Hitler had ordered. It spread quickly through the fighter arm that our 44th Squadron was taking shape at Brandenburg-Briest. Our official nomination was a JV 44.

Steinhoff was in charge of retraining the pilots. Lützow came to us from Italy. Barkhorn, who had scored more than 300 kills* in the east, Hohagen, Schnell, and Krupinski were coaxed out of hospital. Many reported without consent or transfer orders. Most of them had been in action since the

* See footnote, page 266.

first day of the war, and all of them had been wounded. All of them bore the scars of war and displayed the highest medals. The Knight's Cross was, so to speak, the badge of our unit. Now, after a long period of technical and numerical inferiority, they wanted once more to experience the feeling of air superiority. They wanted to be known as the first jet boys of the last fighter pilots of the Luftwaffe. For this they were ready once more to chance sacrificing their lives.

Soon after receiving the first planes we were stationed at Munich-Riem. In the early hours of the morning of March 31, 1945, the JV 44 took off in close formation, and 42 minutes later the planes landed in Munich. They had covered the distance of about 300 miles in record time.

Here in Munich the unit took on its final shape. The Squadron of Experts, as we were called, had as pilots one lieutenant general, two colonels, one lieutenant colonel, three majors, five captains, eight lieutenants, and about the same number of second lieutenants. None of us imagined that we were able to give to the war the much-quoted "turn." The magic word "jet" had brought us together to experience once more *"die grosse Fliegerei."* Our last operation was anything but a fresh and gay hunting. We not only battled against technical, tactical, and supply difficulties, we also lacked a clear picture of the air situation of the floods coming from the west—a picture absolutely necessary for the success of an operation. Every day the fronts moved in closer from three sides. But worst of all our field was under continuous observation by an overwhelming majority of American fighters. During one raid we were hit three times very heavily. Thousands of workers had to be mobilized to keep open a landing strip between the bomb craters.

Operation orders for the ME-262s now changed daily. Conditions in the armament industry were also turbulent. The time of commissioners, special commissioners, ambassadors of the Führer, commissars, and special commissariats had started. All who were to increase production of the industry or to coordinate operations were appointed subordinate to each other, equal to each other, and over each other. From February until March the jet-fighter command went partly over to the SA. From their ranks came the so-called Commissariat of the Führer for Jet Aircraft, a general of the Waffen SS. Hitler had appointed him although Göring in his turn had appointed a Special Commissioner for Jet Aircraft.

Surprisingly I was called by Göring to the Obersalzberg: it must have been somewhere around April 10. To my amazement he received me with the greatest civility, inquired after the progress of our initial actions, and gave me a restricted confirmation that my prediction concerning the use of bombers with the ME-262 in the defense of the Reich had been correct. This indicated that the Reichsmarshal had begun to realize that after all I had been right throughout all those sharp clashes of opinion of the last months. This was the last time I saw Göring.

Four weeks before the collapse of the armed forces the fighter arm was still in a position to represent a factor that could not be overlooked. Operations from Riem started despite all resistance and difficulties. Naturally we were able to send up only small units. On landing, the aircraft had to be towed immediately off the field. They were dispersed over the countryside and had to be completely camouflaged. Bringing the aircraft onto the field and taking off became more and more difficult: eventually it was a matter of luck. One raid followed another.

In this situation the safety of the personnel was paramount and came before any orders to clear the airfield. Each pilot was responsible for his own cover on the airfield and had to dig his own foxhole. When it came to physical work you cannot imagine anything more lazy than a fighter pilot in his sixth year of service. My pilots moaned terribly about the stony ground at Riem. Returning from a mission, I was standing with them on our western airstrip, watching the bombers attacking railway stations in Munich in single waves. Suddenly somebody called, *"Achtung! Bombenangriff!"* Already the ugly finger of death, as we called the markers of the daylight raiders, were groping for our aerodrome. I chased after one of my pilots, who slithered into a nearby hole he had dug for himself. Hellishly narrow, I thought . . . oh, a single fox hole. It was very shallow. Then the first carpet of bombs roared down, passed over our heads. Nauseating, the whistle, the explosion, the blast, the tremor of the ground. A brief pause occurred after the attack of the first formation. I was lying on top of a sergeant. It was Knier. He was shaking, but in answer to my question he insisted that he was no more afraid than I was.

Our hole had a cover. A few splinters had struck this lid with a loud metallic clang. My back was pressed against it. "Knier, what's this on my back?" "100-pound bombs, Herr General," was the prompt reply. I certainly began to shake. Another five salvoes followed at short intervals. Outside there was smoke, debris, craters, fire, and destruction.

All Germans had experienced this during the last years of the war: In the cities, in the factories, on the battlefield, on ships and U-boats: Bombs, Bombs, Bombs! But it was an awkward feeling to be in the middle of a raid and, what is more, to be sheltered by one's own bombs.

During these last weeks of the war we were able to fit out some aircraft with additional weapons, which gave a greater firing power to the ME-262: R4M rockets of 3-cm. caliber, and 500-g. explosivies. A single hit from these was enough to bring down a multiengined bomber. They were fixed beneath the wing in two racks that carried 24 rockets. In a feverish hurry our mechanics and servicing crew loaded up a few jet fighters. I took off in one of them.

In the district of Landsberg on the Lech I met a formation of about 16 Marauders. We called these twin-engined bombers *Halbstarke*. I opened from a distance of about 600 yards, firing in half a second a salvo of 24 rockets into the close flying formation. I observed two certain hits. One bomber immediately caught fire and exploded; a second lost large parts of its right tail unit and wing and began to spiral earthward. In the meantime the three other planes that had taken off with me had also attacked successfully. My accompanying pilot, Edward Schallnoser, who once over Riem had rammed a Lightning because in his excitement he could not fire, waded into the Marauders with all his rockets. That evening he reported back to his quarters, parachute under his arm and a twisted leg.

Our impression of the efficiency of this new weapon was indescribable. The rockets could be fired outside the effective range of the defensive fire of the bombers. A well-aimed salvo would probably hit several bombers simultaneously. That was the way to break up formations. But this was the end of April, 1945! In the middle of our breakup, at the beginning of our collapse! It does not bear thinking about what we could have done had we had those jet fighters, 3-cm. quick-firing cannons, and 5-cm. rockets years ago—before our war potential had been smashed, before indescribable misery had come over Germany through the raids. We dared not think about it. Now we could do nothing but fly and fight and do our duty as fighter pilots to the last.

Service in action still demanded heavy and grievous losses. On April 18, Steinhoff crashed on a take-off but managed to free himself from the burning wreckage of his jet plane with very severe burns. A few days later Günther Lützow did not return from his mission. Long after the end of the war we were still hoping that this splendid officer might not have left us forever. In the same spirit and with the same devotion many more young pilots of our unit fell.

But the fate of Germany was sealed. On April 25 the American and the Soviet soldiers shook hands at Torgau on the Elbe. The last defensive ring of Berlin was soon penetrated. The Red flag was flying over the Ballhausplatz in Vienna. The German front in Italy collapsed. On Pilsen fell the last bomb of the 2,755,000 tons which the Western Allies had dropped on Europe during five years of war.

At that moment I called my pilots together and said to them, "Militarily speaking the war is lost. Even our action here cannot change anything. . . . I shall continue to fight, because operating with the ME-262 has got hold of me, because I am proud to belong to the last fighter pilots of the German Luftwaffe. . . . Only those who feel the same are to go on flying with me . . ."

In the meantime the harsh reality of the war finally decided the question: "Bomber or fighter action by ME-262?" in our favor. The leaders were completely occupied with themselves in Berlin and at other places. Numerous departments, which up to now had interfered with allocation and the operation of jet fighters, ceased to funcion or did not come through any more. Commanders of the bombers, reconnaissance, combat fighters, night fighters, and sundry testing units that had been fitted out with the coveted ME-262 passed their aircraft on to us. From all sides we were presented with jet fighters. Finally we had 70 aircraft.

On April 26, I set out on my last mission of the war. I led six jet fighters of the JV 44 against a formation of Marauders. Our own little directing post brought us well into contact with the enemy. The weather: Varying clouds at different altitudes, with gaps, ground visible in about only three tenths of the operational area.

I sighted the enemy formation in the district of Neuburg on the Danube. Once again I noticed how difficult it was, with such great difference of speed and with clouds over the landmarks, to find the relative flying direction between one's own plane, and that of the enemy, and how difficult it was to judge the approach. This difficulty had already driven Lützow to despair. He had discussed it repeatedly with me, and every time he missed his run-in, this most successful fighter commodore blamed his own inefficiency as a fighter pilot. Had there been any need for more confirmation as to the hopelessness of operations with the ME-262 by bomber pilots, our experiences would have sufficed.

But now there was no time for such considerations. We were flying in an almost opposite direction to the Marauder formation. Each second meant that we were 300 yards nearer. I will not say that I fought this action ideally, but I led my formation to a fairly favorable firing position. Safety catch off the gun and rocket switch! Already at a great distance we met with considerable defensive fire. As usual in a dogfight, I was tense and excited: I forgot to release the second safety catch for the rockets. They did not go off. I was in the best firing position, I had aimed accurately and pressed my thumb flat on the release button—with no result. Maddening for any fighter pilot! Anyhow my four 3-cm. cannons were working. They had much more firing power than we had been used to so far. At that moment, close below me, Schallnoser, the jet-rammer, whizzed past. In ramming he made no distinction between friend or foe.

This engagement had lasted only a fraction of a second—a very important second to be sure. One Marauder of the last string was on fire and exploded. Now I attacked another bomber in the van of the formation. It was heavily hit as I passed very close above it. During this breakthrough I got a few minor hits from the defensive fire. But now I wanted to know definitely what was happening to the second bomber I had hit. I was not quite clear if it had crashed. So far I had not noticed any fighter escort.

Above the formation I had attacked last, I banked steeply to the left, and at this moment it happened: a hail of fire enveloped me. A Mustang had caught me napping. A sharp rap hit my right knee. The instrument panel with its indispensable instruments was shattered. The right engine was also hit. Its metal covering worked loose in the wind and was partly carried away. Now the left engine was hit too. I could hardly hold her in the air.

In this embarrassing situation I had only one wish: to get out of this crate, which now apparently was only good for dying in. But then I was paralyzed by the terror of being shot while parachuting down. Experience had taught us that we jet-fighter pilots had to reckon on this. I soon discovered that my battered ME-262 could be steered again after some adjustments. After a dive through the layer of cloud I saw the Autobahn below me; ahead of me lay Munich and to the left Riem. In a few seconds I was over the airfield. It was remarkably quiet and dead below. Having regained my self-confidence, I gave the customary wing wobble and started banking to come in. One engine did not react at all to the throttle. I could not reduce it. Just before the edge of the airfield I therefore had to cut out both engines. A long trail of smoke drifted behind me. Only at this moment I noticed that Thunderbolts in a low-level attack were giving our airfield the works. Now I had no choice. I had not heard the warnings of our ground post because my wireless had faded out when I was hit. There remained only one thing to do: straight down into the fireworks! Touching down, I realized that the tire of my nosewheel was flat. It rattled horribly as the earth again received me at a speed of 150 mph on the small landing strip.

Brake! Brake! The kite would not stop! But at last I was out of the kite and into the nearest bomb crater. There were plenty of them on our runways. Bombs and rockets exploded all around; bursts of shells from the Thunderbolts whistled and banged. A new low-level attack. Out of the fastest fighter in the world into a bomb crater, that was an unutterably wretched feeling. Through all the fireworks an armored tractor came rushing across to me. It pulled up sharply close by. One of our mechanics. Quickly I got in behind him. He turned and raced off on the shortest route away from the airfield. In silence I slapped him on the shoulder. He understood better what I wanted to say than any words about the unity between flying and ground personnel could have expressed.

The other pilots who took part in this operation were directed to neighboring airfields or came into Riem after the attack. We reported five certain kills without loss to ourselves.

I had to go to Munich to a hospital for treatment of my scratched knee. The X ray showed two splinters in the kneecap. It was put in plaster. A fine business!

The enemy, advancing from the north, had already crossed the Danube at several places. The JV 44 prepared its last transfer. Bär, who had come to us with the remnants of his Volksfighter test commando, took over the command in my place. About 60 jet fighters flew to Salzburg. Orders came from the Reichskanzlei and from the Luftwaffe Staff in Berchtesgaden for an immediate transfer to Prague in order to pursue from there the completely hopeless fight for Berlin. The execution of this order was delayed until it became purposeless.

On May 3 the aircraft of the JV 44 were standing on the aerodrome of Salzburg without any camouflage. American fighters circled overhead. They did not shoot, they did not drop any bombs; they obviously hoped soon to be flying the German jet fighters that had given them so much trouble. Salzburg prepared for the capitulation. The advanced units of Devers' army approached the town. As the rattle of the first tank was heard on the airfield, there was no other possibility left: our jet fighters went up in flames.